DATE DUE

NOV 0 1 2002			
GAYLORD			PRINTED IN U.S.A.

Advising Student Groups and Organizations

NORBERT W. DUNKEL
JOHN H. SCHUH

Advising
Student Groups
and Organizations

JOSSEY-BASS
A Wiley Company
San Francisco

Published by

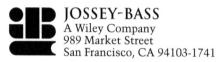

JOSSEY-BASS
A Wiley Company
989 Market Street
San Francisco, CA 94103-1741

www.josseybass.com

Copyright © 1998 by John Wiley & Sons, Inc.

Jossey-Bass is a registered trademark of John Wiley & Sons, Inc.

Jossey-Bass books and products are available through most bookstores. To contact Jossey-Bass directly, call (888) 378-2537, fax to (800) 605-2665, or visit our website at www.josseybass.com.

Substantial discounts on bulk quantities of Jossey-Bass books are available to corporations, professional associations, and other organizations. For details and discount information, contact the special sales department at Jossey-Bass.

We at Jossey-Bass strive to use the most environmentally sensitive paper stocks available to us. Our publications are printed on acid-free recycled stock whenever possible, and our paper always meets or exceeds minimum GPO and EPA requirements.

Jossey-Bass also publishes its books in a variety of electronic formats. Some content that appears in print may not be available in electronic books.

Library of Congress Cataloging-in-Publication Data
Dunkel, Norbert W., date.
    Advising student groups and organizations / Norbert W.
Dunkel, John H. Schuh.—1st ed.
      p. cm.—(The Jossey-Bass higher and adult education series)
    Includes bibliographical references and index.
    ISBN 0-7879-1033-3 (pbk.)
    1. Student affairs services—United States—Administration.
2. Student activities—United States. 3. Faculty advisors—United
States. I. Schuh, John H. II. Title. III. Series.
LB2342.9.D85 1998
378.1'983—dc21   97-21125

HB Printing   10 9 8 7 6 5

The Jossey-Bass
Higher and Adult Education Series

CONTENTS

PREFACE

In preparing this book, we have assumed that people who pursue a career in higher education are interested in interacting with students. To be sure, some individuals plan a career strictly focusing on research or the administrative side of colleges and universities and really do not want to interact on a routine basis with students, but we assume these people are in the minority.

Students can be challenging, fun, and exasperating, and they certainly are unpredictable. They also are an enormous source of energy and optimism, for as each entering group of students begin their careers in our colleges and universities, faculty and staff are able to see the collegiate experience with new eyes. Hopes and dreams are renewed through our new students.

Higher education has been criticized for not putting student learning first (Wingspread Group on Higher Education, 1993), and that criticism certainly can be justified. Other priorities have gotten in the way of student learning, and it may be time to take a fresh look at how faculty (see Boyer, 1990) and others use their time. Indeed, *The Student Learning Imperative* (American College Personnel Association, 1994) proposes that faculty and educational leaders in higher education, including organization advisers, need to develop conditions that motivate and inspire students to devote more time and energy to educationally purposeful activities both in and outside the classroom. Advisers who work with student organizations can help achieve this objective.

Many higher education researchers have come to the inescapable conclusion that students benefit from their involvement in campus organizations. We think the role of the adviser in ensuring this involvement is indispensable; we have written this book to provide a resource for organization advisers so that they can effectively perform their essential role and help students derive the greatest educational benefit possible from their membership in campus organizations.

In many quarters, advising a student organization has been regarded as a peripheral responsibility for faculty and staff. The challenges of working evening hours, having contact with many students, and facing the potential problems associated with advising can create a negative impression on those who are considering an advising assignment. Adviser roles often are unclear or ambiguous. Advisers are assigned substantial responsibility but have limited authority over the organizations they advise. Being an adviser requires specific skills and knowledge to assist groups or organizations through difficult legal issues, complex monetary regulations, and growing student apathy, as well as a solid understanding of how students benefit from their experiences as members of student groups. But all the negative aspects of working with student groups evaporate when one considers the advantages that accrue to advisers who work with students in their organizations.

Among these many benefits are a better understanding of students' lives, an opportunity to observe students' growth and development, and the goodwill that quality advising generates on campus. These benefits motivate many advisers to continue with their responsibilities year after year. In addition, the department associated with the student organization and the institution benefit from skilled advising. Sometimes these benefits are derived over long periods of interaction with students. In other cases, the response of a student to a challenging situation is so positive that it cannot be quantified.

Many people become organization advisers more as a result of chance than because they had planned to serve as advisers as part of their career path. Although student affairs staff members often become organization advisers at some point in their career (Bloland, 1987), other university staff and faculty members become advisers because they are invited by students or assigned the task because no one else in the department will accept it. Advising a student group or organization is not often seen as a prize assignment, particularly by those outside the division of student affairs. Too many advisers find themselves in a role for which they are unprepared, and only good fortune can save them from dealing with a myriad of problems that do not appear to have easy solutions.

Few members of the university community outside of the student affairs staff really understand the amount of growth and development that students experience by being members or leaders of campus organizations. As mentioned previously, the value of belonging to student groups and organizations is well established in the research literature. For example, Pascarella and Terenzini (1991) in their landmark book conclude that students who are members of campus organizations are more likely to be satisfied with their college experience than those who do not participate in campus organizations. Moreover, "alumni are reasonably consistent in reporting that involvement in extracurricular activities, particularly leadership roles, significantly enhanced interpersonal and leadership skill important to job success" (1991, p. 624). Astin (1993) adds that student-to-student interaction, including participating in student clubs or organizations, produces positive outcomes for students.

Considering that membership in student organizations has such tremendous value to students in terms of contributing to their growth and development, institutions of higher education (IHEs) are obligated to provide advisers with the tools they need to enhance the development of the organizations with which they work. McKaig and Policello (1987, p. 45) underscore this point: "The role of the adviser can be an integral element in the success of the student organization and in ensuring that the educational potential of the extracurriculum is realized." Kuh, Schuh, and Whitt (1991) identified examples of organizational advisers playing roles in their study of the factors and conditions that lead to high-quality out-of-class learning experiences for students.

To summarize, we draw three inescapable conclusions: (1) students benefit tremendously from participating in campus organizations; (2) advisers can play a key role in advancing student organizations; and (3) advisers, far too often, are not well equipped for their role. We have written this book as a remedy to the problem implied by the third conclusion.

Audience for This Book

We prepared this book with several audiences in mind. Our primary audience is composed of individuals who have limited experience working with student organizations. Included in this group are faculty members who have teaching, research, and public service as their primary assignments; members of the institution's administrative staff whose functions normally do not include advising student groups; and junior members of the student affairs staff who have not advised organizations as part of their experience. Among this group of junior student affairs staff are graduate assistants and entry-level professional staff in student housing, student activities, and fraternity and sorority life.

One secondary audience includes those staff members who provide training and consultation services to organization advisers. We think that members of the student activities staff, residence life staff, and others who work with group advisers will benefit from the discussions of fundamental concepts for advisers, the practical solutions to problems, and the ideas for training activities we have provided.

Another secondary audience includes those senior administrators who provide oversight for such student affairs units as student activities, residence life, and Greek letter organizations. Included in this group are provosts, chief academic officers, and even presidents. Although most student affairs officers have had experience with student organizations, an increasingly common approach to organizing student affairs is to have the senior student affairs office report to a provost or chief academic officer. In addition, some institutions have chosen to appoint a person with limited student affairs experience to the post of senior student affairs officer. Our suspicion is that provosts, for example, have not had considerable experience as organization advisers. Consequently, we think this book might be useful for them as a way of becoming acquainted with the work that their staff do with campus organizations. We may be overreaching to assume that provosts will read this book from cover to cover, but we do think it would be reasonable for them to read those parts of the book that address the challenges advisers face in the course of their daily work, and to understand that good advising is no different than good teaching or good research. All of these activities require dedicated people who have mastered a body in information and who apply that information in their daily routine.

Finally, we think this book will be a useful reference for graduate students who are preparing themselves for careers in student affairs work. These students will benefit from the concepts introduced here, whether they have direct advising responsibilities or other assignments as graduate assistants.

We offer you one caveat: this is not a book on academic advising, nor has it been prepared for university staff who serve as counselors or who provide other forms of educational or personal assistance. It is written for individuals who advise student organizations on the campuses of colleges and universities. Other sources exist for those interested in learning more about how to help students build schedules, develop their careers, address the developmental problems college students face, and plan the curricular part of their college careers.

Before we go much further, several terms need brief clarification. We use the terms *institution, college,* and *university* interchangeably in this book to mean all institutions of higher education. We also use the terms *student organization* and *student group* synonymously; by these we mean student organizations that are recognized or registered on campus.

Purpose of the Book

Our goal in this book is to describe the knowledge base and skills that are necessary to assist advisers of student organizations in improving their effectiveness. Specifically, our purposes are as follows: (1) to provide a foundation for organization advisers by introducing basic concepts about college students, student groups, and organizations; (2) to describe in detail the general knowledge and information that advisers apply routinely in the course of their work with student groups; and (3) to discuss specific topics that advisers will address on a more occasional basis as they work with student organizations.

Overview of the Contents

As implied by these points, the book is divided into three parts. Part One provides a foundation for group advisers. Chapter One describes the challenges and rewards, both personal and institutional, associated with advising student groups and organizations. Chapter Two provides an overview of student groups and organizations. It reviews several types of groups and organizations that advisers may work with in a college or university setting, and how advisers function in these different groups. We also look at samples of the mission statements and purposes of various organizations, and review the history of where and when student organizations began.

Part Two identifies information and knowledge that advisers will use on a daily basis in their work with student groups. Chapter Three describes the qualities, skills, and knowledge essential for quality advising. It discusses the various roles associated with advising: mentor, supervisor, teacher, leader, and follower. It also looks at recognition and motivation of leaders and members. Chapter Four is devoted to group development and building trust. This chapter discusses building connections with students, understanding group development and group dynamics, and maintaining relationships with students. Chapter Five discusses how advisers can provide academic and career assistance to promote learning and development. This chapter provides information on the referral process, discusses how student career development is influenced by participation in campus organizations, and clarifies role modeling; it also provides information on how values, ethics, and morals development guide the career development process.

Part Three deals with specific issues that advisers will need to address from time to time. Chapter Six provides information on understanding the institution's relationship with student groups and organizations. We look at involvement with other campus constituencies and with campus officers, and explore the role of campus organizations in the life of the institution. Chapter Seven discusses financial management and budget information. This chapter outlines the budget process, presents a balance sheet, and describes simple fund accounting. It also includes information about developing financial resources. Chapter Eight provides basic legal information. It discusses constitutional issues, risk management, and issues and concerns related to the use of alcoholic beverages. Chapter Nine describes how to deal with conflicts and other problems associated with the organization or individual members and suggests various campus resources for resolving these kinds of problems. Chapter Ten provides advisers with tools for evaluating their work and for evaluating the "health" of their student organizations. It provides additional activities, resources, and information for advisers to ensure that they function at a high level of effectiveness. Chapter Eleven includes additional recommendations for practice and for keeping advisers' skills up-to-date.

How to Use This Book

Obviously, if time permits, you will benefit most by reading the book from cover to cover. However, we offer an alternative for those who choose to read the book in parts. Everyone should read the first five chapters; they provide an excellent foundation for the adviser and strong recommendations for working with groups on a day-to-day basis. As we have already discussed, the balance of the book addresses specific issues that undoubtedly will arise during the course of an academic year but that are unlikely to be a part of the regular activities of the organization. For example, budgets work in a cycle, and when it is time to prepare the budget for the next year, your review of Chapter Seven will be quite helpful.

You will find case studies, samples of forms, checklists, and other materials throughout this book. We encourage you to discuss these materials with colleagues, complete the exercises, and use the cases to get the most out of the information provided by the text.

Acknowledgments

Many people assisted us in developing and producing this book. We want to acknowledge M. Lee Upcraft for his feedback as we developed the concept for the book. Diane Porter, Russ Fromen, and Jim Conneely deserve our thanks for reviewing manuscripts.

We want to express our appreciation to Gale Erlandson, senior editor for the Higher and Adult Education Series at Jossey-Bass, for assisting us through the publication process, and for giving us her insightful feedback.

Norb Dunkel wishes to recognize the help of the many advisers he contacted for examples of materials and information. He also thanks Jim Grimm for his unwavering support of student involvement and representation at all levels and Kathy Smith for her assistance in troubleshooting word processing problems. Finally, he wishes to thank his wife, Kim, and his son, Nicholas, for their patience and support in allowing him to travel and teach while he served as an adviser.

John Schuh wishes to thank Marcia Stevens for reviewing the manuscript while it was in the production process and Ginger Cox for her tireless support in developing the manuscript. He also thanks his wife, Linda, and his daughter, Kim, for their continuing encouragement of his writing and editorial projects.

September 1997

Norbert W. Dunkel
Gainesville, Florida
John H. Schuh
Ames, Iowa

THE AUTHORS

Norbert W. Dunkel is associate director of housing for staff and student development at the University of Florida, Gainesville, Florida. He has held various administrative positions at South Dakota State University and the University of Northern Iowa. He serves as the founding coeditor of the *Florida Perspective,* a journal for student affairs; he cofounded the National Housing Training Institute and has served as codirector for seven years. He has authored several articles and chapters, and served as an associate editor for *The College Student Affairs Journal* and as editor of *The Journal of College and University Student Housing.* Dunkel is coeditor (1993, with Cindy Spencer) of the book *Advice for Advisors: The Development of a Residence Hall Association,* now in its second edition.

Dunkel has served as a student organization adviser for the past sixteen years, and he currently serves as the adviser to the University of Florida Inter-Residence Hall Association. He served as adviser to the Florida Association of Residence Halls (FARH) from 1991 to 1995. He teaches a graduate course at the University of Florida on advising student organizations. He was inducted into the South Atlantic Affiliate of College and University Residence Halls (SAACURH) Adviser Hall of Fame and the Association of Alumni and Friends of the National Association of College and University Residence Halls (NACURH). Dunkel was the first recipient of the FARH Adviser of the Year Award, named in his honor in 1992, and in 1996, he was awarded the SAACURH and the NACURH Daniel Hallenbeck Awards for Career Service.

John H. Schuh is professor of educational leadership in the College of Education at Iowa State University. Previously, he has held administrative and faculty appointments at Arizona State University,

Indiana University, and Wichita State University. He is the author, coauthor, or editor of more than 125 publications, including eleven books and monographs. He is the author of *Involving Colleges* (1991, with George Kuh, Elizabeth Whitt, and Associates) and *Assessment in Student Affairs* (1996, with M. Lee Upcraft). He has been editor and chair of the American College Personnel Association Media Board and a member of editorial boards of the Association of College and University Housing Officers-International (ACUHO-I), the American College Personnel Association (ACPA), and the National Association of Student Personnel Administrators (NASPA).

Schuh has received awards for research and publications from ACPA and NASPA and for leadership and service from ACPA and ACUHO-I. He has served on the governing boards of ACUHO-I, ACPA, and NASPA. He is an honorary member of the Indiana University Residence Halls Alumni Association and the Wichita State University crew team. Schuh received the Dorothy C. Miller Award for outstanding contributions to the Wichita State University Greek system. He was awarded a Fulbright grant to study higher education in Germany in 1994.

Advising Student Groups and Organizations

PART ONE

What Advising Offers and Requires

CHAPTER 1

Challenges and Rewards of Advising

Students benefit substantially from being involved in campus organizations. Astin (1985, p. 133) states that "students learn by becoming involved." He defined a highly involved student as "one who . . . devotes considerable energy to studying, spends a lot of time on campus, participates actively in student organizations, and interacts frequently with faculty members and other students" (p. 134). *The Student Learning Imperative* adds that "serving as an officer of a campus organization or working offer opportunities to apply knowledge obtained in the classroom and to develop practical competencies" (American College Personnel Association, 1994).

Involvement in student organizations also provides challenges and rewards for you the adviser. On the one hand, some advisers are actively involved with their students and enjoy their interaction immensely. Some advisers work with debate teams and travel every weekend to various contests; others enjoy white water rafting with their organization or having lunch at the dining center with the executive officers. On the other hand, some advisers have such a negative experience that after one term they refuse to advise another student organization.

Regardless of why you have become an adviser—be it a role freely chosen or one thrust upon you—an understanding of the challenges and rewards of advising will help you fulfill your responsibilities more effectively. This chapter summarizes the challenges and rewards—for the institution, the organization, the adviser, and the student—of being involved in and working with student organizations, and at several points directs your attention to other chapters for in-depth discussion of specific issues.

Challenges _____

Institutions, organizations, advisers, and students face a variety of challenges related to student groups. We look at each of these challenges in detail.

Institutions

Faculty and practitioners in student affairs units know the benefits students experience by being involved in campus organizations, but it is nevertheless an institutional challenge to educate the greater campus community about the benefits of student involvement in organizations. We strongly recommend that you read *Achieving Educational Excellence* (Astin, 1985), *How College Affects Students: Findings from Twenty Years of Research* (Pascarella and Terenzini, 1991), and *What Matters in College?* (Astin, 1993). These three books are central to understanding the rewards and benefits that an institution can gain from having involved students. Consequently, the first challenge faced at an institutional level is to ensure that the knowledge of the benefits and rewards described in these books is distributed widely among faculty and staff.

A second institutional challenge is to develop and maintain a legal safety net for organizational activities, programs, and travel. Student organizations work with contracts and agreements, travel extensively throughout the country and world, and participate in such high-risk activities as skydiving, white water rafting, and mountain climbing. The institution must have staff assigned to assist organizations with complex contractual agreements, to assist in providing safe transportation, and so on. Colleges are facing increasingly complex liability and risk management questions; the campus legal counsel can assist in many aspects of this institutional challenge. (Chapter Eight provides detailed information on selected legal issues of advising.)

A third institutional challenge is the increased need to find the supplies and the meeting and office space to enable student organizations to function. Student activity fees enable many institutions to construct and maintain a central suite of offices for students. Typically this suite is located in a student union. Student committees allocate the office space. Student organizations, in turn, provide their own office equipment and supplies.

Meeting space for student organizations is increasingly difficult to find. Institutions are struggling to balance the assigning of meeting rooms for conferences and other revenue-generating activities with the needs of student organizations. Many institutions use classroom space during off hours for student organization meetings. In other circumstances, student organizations are finding it necessary to move their meetings to off-campus facilities.

Another institutional challenge is to clarify for the public the distinction between registering organizations versus recognizing them. Members of the general public often complain about student organizations that appear to run contrary to the mission of the institution. Whereas private institutions can take a more restrictive position regarding which student organizations may be allowed to be "recognized" by the institution, public institutions tend to follow a procedure of "registering" student organizations. At times some members of the public consider the mere existence of a particular organization an affront to the use of tax dollars. The general public may not possess a clear understanding that the institution only registers the organization and does not recognize (or approve) the organization. We explain the registration process in detail in Chapter Three. The challenge for institutions is to communicate with the public regarding the educational mission of the institution. For example, this mission may include providing a means of dialogue and debate, thus allowing students an opportunity to explore the value of an organization that appears to offend others.

The fifth institutional challenge is to bring campus leaders together for discussions of events, problems, and the life of the college. Institutional leadership should understand that the students are some of the best sources of feedback and insight for the institution. Students can provide valuable information on academic advising, campus safety and security, career planning, and parking.

Many institutions have invited students from select student organizations to provide this information. The leaders of these institutions have discovered the value of establishing relationships with a student constituency that can later be helpful when a campus crisis occurs and the students are needed to assist in distributing information, making public statements, or sharing a podium during a press conference. (Chapter Six discusses the relationships that student organizations have with the institution.) Thus, another institutional challenge is to understand the ongoing value and resources that student organizations and their membership can provide to the college.

A final institutional challenge is to educate the members and officers of student organizations about the requirements for holding an elected position and the priority the institution places on students' academic commitment. Institutions, primarily through the student activities office, maintain the information necessary for determining officer eligibility. As the number of student organizations has swelled to over five hundred on some campuses, institutions face increasing difficulty in reviewing records for eligibility. Some organizations have specific eligibility requirements for students to be members or to serve as officers (or both). In these cases, it is the institution's responsibility to review the officers' or members' grade-point averages and class loads, because student records cannot be revealed to student organizations under current privacy laws.

Organizations

One of the greatest challenges for a student organization is to recruit and retain an adequate membership base. Recruiting is less of a concern for some organizations because of the nature of their activities. For example, military or recognition organizations have a direct academic linkage that serves as an organization's entry point. Others, such as intramural sports groups, experience substantial student interest and may have to limit the number of participants. Still other organizations, such as fraternities and sororities, have an elaborate process of rushing, tapping, and being oriented into the organization.

For many special-interest student organizations, recruitment and retention are vital, ongoing concerns. The organization may spend time at student organization program fairs or spend money on ads, or they may produce slide and film shows to publicize their organization. Because so few students may be interested in a specific special interest, the organization must publicize to the broader student body to attract members.

Securing funding to meet the organization's needs is another challenge. Some organizations receive direct funding from student activity fees, student government allocations, membership dues, or foundational accounts and trusts. Most student organizations, however, spend time raising funds and soliciting for money to operate on even the most frugal budgets. Chapter Seven provides a number of suggestions about fundraising to support student organizations.

Auditing financial records and maintaining fiscal responsibility also are organizational challenges. Providing oversight for the budget is crucial. Many institutions require audits of accounts through a student government or student activities general accounting office. More often, this responsibility is given to the organization's treasurer, with additional oversight provided by the adviser. Again, Chapter Seven provides guidance for this challenge.

Another organizational challenge is to identify and train individuals to advise student organizations. To be recognized or registered on most campuses, an organization must have an adviser. Granted, most organizations select their adviser on the basis of the interest the person has in the organization. Other organizations inherit advisers who serve in that capacity due to the responsibilities of their positions. They have little or no input into the selection of their adviser. Still other organizations have great difficulty finding a faculty or staff adviser due to the controversial nature of the organization or its values, or because of the embarrassment an adviser might experience by being associated with the organization.

Another challenge for the organization is to make an active effort to involve the adviser in meetings and activities. Some organizations encourage their advisers to attend all their meetings and activities, whereas others appear to work in a vacuum, failing to communicate the dates and times of meetings to their adviser. In order for advisers to be effective, they must be able to attend and, to a certain level, participate in organizational meetings and activities.

A difficult challenge for some organizations is to understand that they are a part of the institution and therefore must comply with the policies and procedures of the institution. Often these policies and procedures require organizations to submit timely and proper paperwork to maintain organizational eligibility, budget oversight, or officer rosters. This challenge is especially difficult for disorganized or unorganized student groups. Organizations not receiving funding from the institution may have the perception that they do not owe the institution anything and consequently do not need to submit anything to the bureaucracy of the institution. An adviser can assist in both these matters by providing direction for the organization and clarity of purpose.

A final challenge for organizations relates to one mentioned in our discussion of institutions. The organization must monitor activities and events for liability and risk management implications. As an institutional representative, the adviser serves an important function by reviewing planned organizational activities and events. An adviser's knowledge of the details of the activities and events is of even more importance when contracts, travel, or other potential risks to students are involved.

Advisers

In your work as an adviser, one of your greatest challenges is managing your time and not becoming overcommitted to the organization. The students and the organization can be very demanding of your time. Attending weekly meetings with the student organization president, the executive board, and the organization itself; attending a couple of activities or events each week; making phone calls; attending individual meetings with students in the organization; and writing letters of reference and recommendation—these activities collectively can take a considerable amount of time. You need to set expectations early as to your ability to attend meetings, events, and activities. Chapter Three provides additional information on the demands placed on advisers.

The typical training of the adviser is minimal. Some advisers refine their skills by taking advantage of professional organizations and associations to attend programs and listen to speakers. Others will use the organization's manuals or notebooks to provide advising information. Still other advisers have developed a proven advising technique over many years of experience or have applied their knowledge of supervision to the role of advising. Chapter Three provides detail on the skills common to both supervising and advising.

Graduate courses are emerging that focus on advising student groups and organizations. An example of this kind of course is one offered at the University of Florida through the Department of Counselor Education. Most advisers use a combination of these various approaches. The campus student activities office and the central office of an organization's national association are excellent places to start in identifying adviser training opportunities to overcome the challenge of lack of training.

Another challenge for you is to clarify for members what your role is in the organization. Students will have their own ideas; your role should be discussed as soon as possible following the election of officers. Following a discussion of everyone's expectations, it is also important to discuss what you and your office staff can provide, how to communicate effectively among the members, the executive board, and yourself, and the time and stress management of the member, executive board, and adviser positions. Chapter Three provides some activities to assist in the discussion of these issues.

Another challenge for you is to avoid becoming overcontrolling in the organization's matters. The organization is for the students, and decisions should be made by students. An adviser who begins to take control by making decisions or running meetings runs the risk of having the students vote with their feet by leaving the organization or ostracizing the adviser. Most faculty and staff advisers play supervisory roles, and their practice and experience as supervisors is helpful for providing direction, assisting in the decisions, and facilitating meetings. Advisers must step back and allow the students the opportunity to run their organization. Some circumstances can arise in which you should take more directive action. Chapter Eight, on legal issues, provides detailed information on the matters in which the institution might be liable and that would necessitate your intervening. Chapter Seven discusses circumstances in which the financial integrity of the institution would be at risk, necessitating your taking action. In most situations, these matters can be worked out with the organization's president or executive board in advance of the program, activity, or meeting.

Another challenge for you is to be aware of decisions and action taken by the organization. Some advisers are not able, for a variety of reasons, to attend the organizational or executive board meeting and therefore will miss some of the decisions being made by the organization. It is nonetheless the responsibility of the adviser to be aware of the decisions that are made in order to respond to questions, to ensure that financial and legal issues are properly addressed, and to better understand the climate and attitude of the organization and its members. You can stay informed about decisions by meeting on a weekly basis with the organization's president, by reading minutes, or by communicating via e-mail with the president or secretary.

Finally, you can be challenged to be patient in the growth and developmental processes of students. It may seem easier simply to make decisions for the organization and quickly provide solutions and results. However, you need to ask yourself how membership in the organization will augment the students' education. If you allow students the opportunity to discover answers themselves and to attempt different approaches or techniques to group development, the students will benefit. This process entails patience and the ability to sit back and allow the process to take its course. Trial and error can be a valuable approach to student and organizational development without harm to the student, organization, or institution.

Students

Astin's research (1993) found several challenges for students related to their involvement in campus organizations. He determined that involvement in a social fraternity or sorority has a negative effect on liberalism; participating in intercollegiate sports has a negative effect on students' performance on three standardized tests (GRE Verbal, LSAT, and NTE General Knowledge), and requires a substantial amount of time for competition at the intercollegiate level;

and working on class group projects has a negative effect on students' performance on the GRE Verbal test. Kuh and Lund (1994, p. 11) found that "participation in student government was negatively correlated with the development of altruism."

Another challenge to students, whether they are members of the executive board or members of the organization, is for them to make an active attempt to establish a relationship with you. You may be new to the organization, or you may have been involved as an adviser for many years. In any case, the student's challenge is to work with you to identify expectations and roles. This relationship building is a process that continues throughout the year. Chapter Three provides detailed information on the relationship- and team-building processes.

Students are challenged to establish a system of communication that benefits and provides information to the organization. Student organizations thrive on continuous communication among the executive officers and members, the adviser and executive officers, the organization and institution, and perhaps the members and their constituency. Communication can be facilitated through technology (for example, e-mail, the World Wide Web, voice mail networks), the distribution of agendas and minutes of the meetings, discussions during meetings, and the mail. Students are challenged to develop an effective means of communication in order that all members and other interested parties receive proper and timely information.

A difficult challenge for students is to balance the time needed for their academic responsibilities and for the extracurricular activity of a student organization. You should be in a position to provide the information, resources, and referrals necessary to assist students in achieving this balance. Some advisers work individually with students to complete a time management analysis. Chapter Five provides information and activities for you to use with your students.

A final student challenge is to be patient with the institution's decision-making processes. Colleges and universities, whether public or private, all have complicated systems of accounting for funds, submitting paperwork for travel, and making room reservations. You can help students work their way through these institutional procedures. In addition, you are in a position to provide information and clarification on these lengthy procedures. You can identify the faculty or staff on campus who will visit with students to hear about their needs or who might help to accelerate the administrative processes. However, students should not rely on you for all the answers or shortcuts in solving their problems.

Rewards

Let us turn now to the wide variety of rewards that institutions, organizations, advisers, and students can enjoy as part of their experience with student groups.

Institutional Rewards

An institution's ability to attract and recruit new students is greatly increased by the visibility and involvement of students in organizations. Some of the more visible student organizations lead summer preview and orientation programs for new and prospective students and their parents. Other organizations work throughout the academic year as student diplomats to host tours and speak to prospective students and their parents. These student organizations have as their primary purposes advancing the institution and providing information to campus visitors for the recruitment of students. Many other student organizations (such as military, collegiate sports, and special interests) use their visibility or connection to academic programs to recruit students to the institution. Involvement in recruitment programs can be found in many other student organizations' purpose statements.

Improved retention is another institutional benefit of students' involvement in organizations. We know that "learning, academic performance, and retention are positively associated with academic involvement, involvement with faculty, and involvement with student peer groups" (Astin, 1993, p. 394). Academic involvement includes time allocated to studying and doing homework, courses taken, and specific learning experiences. Involvement with faculty includes talking with faculty outside of class (for example, as part of involvement in student organizations), being a guest in a professor's home, or working on a research project. Involvement with student peer groups includes "participating in intramural sports, being a member of a social fraternity or sorority, . . . being elected to a student office, and hours spent in socializing or in student clubs or organizations" (p. 385).

Another benefit to the institution is to have students serve on various advisory boards and committees to provide feedback for institutional events and projects. Many institutions request that students from various organizations serve as representatives on search committees, athletic advisory committees, student union boards, concert committees, budget advisory committees, or even governing boards. The feedback and insight that students provide the institution come directly from the consumer through a student organization.

A similar reward is to have key student organization leaders meet with campus administrators, faculty, and staff during times of crisis to provide feedback and assistance to the institution. In the past few years, serial killings, major fires, plane accidents, and natural disasters have occurred on college campuses. The individuals who have lost their lives included students, faculty, and staff. These events and their aftermaths are difficult periods for the campus. The director of the counseling center on a campus that experienced multiple homicides observes, "The absolutely outstanding cooperation of our student leaders, particularly the student body president, enabled us to get valuable student feedback and perspectives, and provided strong leadership for students" (Archer, 1992). Involving key student leaders from such organizations as the residence hall association, fraternities and sororities, student government, the Hispanic-Latino student association, or the black student union can help the institution plan memorial ceremonies, improve educational approaches to safety and security, or publicize enhanced services. In addition, student organizations can be involved in press conferences to help reassure students and answer questions.

Organizational Rewards

Naturally, the primary organizational reward is in providing students with an opportunity to participate in an enjoyable activity or to achieve a valuable purpose. Students participate in organizations, in part, to gain a sense of acceptance by their peers. Astin (1993) asserts that the peer group is the most potent source of influence on students' growth and development during their college careers. If students discover an organization that provides a common interest or academic theme to their liking, they may feel a greater sense of acceptance. The organization's reward is a group of students with common interests, enjoyment, or goals.

Another organizational reward is the opportunity to contribute to the tradition and history of the institution and organization. Many student military, sports, Greek letter, and honorary organizations have a rich history within an institution. The organizations may sponsor homecoming events, such as the student-produced Gator Growl at the University of Florida, a comedy, skit, and light show pep rally in the football stadium, which attracts over eighty-five thousand students; career expositions; or major institutional events, such as VEISHEA at Iowa State University. "VEISHEA is an acronym for each of the colleges in existence at the time the festival was founded [in 1922]" (Schuh, 1991, p. 40). Another example of a campus event is the original cardboard boat races at Southern Illinois University in Carbondale, sponsored by an engineering club. These types of events provide some student organizations with the opportunity to contribute to the tradition and history of the college.

Another organizational reward is in the fulfillment of the organization's purpose. Some organizations advance an area of study or research, provide feedback to the institution, prepare students for military service, provide recreation, or represent students of a particular constituency. A student organization that fulfills its purpose provides one of the greatest rewards possible. When student leaders can keep their organization involved in matters within its stated purpose, the organization maintains strong leadership and meets its goals. When a student organization discovers it necessary to pursue other meaningful purposes, the students must know and understand how to revise their constitution, adjust purpose statements, or redirect the resources available to them.

Adviser Rewards

One of the several rewards for you as an adviser is being able to observe the development of students during their college matriculation. You have the opportunity to work with incoming students and, in many cases, observe them in and out of classroom environments over the course of several years. You can feel the students' excitement as they too discover an organization. It is rewarding to observe the students as they move from membership to leadership roles, or from being reserved to participating fully.

Another reward for you, one that is seldom sought, is to be recognized by the institution, organization, and students for a job well done. Letters from students ten years after they graduate, a plaque from the executive board at the conclusion of the year, a distinguished service award from the institution, an advising award from the organization's national association, or a thank you from a student—all these are possible (usually unexpected) rewards for your involvement in a student organization.

You should feel flattered in serving as a reference for students. When a student approaches you for a reference, it means that in the student's eyes, a relationship exists between you and the student. At certain times of the year the request for references can be inordinately heavy; however, the reward in being asked to complete a reference far outweighs the work involved in providing it.

A very fulfilling aspect of being an adviser is in serving as a mentor for students. Either you or the student can initiate the mentor relationship. Maintaining contact with certain students during their academic career or providing them assistance following their graduation can be very rewarding to a mentor in an advisory capacity. Chapter Three provides detail about the mentoring role and also identifies activities that you and students can undertake.

Another reward for you is the opportunity to be able to observe the fads, cultures, and subtle changes that occur in student life. You sometimes are among the few individuals on campus who possess a sense of campus activities and attitudes. In the course of attending meetings, going on trips with the organization, or attending evening activities, you will find it easy to observe and note the language, dress, and nonverbal communication of the students along with the various messages and nuances of their interaction. Your being able to relate enables better understanding of students, which in turn helps you as you work with the organization, academic department, or institution on student problems and concerns.

Advising also provides an opportunity to teach, lead, and coach students involved in student organizations. You may present programs to the organization's membership or executive boards; facilitate leadership development programs for members; take members and executive boards on retreats and workshops; or involve the members in community service or volunteer service. These types of activities allow you to practice your teaching, leading, and coaching skills. Chapter Three provides detailed information and activities for each of these advising roles.

Another reward is an opportunity to form networks with colleagues involved as advisers of similar organizations. Traveling to professional or student-oriented conferences allows you the opportunity to visit with colleagues with similar interests. These trips and collegial relationships not only rejuvenate you but also help create a network to rely on for resources and information. Some organizations have highly developed regional, national, or international associations for advisers, separate from the students. These organizations provide you a forum in which to openly discuss problems and present views. Similarly, an increasing number of computer discussion groups are available for advisers of different organizations. These groups provide a more global opportunity to discuss topics and access resources without even leaving the office. Chapter Two provides summary information on different types of student organizations as well as on the professional organizations available to you.

The opportunity advising provides to serve the institution is yet another reward. Many faculty are evaluated on the basis of their teaching, research, and service. Serving as a faculty adviser to an organization enriches the service component of a faculty member's annual dossier. This reward is peripheral to the many others you will realize as an adviser, but is nonetheless important for those faculty who have tenure or other related compensation considerations tied, at least in part, to institutional service.

A final reward for you is the opportunity to participate in an organization whose purpose you enjoy. For many faculty and staff, the work of their profession leaves little time for additional special interests. However, among the wide variety of student organizations that exist, you can often find one whose activities or purpose complements your interests.

Student Rewards

As we have already discussed, the rewards or benefits students gain through involvement in extracurricular activities have been studied extensively. Astin (1993) reports that membership in a social fraternity or sorority has positive effects on leadership abilities; participating in intramural sports has a positive effect on physical health, alcohol consumption, and attainment of the bachelor's degree; and participating in collegiate sports has positive effects on physical health, leadership, and satisfaction with student life. Pascarella and Terenzini (1991) conclude that learning and personal development are enhanced when students are involved in educationally purposeful extracurricular activities. Kuh and Lund (1994, p. 10) observe that involvement in student government "was the single most potent experience associated with the development of practical competence." *Practical competence* in this case is defined as skills that employers are seeking, in such areas as decision making, leadership, cooperation, and communications. Kuh and Lund also report that participation in student government contributes to the development of self-confidence and self-esteem.

Student rewards include being recognized by the institution, organization, or adviser; meeting new people and discovering new friends; gaining new skills that can be transferred to their careers; networking with faculty, staff, and employers through contacts gained in the student organization; enjoying the personal satisfaction of completing tasks and projects that have received a positive evaluation; and serving as a campus resource to parents, faculty, staff, and other students.

Students also benefit when they learn skills while working with the organization that can be transferred to their career. Chapter Five provides an exercise in identifying these transferable skills.

CHAPTER 2

Overview of Student Groups and Organizations

As an adviser you should understand the purpose and mission of the specific organization with which you work; you will also benefit from an overview of the many types of organizations, their purposes, and the role advisers play in each type.

Thousands of different organizations exist on college and university campuses involving hundreds of thousands of students. In this chapter we identify various types of college and university student groups and organizations. We have developed the following taxonomy of organizations: student government, Greek letter, residence hall, honors and recognition, military, sports, departmental, and special interest. Our description of each category includes its purpose and history, the type of person who typically advises that kind of organization, and the various associations that provide services and direction. We look first at the purpose and role of the student activities office; on most campuses this office coordinates the registration of student groups and organizations. In addition, we provide the general requirements for registering versus recognizing an organization.

The Role of the Student Activities Office

Extracurricular activities typically are coordinated by an office of student activities or by similar administrative units. These activities range from attending concerts and building homes to white water rafting and listening to a speaker; they provide students an opportunity to volunteer, participate, and lead. Student activities normally will provide students with an opportunity to continue the socialization process, participate in group interaction and relationships, and develop leadership skills (Mueller, 1961)

The history of student activities can be traced to the American colonial period, prior to the development of the first Greek letter organizations. Early student activities were based on religious themes and strong discipline. They evolved to include literary organizations, debating societies, and athletic clubs that organized social events, debates, or sporting contests. As the Greek letter organizations, honors organizations, recognition societies, student government, and intercollegiate athletics developed, so did the view that institutions needed to employ professionals to advise student activities. "The student affairs staffs now included such titles as director of student activities, director of counseling, as well as the original title of dean of women, dean of men" (Saddlemire and Rentz, 1988, p. 264).

The National Association for Campus Activities (NACA) was formed in 1960 and has evolved into the nation's largest organization of campus activities programmers. At first, NACA conferences were held so that colleges could collectively book performers and attractions. Throughout the years this organization has expanded to keep pace with current educational and student needs. NACA's purpose is "serving colleges and universities, . . . inspiring excellence in student leadership development and programs outside the classroom, advancing the campus activities profession, and enhancing a marketplace. The Association accomplishes its mission by providing educational and business opportunities, resources, and services for college students, staff, and suppliers" (National Association for Campus Activities, 1996, p. 175).

The NACA national conference and eleven regional conferences are developed to support the service and resource aspect of this mission. The conferences include three different elements. First, the showcase provides a stage for bands, comedians, and other performing artists to perform in front of students and staff who might wish to contract their act. The national conference showcases approximately eighty acts. Second, there are numerous education programs presented by faculty, practitioners, and students. These programs provide information on how to work with agents, do publicity, and turn a cafeteria into a performance site. Third, there is an exhibit marketplace where vendors, agents, and businesses meet with conference participants.

Many student activities offices across the country are responsible not only for the development of a calendar of events for the campus but also for providing structure for campus organizations. The student activities office provides services and support to the organizations while allowing them the freedom to fulfill their purposes. Many campuses register their student groups and organizations. Registering the student groups and organizations provides assurance of consistency to the institution (Craig and Warner, 1991). Providing institutional consistency throughout the registration process usually requires that each student group or organization (1) submit a constitution, complete with mission statement, membership requirements, and voting procedures; (2) provide a list of the executive board officers, who must meet minimum academic and disciplinary standards; and (3) report the name of the faculty adviser. A student group or organization fulfilling the registration process may then be eligible to reserve institutional space for meetings and events, receive money from the student government, or secure office space in a student activities center. As discussed earlier, private institutions may not only register student groups and organizations but also recognize the group or organization as one that supports and sustains the institutional mission.

Student activities centers often provide training for students and advisers, resources for program development, personnel to handle institutional contract management for performers and attractions, oversight for maintaining the minimum institutional standards for students to remain eligible to serve in leadership positions in student organizations, facilities for office and meeting space, and staff with experience to assist student organizations with their group development and motivational problems.

Characteristics of Typical Student Organizations

As mentioned in the introduction to this chapter, there are several categories of student organizations: student government, Greek letter organizations, residence hall organizations, honors and recognition organizations, military, sports, departmental, and special-interest organizations. We discuss each type individually in the following sections.

Student Government

"Beginning at Amherst College in 1828, undergraduate students have sought to be involved with the governance of their institutions. While their 'House of Students' was short lived, this early organization ushered in the student government movement in American higher education" (Keppler and Robinson, 1993, p. 36).

These early forms of student government were centered around issues of disciplinary control, and maintenance of residence halls; they also held a consultative role with faculty to structure student government organizations. These organizations had elected officers but were not empowered with decision-making ability (Horowitz, 1987). From the austere beginnings of student government evolved today's organizations, which deal with such major issues as student apathy, rising tuition, budget cuts, campus parking, and multicultural awareness (Keppler and Robinson, 1993).

Some highly visible student governments are involved in numerous aspects of college and university life and have oversight of millions of dollars. Cuyjet (1985) surveyed student government presidents and advisers to determine the role that student government plays on campuses. The presidents and advisers reported that student government provides the official representation of the student body to the administration and faculty. However, they indicated that student government has little influence on the major decision-making councils on campuses.

The purpose of student government varies from campus to campus. For example, the purpose statement of the student government of the University of Florida reads:

> We, the members of the Student Body of the University of Florida, desiring to: provide a form of government for the supervision of student activities; provide a forum for the expressions of student views and interests; maintain academic freedom, academic responsibility, and student rights; improve student cultural, social, and physical welfare; develop better educational standards, facilities, and teaching methods; help promote national and international understanding and fellowship at the student level; and, foster the recognition of the rights and responsibilities of students to the school, the community, and humanity; do hereby establish this Constitution [Student Government, 1996, p. 1].

The organizational statement is that of a highly complex organization with a wide variety of purposes, interests, and activities.

Student governments can be highly complex organizations that include a student body president; a vice president overseeing cabinet directors; a treasurer supervising financial assistants, auditors, and general accounting office personnel; a chief of staff who coordinates various central office staff and campuswide projects and programs; an honors court chief justice overseeing academic dishonesty procedures; a senate president coordinating the senate proceedings; and other agencies that contract with a student government, such as performers, attractions, yearbook staff, and so forth.

Campus business services, student affairs, and auxiliary services have traditionally been viewed as the campus service providers.

Student government also is an important service provider. Cuyjet (1994) examines student government issues and services and finds that in student government, the most important issues and services are general student apathy, allocation of student activity fees, activities programming, availability of classes, participation in college or university governance, race relations on campus, representation on campuswide committees, rising tuition, safety on campus, and recycling and the environment. Cuyjet also observes that even though the preceding list included the most prevalent issues and services, students also addressed administrative and faculty salaries, organizing national lobbies, drug use and testing, enrollment ceilings, faculty and staff collective bargaining, admissions standards, legal aid, day care for student families, graduation standards, and community homelessness. The breadth of involvement of student governments in issues and services on campuses reflects a strong interest in wanting to evaluate and influence contemporary issues and services.

Boatman (1988) identifies four essential components of a strong student government. The first component includes being party to information similar to that which the faculty and employees receive, having information that provides clarity to the institutional structure, and receiving information regarding the relationship of other campus student organizations to the student government. The second component includes access to high-level administrators, involvement of students on all levels of committees and boards, and provision for general social interaction with faculty and staff. The third component is a shared respect between student government and faculty and staff, between student government and the press, and between student government and the general student body. The final component of a strong student government includes an organizational structure that allows for proper representation throughout the various forms of campus governance, a clear system of student leadership development, and an atmosphere in which students and staff communicate as colleagues.

Advisers to student governments include the vice president for student affairs, the dean of students, the student activities staff, faculty, and graduate students. Boatman (1988) identifies some of the characteristics and skills of an ideal student government adviser: (1) having the ability to develop a relationship with students (for example, appreciating students, being supportive and sensitive); (2) being an informed resource person (for example, having information regarding home and peer institutions, being involved in associations and aware of current issues); (3) having institutional credibility (for example, having access to and credibility with high-level decision makers, being a skilled advocate, and having time in the midst of his or her responsibilities to advise); (4) being a positive role model (defined as modeling creative problem solving, demonstrating a positive approach, modeling a balanced life, and modeling an appreciation of diversity); and (5) having adaptive skills (for example, patience and tolerance). Advisers have the challenge of working with diverse students possessing numerous motives for their involvement in student government.

Greek Letter Organizations

The American college and university fraternity system has been established for over two hundred years. It represents hundreds of sorority and fraternity chapters in which thousands of students are members. The fraternity system makes up one of the largest categories of student organizations represented on college and university campuses today. Phi Beta Kappa, founded at the College of William and Mary on December 5, 1776, was the first Greek letter organization on an American campus. Two years later, Phi Beta Kappa founded chapters at Yale University and Harvard University (Owen, 1991). Since the founding of Phi Beta Kappa, chapter membership in other fraternities continued to expand with chapters for men and women; African American, Hispanic-Latino, and Asian students; honor students; students involved in civic affairs; and students who are campus leaders.

Men's Groups.   The Phi Beta Kappa chapter at the College of William and Mary was not only the first Greek letter organization on an American college campus but also the first scholarly organization for men. In the mid-1850s, the development of men's organizations with a literary emphasis began. In 1917, a chapter of Delta Phi was established at Washington (now Trinity) College, initiating what would become an explosive expansion in chapter development throughout eastern America (Owen, 1991).

Many of the men's organizations (fraternities) are members of the National Interfraternity Conference (NIC). Founded in 1909, the NIC now represents over 400,000 students from more than eight hundred campuses throughout the United States and Canada. These campuses host approximately 5,200 fraternity chapters (Owen, 1991). The purpose of the NIC "shall be to promote the well-being of its member fraternities by providing such services to them as the House of Delegates may determine, these services to include, but not be limited to, promotion of cooperative action in dealing with fraternity matters of mutual concern, research in areas of fraternity operations and procedures, fact-finding and data gathering, and the dissemination of such data to the member fraternities. Conference action shall not in any way abrogate the right of its member fraternities to self-determination" (cited in Owen, 1991, p. I-29).The NIC provides a variety of services to its membership including organizing a number of regional and national conferences; developing various publications; providing a foundation for distribution of money for research; and staffing the NIC office in Indianapolis, Indiana.

Women's Groups.   Women's fraternities began with Alpha Delta Pi, founded as the Adelphean Society in 1851. Pi Beta Phi came into being in 1867 as the first organization of college women established as a national college fraternity. Kappa Alpha Theta was organized in 1870 as the first Greek letter society for women (Owen, 1991, I-12). Gamma Phi Beta, founded in 1882, was the first women's organization named as a sorority. Even though other women's groups were previously founded, they were incorporated as fraternities.

Many of today's sororities belong to the National Panhellenic Conference (NPC). The purpose of the NPC is "to foster interfraternity relationships, to assist collegiate chapters of the NPC member groups, and to cooperate with colleges and universities in maintaining the highest scholastic and social standards" (cited in Owen, 1991, p. I-37). Beginning in 1902 as the Intersorority Conference, the NPC now represents twenty-six women's fraternities. The NPC offers a variety of services to its members, including regional and national conferences, publications, and a full staff at the national office in Indianapolis.

Greek Letter Professional Groups.   In 1909 the black Greek letter movement began as a means "by which cultural interaction and community service could be maintained" (cited in Owen, 1991, p. I-41). Community service and cultural interaction were formalized as purposes in 1930, when the National Pan-Hellenic Council (NPHC) was established; it now represents eight national Greek letter community service fraternities and sororities. Over 900,000 affiliated members belong to the NPHC. The NPHC councils "are designed to assure that member organizations maintain their distinct identity of promoting and providing community services. NPHC organizations embrace a service for life philosophy and aim to assure the continuance of social action, political empowerment, and economic development" (cited in Owen, 1991, p. I-43).

The Professional Fraternity Association (PFA) began in 1977 with the consolidation of the Professional Panhellenic Association and the Professional Interfraternity Conference. The purpose of the PFA "shall be to advocate and encourage excellence in scholarship;

advancement of professional and interfraternity ethics; cooperation among member fraternities for the advancement of fraternal ideals, and loyalty to alma mater" (cited in Owen, 1991, p. I–46). Thirty-four professional fraternities are members of the PFA; their central office is located in Indianapolis.

Faculty advisers of fraternities and sororities come from all areas of college and university academic and student affairs. Most advisers are alumni or alumnae of the fraternity or sorority they advise. Their prior experience provides them with a knowledge of the culture, organization, rituals, and history of the fraternity or sorority.

Fraternity executives also may belong to the Fraternity Executives Association (FEA). The FEA was organized in 1930 in an effort for chief executives of fraternities and sororities to discuss mutual problems and concerns. The FEA "shall at all times be operated exclusively to further the common business interest of the members of the Corporation by promoting, supporting, and encouraging the free discussion and exchange of ideas relating to college fraternal organizations" (cited in Owen, 1991, p. I-56). The FEA sponsors an annual national conference at which currently seventy-five voting members participate in developing the association.

Campus advisers to men's and women's fraternities may belong to the Association of Fraternity Advisors (AFA), mentioned earlier. Founded in 1976 in Indianapolis, the AFA has approximately one thousand regular and affiliate members. The AFA leadership is composed of elected executive officers working with a central office in Indianapolis. The purpose of the AFA is "to provide for the cooperative association and professional stimulation of those persons engaged in the advisement of fraternities and sororities; to formulate and maintain high professional standards . . .; to provide a forum through publications, conferences, and informal interactions for the sharing of ideas and concerns . . .; to stimulate educational programming and student development concepts within local chapters . . .; to promote research and experimentation . . .; to encourage interested and qualified persons to seek student personnel positions in postsecondary educational institutions . . .; and to maintain positive and supportive working relationships with related professional student affairs associations, with national fraternity and sorority organizations, and with national interfraternity organizations" (cited in Owen, 1991, p. I-62).

Realizing that they would benefit from meeting to discuss their common interests, the editors of NPC and PFA publications organized the College Fraternity Editors Association (CFEA) in 1923. The purpose of the CFEA is "to stimulate and encourage those engaged in college fraternity journalism and communications; to form a center for the communication and exchange of views of all those interested in fraternity communications; to establish a community of interest through personal contacts; to raise the standard of fraternity journalism and communications; to publish information helpful to its members; and generally to do those things that will aid in elevating our profession and tend toward an intelligent understanding of the general college and professional fraternities and sororities and honor societies by administrators, students, and the general public" (cited in Owen, 1991, p. I-70). The CFEA, which currently has approximately 450 members, also hosts an annual conference.

Residence Hall

Campus housing accommodations have been provided for students since Oxford and Cambridge developed residential colleges in the thirteenth century. Male students living in the early residential colleges were to be educated as gentlemen scholars (Rudolph, 1962). In American higher education, residential components accompanied the founding of institutions across the country. In 1890, for example, President Eliot of Harvard University split classroom responsibilities from the student relations outside the classroom and created the first dean of men position (Cowley, 1937). This development and the growth of student government organizations allowed students in residence halls increased opportunities for beginning residential governing bodies.

Campuswide residence hall associations (RHAs) were established at many colleges and universities in the early twentieth century. In 1954, the Midwest Dormitory Conference was founded at Iowa State University by Iowa State University, the University of Colorado, the University of Missouri, and the University of Northern Iowa, to encourage the exchange of ideas and information. In 1961, the Inter-Mountain Residence Hall Association (IMRHA) affiliated with the Association of College and University Residence Halls to form the National Association of College and University Residence Halls (NACURH). Its purpose is to "design and facilitate programs and informational services to promote the educational goals of residence hall students through discussion groups, seminars, and speakers at the annual conference and other means of information exchange throughout the year" (cited in Stoner, Spain, Rasche, and Horton, 1993, p. 169).

Today, NACURH has over 450 affiliated member institutions, hosts an annual conference of approximately 2,300 delegates, has eight regions in the United States and Canada, and is the largest student-operated organization in the country. NACURH offers a variety of services to institutions, including several publications; honorary recognition to students through the National Residence Hall Honorary (NRHH), peer substance abuse programs delivered by the Student Action Teams (SAT), and central resources from the National Information Center (NIC). All of these services are located on university and college campuses and staffed by student leaders and volunteers.

There are also many statewide residence hall organizations. These state organizations are similar to NACURH regional organizations in that they have a state board of directors, various committees, and an adviser from a member institution. One example of a typical purpose of a state association is "to involve all state institutions, to unify the state, increase communication, be a support network, provide conferences for planning and programming, and to have a state directory resource list" (Florida Association of Residence Halls, 1996, p. 1). State associations typically host an annual conference, and in some cases hold a leadership mini-conference for the residence hall associations' executive board members.

Institutionally, RHAs traditionally are organized with an executive board consisting of a president, vice president, secretary, treasurer, and adviser. The RHA may be structured in one of three ways: (1) an area or building government with a central RHA, (2) a central RHA with representatives from individual buildings or areas, or (3) an area or building government with no central RHA. The RHA often is responsible for creating programs, forming policy, addressing quality-of-life issues for the residence hall program, allocating money, and recommending contracts and vendors (Verry, 1993).

The advisers of the hall, area, institutional, state, regional, and national organizations are exclusively from campus housing staff. The advisers may hold positions as chief housing officers; senior, mid-level, or entry-level professionals; or graduate staff. Osteen (1988) recommends an advising model in which the campuswide RHA is advised by a central housing office staff member, the area governing body is advised by an area staff member, and the hall-level governing body is advised by a hall staff member. Komives and Tucker (1993) confirm the validity of this approach in their national study of successful RHA themes. They also find that to be successful, RHAs must establish a system of leadership training and have a clearly focused purpose, staff committed to student involvement, several sources of funding, and a system of recognition and rewards.

Because advisers to RHAs are exclusively housing staff, many of these advisers belong to the Association of College and University Housing Officers-International (ACUHO-I). This association, founded in 1950, provides professional development; policy assistance; and resources through the annual conference, publications, drive-in workshops, institutes, and consulting services. Close to one thousand institutions are affiliated with ACUHO-I. The ACUHO-I central office is located in Columbus, Ohio.

Honors and Recognition

Honors and recognition societies have a rich history on college and university campuses. The number of honors and recognition societies rapidly grew in the early 1900s. In 1925, a meeting held in Kansas City was the first formal gathering of eighteen such organizations (Owen, 1991, p. I-50). This early meeting provided the platform upon which the Association of College Honor Societies (ACHS) was formed. Today, approximately seventy honor societies and forty recognition societies are members of the ACHS. The association archive has been established at Muhlenberg College in Allentown, Pennsylvania.

The purpose of the Association of College Honor Societies is "to act as the coordinating agency for college and university honor societies . . .; to provide facilities for the consideration of matters of mutual interest, such as administrative problems, establishment and maintenance of scholastic and other standards, membership costs, functions of honor societies, and prevention of undesirable duplication and competition among honor societies; to define honor societies of the several types and to classify existing societies into their proper categories under these definitions; to cooperate with college and university faculty and administrative officers in developing and maintaining high standards and useful functions within honor societies which are organized or seek to be organized; and to collect, publish, and distribute information and data of value to honor societies, colleges and universities, and publishers of directories and journals" (cited in Owen, 1991, p. I-52).

The ACHS draws a distinction between honor societies and recognition societies. An honor society is "an association of primarily collegiate chapters whose purposes are to recognize and encourage high scholarship and/or leadership achievement in some broad or specialized field of study" (cited in Owen, 1991, p. I-51). A general honor society is defined as "one which receives into membership individuals from one or all schools and colleges of an institution who have achieved high scholarship and who fulfill such additional requirements of distinction in some broad field of study, research, and culture or in general leadership as the society has established" (cited in Owen, 1991, p. I-51). Examples of honor and general honor societies are Mortar Board Senior Honor Society (service, scholarship, and leadership), Phi Kappa Phi (scholarship), Order of the Coif (law), Gamma Theta Upsilon (geography), Tau Beta Pi (engineering), Alpha Lambda Delta (freshman scholarship), and Phi Alpha Theta (history).

A recognition society is defined as one that "confers membership in recognition of a student's interest and participation in some field of collegiate study or activity, with more liberal membership requirements than are prescribed for general and specialized honor societies. Accordingly, recognition societies are not eligible for membership in the Association of College Honor Societies" (cited in Owen, 1991, p. I-54). Examples of recognition societies are Blue Key (student activities), Scabbard and Blade (military), Sigma Delta Psi (athletics), and Beta Beta Beta (biology).

The advisers of the honors and recognition societies generally are from the faculty and staff of the college. Often these advisers are alumni or alumnae of the society or are faculty in the department the society represents, or they are inducted as honorary members of the society they advise.

Military

Student military organizations were founded over two hundred years ago, when the concept of military training was integrally linked to institutions of higher education. These organizations "within degree-granting institutions of higher learning" possessed the underlying philosophy "to educate citizens in the principles and fundamentals of war" (Army ROTC, 1996, p. I-1). As these organizations evolved from earlier philosophies and structures, the Reserve Officer Training Corps (ROTC) emerged. Today's ROTC is organized with three separate branches: the Army ROTC, Air Force ROTC, and Navy-Marine ROTC.

Advisers to the individual programs at institutions are military officers who serve as instructors in the ROTC program. The advisers generally are assigned an incoming class, and work with the class members during their four-year education. The advisers work closely with the students, assisting them with personal, career, academic, and military service concerns. Students involved in these programs also may be involved in civic volunteer activities, color guard and drill teams, intramural sports, student government, or any other university and college student organization.

Navy-Marine ROTC.   The Navy-Marine ROTC (NROTC) was established "to develop midshipmen morally, mentally, and physically and to imbue them with the highest ideals of duty, honor and loyalty in order to commission college graduates as naval officers who possess a basic professional background, are motivated toward careers in the naval service, and have a potential for future development in mind and character so as to assume the highest responsibilities of command, citizenship, and government" (Navy-Marine Corps ROTC, 1997, p. 1).

As of January 1997, sixty-eight universities and colleges were hosts to NROTC programs in all fifty states and the District of Columbia, Panama Canal Zone, Virgin Islands of Puerto Rico, and Guam. Students who begin an NROTC program enter as midshipmen appointed to the U.S. Naval Reserve. During the four-year college matriculation, midshipmen take courses in military science and tactics, and in the history and traditions of the Navy. In the summer, midshipmen take part in one or more cruises. On completion of the four-year program, a graduate receives a commission in the Navy or Marine Corps.

The battalion is the organization for the freshmen through senior classes. The battalion is further organized into companies commanded by a midshipman or officer candidate (OC) with the rank of midshipman captain, assisted by an executive officer and staff. These students are responsible for all battalion events and activities.

The NROTC program was founded in 1926, and since 1946 more than seventy thousand men and women have received their commissions through the Navy-Marine ROTC.

Air Force ROTC. The Air Force ROTC is "designed to recruit, educate and commission officer candidates through college campus programs based on Air Force requirements" (United States Air Force, 1996, p. 1). The first Air Force ROTC units were established between 1920 and 1923 at the University of California at Berkeley, Georgia Institute of Technology, the University of Illinois, the University of Washington, Massachusetts Institute of Technology, and Texas Agricultural and Mechanical College. Following World War II, General Eisenhower signed General Order No. 124, establishing Air Force ROTC units at seventy-eight colleges and universities throughout the nation. Women were enrolled in the commissioning program in 1956. The 1964 ROTC Vitalization Act established scholarships (United States Air Force, 1996).

As of January 1995, there were Air Force ROTC units at 146 colleges and universities in forty-five states and the District of Columbia and Puerto Rico. Additionally, 699 separate cross-town enrollment programs in other institutions of higher education were supported by one of the 146 host institutions. Students beginning the program enroll as cadets attending courses in general military science. After completing the first two years of course work, and upon being selected, students may enter the professional officer course, continuing with attendance at a four-week summer field training program and leadership laboratory. Upon graduation, "all cadets are enlisted in the Air Force Reserve and assigned to the Obligated Reserve Section" (United States Air Force, 1996, p. 2).

Army ROTC.   The Army ROTC maintains a philosophy that "dates back to the colonial times when the colonial frontiersman accepted responsibility to take up arms for his own and his neighbors' common defense. Since the emergence of our nation we have been dedicated to the proposition that national defense is a responsibility of citizenship and that those men and women to whom our society has offered a higher education incur the responsibility of leadership. It is through the Army ROTC program that this philosophy is formalized and implemented" (Army ROTC, 1996, p. I-1).

Army ROTC began when the concept of military training was introduced into institutions of higher education in 1819; Captain Alden Partridge, a West Point graduate, founded the American Literary, Scientific and Military Academy (now Norwich University). He is regarded as the "Father of AROTC." The Virginia Military Institute in 1839 and the Citadel in 1842 were the next degree-granting institutions established. In 1908, Congress authorized the appointment of doctors as reserve officers in the Medical Corps. In 1916, the National Defense Act formally established the Army ROTC for emergency duty. Since 1916, two other acts have affected the Army ROTC: the 1955 Reserve Forces Act establishing reserve commissions and the 1964 ROTC Vitalization Act establishing scholarships (Army ROTC, 1996).

Army ROTC programs are found at 353 colleges, universities, and junior colleges in all fifty states and Guam and the District of Columbia (Army ROTC, 1991). Students enter the program as cadets. Typically, cadets take four years to complete their program. The combined cadet corps of freshmen through senior classifications represents the battalion. The cadet corps is further organized into companies, platoons, and squads, each with a student commander or leader.

Over two hundred institutions participate in Scabbard and Blade, an Army ROTC national honorary society. Founded in 1904 by five cadets at the University of Wisconsin, Scabbard and Blade raises the standards of education and encourages good leadership and fellowship among the detachments (Army ROTC, 1996).

Sports

Student involvement in organizations providing leisure, fitness, and sports has exploded on college and university campuses in the past twenty years. Student interest has been the impetus for the funding of multimillion-dollar facilities, extensive graduate and professional staffing, transportation systems, and equipment purchases in order to support the wide variety of sports organizations available to students.

During the eighteenth century, members of the upper class on the East Coast developed club sports in the European tradition, representing such interests as bridge, chess, rugby, and sailing. In 1734, the Jockey Club was formed in Charleston, Virginia, marking the founding of the first recognized recreational sport. During the nineteenth century, as the working class found additional time for recreation, sports clubs such as baseball, archery, and track and field were organized. In 1814, Georgetown University permitted students to swim, box, fence, and play handball. The YMCA was founded in 1851 and the YWCA in 1866, to provide facilities and activities for informal sports such as bike riding, roller skating, and "early bird" swimming (Bayless, Mull, and Ross, 1983).

Interest in physical education grew as public education became established. By the end of the eighteenth century, teacher training for physical education was institutionalized. In 1913, "the first organized intramural sport program with a faculty adviser began, when the University of Michigan and the Ohio State University, offered intramural competition in various sports. Dr. Elmer Mitchell, the 'Father of Intramurals,' authored the first intramural textbook in 1925" (Bayless, Mull, and Ross, 1983, p. 135). During the twentieth century, sports proliferated on college and university campuses.

Sports programs were established by students to meet the varying needs of traditional and special-interest groups. *Student organizations involved in sports* is a collective term comprising four different types of sports: (1) instructional sport, or the teaching of skills and strategies for the purpose of educating participants; (2) recreational sport for the participation and fun of involvement; (3) athletic sport for achieving excellence in performance further defined as winning; and (4) professional sport, which places a higher priority on entertainment and financial rewards (Bayless, Mull, and Ross, 1983).

Recreational sports are further divided into four separate categories: informal sport, a self-directed activity; intramural sport, which involves structured contests and tournaments limited to the institution from which it was originated; extramural sport, which involves structured contests and tournaments between different institutions; and club sport, which involves groups organized because of a common interest in a particular sport (Bayless, Mull, and Ross, 1983).

One other way of classifying student sports is by the type of competition. Team sports include soccer, rugby, and basketball. Meet sports include track, swimming, and gymnastics. Dual sports include tennis, handball, and racquetball. Individual sports include skiing, fencing, and target shooting. Special event sports are represented by activities such as new games or superstar competitions (Bayless, Mull, and Ross, 1983).

An example of a purpose statement for a sports club is that of the University of Wisconsin-LaCrosse Women's Rugby Football Club (1996, pp. 1–2):

> To promote women's rugby in all its aspects within the university; to ensure that women's rugby played within the university system is played in accordance with the laws of the game of Rugby Football and the declaration of Amateurism of the International Rugby Football Board; to acquire property and money in order to carry out the union's purposes; to work toward the formation of a national women's rugby union with the same purposes as this union; and that the rules and regulations of the UW-L Rugby Football Club shall be followed when not inconsistent with the rules and regulations of UW-LaCrosse.

Another example of a purpose statement for an informal club is from the Ball State University Country Kickers Dance Club (1997, p. 1). Its purpose is to "promote the teaching of American Country dances and traditions by providing formal dance instruction and recreational dancing."

As the demand for trained personnel increased, so too did interest in forming a collective organization. In the 1950s, the National Intramural Association was formed; in 1975, the organization was renamed the National Intramural-Recreational Sport Association (NIRSA). The purpose of NIRSA "is to provide for the education and development of professional and student members and to foster quality recreational programs, facilities, and services for diverse populations. NIRSA demonstrates its commitment to excellence by utilizing resources which promote ethical and healthy lifestyle choices" (National Intramural-Recreational Sport Association, 1996b, p. 1).

NIRSA now represents nearly 650 institutional, 1,700 professional, 725 student, and 100 associate members, serving more than twelve million sports participants throughout the world (National

Intramural-Recreational Sport Association, 1996a). The NIRSA national center office is located in Corvallis, Oregon.

Advisers of student sports organizations may be involved in a variety of capacities. Some may work with a specific student organization. These advisers generally have a special interest as a participant or proponent of the sport that the organization addresses. Others may serve on an advisory council or board that conducts studies; serves as a liaison between staff, students, administrators, and participants; makes recommendations regarding policy and procedure; or serves as a sounding board to influence decisions (Bayless, Mull, and Ross, 1983).

The roles and responsibilities of advisers vary widely in sports organizations. For example, the adviser of the Ball State University Country Kickers Dance Club serves in an advisory capacity to the executive and does not have voting rights (Country Kickers Dance Club, 1997). The adviser of the University of Wisconsin-LaCrosse Women's Rugby Football Club "advises and stimulates interest in the organization; provides guidance in the development and implementation of programs and activities; serves as liaison between the University and the organization, interpreting, if necessary, University policy or philosophy; and attends meetings and activities regularly" (University of Wisconsin-LaCrosse Women's Rugby Football Club, 1996, p. 5).

Students continue to create new sports organizations to explore their interest areas. Across the country more than four hundred sports organizations are registered on campus organization lists.

Departmental

Numerous student organizations are associated with academic departments. These student organizations can be traced back to the literary and debate clubs of the early nineteenth century. Throughout the years, students became increasingly invested in their academic departments as sources of academic assistance, career planning information, and conferences and meetings. Students within departments have a common course of study and naturally associate with one another in class. The various departmental student organizations that have been founded and registered on campuses range from geology and botany clubs to public relations societies and theater troupes.

An example of a purpose statement for a departmental student organization is the Appalachian State University Public Relations Student Society of America. Its purpose is "to encourage the understanding of current theories and procedures in the practice of public relations; to provide students of public relations an opportunity to become acquainted not only with their peers, but with professional practitioners as well; to encourage students to adhere to the highest ideals and principles of the practice of public relations and to instill in them a professional attitude; the purpose and objectives of this chapter shall be consistent with the policies and procedures and under the authority of the Appalachian State University governing clubs" (Public Relations Student Society of America, 1996, p. 1).

The University of Wisconsin-LaCrosse chapter of the American Marketing Association is another example of a departmental student organization. Its purpose is as follows:

> To represent the ideals of the AMA to the fullest while providing our members with opportunities to realize their marketing potential within AMA; to develop sound thinking in marketing theory and more exact knowledge and definition of marketing principles; to develop better public understanding and appreciation of marketing problems; to encourage and uphold sound, honest practices, and to keep marketing work on a high ethical plane; to promote friendly relations between students, faculty, and business people; to encourage participation in group activities, events, and projects that will enable the students to enhance their marketing skills; and to establish networking through speakers at chapter meetings and conferences [University of Wisconsin-LaCrosse American Marketing Association Collegiate Chapter, 1996, p. 1].

Another example is from the University of Florida Geomatics Student Association (1996, p. 1): "dedicated to the purpose of maintaining and promoting the status of surveying and mapping as an ideal profession, the Surveying and Mapping Student Chapter (GSA) was organized to recognize the characteristics of an individual, deemed to be fundamental to the successful pursuit of a surveying and mapping career, and to aid in the development of those characteristics in the Geomatics student."

Advisers to departmental student organizations almost exclusively come from departmental faculty. The responsibilities of the adviser can be quite different from one departmental student organization to another. In the case of the Public Relations Student Society of America (PRSSA), the faculty adviser "shall teach at least one, but not all, of the public relations courses listed on the application for a PRSSA charter, who shall be recognized as the official faculty representative in and to the chapter and who shall act as the official link between the student chapter and the PRSSA" (Public Relations Student Society of America, 1996, p. 2). The Appalachian State University PRSSA additionally requires one or two professional advisers "who are members of the PRSSA, at least one of whom must be a member who is accredited, who shall represent the practice rather than the academic" (Public Relations Student Society of America, 1996, p. 2). The person advising the University of Wisconsin-LaCrosse American Marketing Association Collegiate Chapter (1996, p. 3) "must be a professional member of the Association; will serve for at least one full school year, shall attend the meetings of the collegiate chapter, and shall aid and advise the group on matters under consideration; shall be responsible for the continuity of records and other property of the collegiate chapter; . . . and shall be the official contact with the AMA Headquarters."

The Geomatics Student Association at the University of Florida (1996, p. 1) requires the adviser to "act in an advising capacity to the chapter"; he or she "is morally obligated to make the chapter officers aware of their duties. The adviser shall serve as the custodian of the chapter's rituals and paraphernalia."

Departmental student organizations may belong to regional, national, or international associations, which often host conventions. These larger gatherings provide students with opportunities to improve their leadership skills, develop networks with companies and agencies, listen to keynote speakers, and present papers and programs to colleagues.

Special Interest

The special-interest category comprises the greatest number and diversity of student organizations. Throughout the years, students exposed to fads, subcultures, new games, media, and new ideas formed a wide variety of new student organizations. A few examples of special-interest student organizations are radio stations; lesbian, gay, and bisexual organizations; Habitat for Humanity; environmental action; and model railroading.

A number of spiritual and religious student organizations work closely with various campus ministries. Students participating in the New Center, Hillel, Inter-Varsity Christian Fellowship and so forth bring a common spiritual goal to their organizations. The support provided through these student organizations helps satisfy students' religious and spiritual needs. Advisers may be clergy from the community, or faculty and staff from the campus who have similar spiritual interests.

Ethnic and cultural organizations are an important segment of student life on campus. Hispanic and Latino student associations, African American student associations, Asian student associations, Caribbean student associations, and the like provide students with similar racial and ethnic heritages the opportunity to enjoy common interests. These student organizations have been able to identify their issues and concerns and to work collectively in securing the necessary resources to support academic centers, museums, retreats, programming, and activities. These groups receive funds allocated from the campus student government or campus general operating accounts in addition to funds contributed by members or raised by the group. Advisers to student ethnic and cultural organizations commonly share the racial or ethnic identity of the members. Campus administrators, faculty, or staff commonly serve as advisers. These organizations play an increasingly important role in the life of their college. The organizations assist campus officials in identifying student academic and social needs. Moreover, they often are able to assist in student recruitment and retention. It is likely that new student organizations will be formed in the future in part "because of the growing awareness that no set of categories can adequately reflect the full array of students. Further subgroups will emerge, both in regard to student background and situational differences" (El-Khawas, 1996, p. 74).

An example of a special-interest student organization is Ball State University Medieval Recreations, formerly known as the Society for Creative Anachronism. The organization's purpose is "to provide and promote active study and recreation of portions of pre-16th Century Western European history and activities" (Medieval Recreations, 1997, p. 1).

People for Animal Liberation is a student organization at Appalachian State University. This special-interest organization was formed "to promote harmonious living between all animals, human and non-human. The group will seek to actively educate the campus and community about animal rights issues. We will also provide a setting for open discussion on animal rights issues and vegetarianism" (People for Animal Liberation, 1996, p. 1).

Another example of a special-interest student organization is the Fantasy Roleplaying Club. Their purpose is as follows: "to promote the teaching and playing of any games leading to the enhancement and furtherance of role playing gaming; to originate, arrange, provide, and distribute, with or without compensation, games, pamphlets, magazines, and other literature; to originate, arrange, sponsor, and hold meetings and conventions, lectures and talks, for the further advancement of gaming; and to attend tournaments, conventions, lectures, competitions, and other activities related to gaming" (Fantasy Roleplaying Club, 1992, p. 1).

The role of the adviser and the range of the adviser's responsibilities in these organizations varies. For the People for Animal Liberation, the adviser "shall attend meetings whenever possible, shall assist in providing guidance and planning to the organization in its attempt to fulfill the previously stated goals. The faculty adviser shall also provide guidance in assuring adherence to the policies of [Appalachian State University]" (People for Animal Liberation, 1996, p. 3). For the Fantasy Roleplaying Club, the adviser "shall have no responsibilities other than to counsel the executive board or membership on various activities as the club is considering" (Fantasy Roleplaying Club, 1992, p. 1).

Many campus student organizations may be members of larger state, regional, national, or international associations; these larger associations will have an adviser working with them. Advisers of the campus organizations and larger associations tend to be campus faculty members, administrators, or staff members who have a specific interest in the organization. The adviser can play an integral role in officer and member training and other programming of the special-interest group. For instance, in a religious student organization, the adviser may be a campus minister. The campus minister not only advises the executive board on institutional matters but also may instruct the organization in spiritual matters. The level of involvement required and responsibility assumed by the adviser is likely to come from the organization's constitution or purpose statement, or may be negotiated with the organization's leaders and members.

PART TWO

Essential Knowledge and Skills

CHAPTER 3

Roles and Functions
of Advisers

In this chapter we identify the qualities, skills, and knowledge you will find essential in your routine work with student groups and organizations. We provide information about constitutions and the various roles you will adopt or work with as an adviser: mentor, supervisor, teacher, leader, and follower. We also discuss at length a critical aspect of advising, namely, motivating students. Throughout the chapter, we have provided examples of forms, schedules, and case studies to use for training and for maintaining the group.

Constitutions

The constitution is the most important organizational document. It gives the organization and membership purpose, direction, and guidance. The document is not intended to be static; rather it should be reviewed periodically so that it fits the need of the contemporary student group. The language should be clear and concise, leaving little to interpretation. Depending on the complexity of the student organization, the constitution may be only one page in length. More complex organizations have fifteen- to twenty-page constitutions. Whether an organization is new and in the process of creating a constitution, established and undertaking a periodic review of its constitution, or established and reviewing the constitution for the first time in twenty years, the organization's constitution must include several important components, as shown in Exhibit 3.1.

Whether an organization is framing or revising a constitution, several issues should be considered by the organization's leaders. First, the constitution should include all the elements required by the campus office that registers student organizations. Second, if the organization is the custodian of a foundation account, scholarship, or fellowship funds, there should be information about how funds will be distributed if the organization is dissolved. Third, a constitutional committee should be identified by the organization's president to review the document periodically. Fourth, the adviser should meet with the committee to provide historical perspective and advice on legal or financial matters, and to listen to discussion. Finally, the constitutional approval process should be reviewed by the committee to gain an understanding of the time involved for constitutional approval. This process can vary from campus to campus, but in most cases the constitution is approved by a committee, presented to the membership, and adopted by a two-thirds vote of the membership. The constitution then is sent either to the student activities office or to whatever campus organization registers student organizations, where it is kept on file. As adviser, you should have a copy of the constitution and should review it at least annually to stay informed as to its contents.

Adviser Roles

You must play numerous roles while working with individual students and student organizations. Naturally, you will be most comfortable in the role with which you are most familiar; however, you must understand that although comfort in a specific role may diminish your sense of needing to know about other roles, student groups and organizations will continually challenge you to assume and work with various roles depending on you or your situation. If you understand the variety of roles, take time to practice techniques associated with the various roles, and work with student groups and organizations to reach a collective agreement as to your limitations and expectations of the roles, you will be much more effective in your work with student groups. Let us look now at these essential roles.

Mentor

Faculty and staff members who have worked with student groups and organizations can identify many students who attribute their

Exhibit 3.1. Elements of a Constitution

Constitution of the _____ club of _____

Article I: Name

Section 1: The name of this organization shall be _____

_____.

Article II: Purpose

Section 1: The purpose of the _____ club is to _____

_____.

Article III: Officers

Section 1: Officers serving as the Executive Board shall be the President, Vice President, Secretary and Treasurer.

Section 2: The term of office for Executive Board members shall be one year or until their successors are elected.

Section 3: Executive Board members must be in good standing with the institution.

Section 4: The Adviser shall be a member of the institution's faculty or staff. The Adviser has no vote in the organization.

Article IV: Membership

Section 1: Membership is open to any student. [The sections for this article will vary according to the particular needs of the organization.]

Article V: Election of Officers

Section 1: Election of officers will occur at the last meeting of the spring term.

Section 2: Each member in attendance at the last meeting of the spring term shall be accorded one vote per office.

Section 3: All elections will be held by secret ballot.

Section 4: A simple majority vote will constitute an officer election.

Article VI: Meetings

Section 1: All meetings will be held on the second and fourth Tuesday of each month at a time and place to be determined by the organization.

Section 2: All members must attend a majority of the meetings held during the year to be eligible to vote at officer elections.

Article VII: Amendments

Section 1: Amendments to this constitution shall be adopted by a two-thirds vote of the members present at a regular meeting following the meeting at which the proposed amendment was distributed.

success to the relationship they have developed with their adviser. This relationship may continue for many years. Mentoring can be defined as a one-to-one learning relationship between an older person and a younger person based on modeling behavior and on an extended, shared dialogue (DeCoster and Brown, 1982).

The mentor can be characterized as a person having (1) a knowledge of the profession; (2) enthusiasm for the profession and its importance; (3) a genuine interest in the professional and personal development of new professionals; (4) a warmth and understanding in relating to students and staff in all types of settings; (5) a high yet achievable standard of performance for self and others; (6) an active involvement in and support of professional associations; (7) an honest emotional rapport; (8) the available time and energy to give freely to others; (9) the time to stimulate others to extend themselves intellectually, emotionally, and professionally; (10) the initiative to expose others to a select but broad-based network of professionals who can help with development of the new professional; and (11) the care to guard young professionals from taking on too much too soon in their career.

Odiorne identifies five qualities that characterize good mentors (adapted from a citation in Schuh and Carlisle, 1991, p. 505):

- Good mentors have been successful in their own professional endeavors.
- Good mentors behave in ways worthy of emulation.
- Good mentors are supportive in their work with subordinates. They are patient, slow to criticize, and willing to work with those who are less well developed in their careers.
- Good mentors are not afraid to delegate tasks to colleagues and are not threatened by others who exhibit talent and initiative. They provide support for protégés who have been unsuccessful and provide plenty of praise for those who have been successful.
- Good mentors provide periodic, detailed, and honest feedback to the protégé.

Boatman (1986) suggests that student leaders can play an integral role in developing the environment in which an effective peer mentoring relationship can take place. This relationship allows students to direct the leadership development of their peers. Peer mentoring relationships can serve as a supplement to the more traditional adult-protégé relationships on campuses.

Exhibit 3.2 is a mentor activity that you can use with students to assist them in identifying mentors. You can use the form with individuals or with several organization members, with the executive board, or as an adviser training activity. Exhibit 3.3 is a case study about mentoring. You can use this progressive case study with executive boards, representative bodies, or advisers.

Supervisor

Although some writers would disagree (for example, Kowalski and Conlogue, 1996), we believe that there are far more similarities than differences between advising and supervising. Dunkel (1996) identifies the components of a supervisory cycle (see Figure 3.1); many of these components are transferable to effective advising. The six stages of the supervisory cycle are team building, performance planning, communication, recognition, self-assessment, and evaluation.

Team Building.   In team building, your role is to work with the president and executive board soon after their appointment or

Figure 3.1.
The Supervisory Cycle

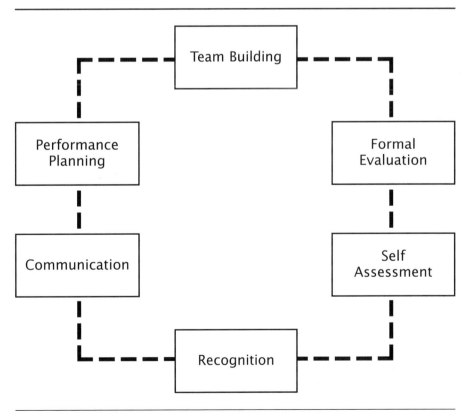

Source: Jardine, 1996; Carr, 1995. Used by permission.

Exhibit 3.2. Mentor Activity

Directions: Give a copy of the sheet to each student, allowing him or her ample time to complete the questions prior to a facilitated discussion.

Facilitator Questions

1. Are you still in contact with these individuals?
2. As you review the names, are there consistencies in their gender, race, or age?
3. What traits do these individuals have in common?
4. Who initiated each of these relationships?
5. What characteristics do these individuals possess that you have tried to emulate?
6. Can you identify other thoughts regarding these individuals?

Identify those individuals who have guided or assisted you with the following:

Your academics

Your career

Your spirituality

Your special interests and hobbies

Your family

Exhibit 3.3. Mentor Case Study

Directions: You can use the following progressive case study with groups of five or six students or advisers. Distribute the initial case to the participants and allow them time to complete the first two questions. When the questions are completed, take ten to fifteen minutes to discuss participants' answers. Following discussion, hand out the first update and again allow time to complete the questions that follow; continue with the second and third updates in the same way. To finish the activity, allow the participants time to complete the final questions prior to discussion.

Initial Case

You graduated with a master's degree in college student affairs two years ago. You are a single white male working as a full-time copyeditor for the university press. It is fall term, and you are beginning your third year as adviser to the Journalism Club. The Journalism Club is one of two hundred recognized student organizations at the university.

Your executive board of five students was elected four weeks earlier, and the students have already participated in a training program to familiarize them with their responsibilities as officers. The president, Cathy Smith, a white female in her junior year, has asked if she could visit with you for an hour to discuss her journalism career, stating that you know all the right people and have all the answers.

1. As the organization's adviser, what are your questions at this point in the situation?

2. What actions do you take at this point in the situation?

Update One

You have met with Cathy Smith and discussed the options she is interested in pursuing in journalism. She has asked you to review her résumé and serve as a reference for her. You have agreed to review her résumé, but you are uncomfortable in serving as a reference because you really do not know her.

1. As the organization's adviser, what are your questions at this point in the situation?

2. What actions do you take at this point in the situation?

Update Two

You have decided not to serve as a reference and have told Cathy the reason why. She appears to understand and instead has now asked you if you would call two or three publishing companies to open some doors in order for her to secure an internship next summer as a copyeditor.

1. As the organization's adviser, what are your questions at this point in the situation?

2. What actions do you take at this point in the situation?

Update Three

You have decided to call the company you interned for as a graduate student. You have told Cathy that you would make that call after you have had an opportunity to review some of her copyediting work. Upon review of her work, your sense is that she does not possess the level of skills you believe are necessary in order to do quality work.

1. As the organization's adviser, what are your questions at this point in the situation?

2. What actions do you take at this point in the situation?

Final Questions

1. What departments, agencies, or people should have been involved in this situation?

2. What kind of follow-up is necessary in this situation?

3. What other strategies could this mentor have employed in this situation?

4. Have you experienced a similar situation as an adviser?

election. Team building establishes relationships that will enhance the ability of the organization's leadership, members, and adviser to work together. It is important for you to understand your strengths and weaknesses, work styles, and relationships with authority, and any intervening variables that affect your ability to work. Student leaders need to understand their pressures, strengths and weaknesses, work styles, goals, and ability to feel empowered, and any circumstances that affect their ability to work. A meeting between you and the student leaders to identify and discuss these factors will help establish a relationship of open communication and understanding. Exhibit 3.4 is a teamwork activity that executive board members can use to generate and discuss techniques to improve the symptoms listed.

A team-building retreat or workshop is essential. Teamwork does not occur by accident. It is intentional, genuine, and active. In the interest of saving space we will use the terms *retreat* and *workshop* interchangeably, although we recognize that there are some inherent differences between the two. Student organization leaders can work with you to plan a productive retreat.

To begin the workshop process, the planners need to identify the desired outcomes of the activity: Are they to be focused on socializing, formulating a strategy or plan, discussing membership recruitment (Blank and Kershaw, 1993), or something else? Second, planners should identify a location that provides a special environment. Finding a location away from campus and free of interruptions is vital to a productive retreat. Camps, conference centers, or rustic inns that charge modest fees can usually be found a short distance from many campuses. Third, planners need to build in a structure for the retreat. The environment will provide an informal, comfortable setting; a schedule that allows for time on task, breaks, meals, and casual free time will provide the needed structure. Fourth, you and the officers need to identify each person's roles and responsibilities. Identifying the facilitator of activities and the coordinators for meals is important in preparing for the retreat. Planners should also consider using a team-building activity early in the retreat schedule. The environment and atmosphere of working together away from campus will accomplish part of the team-building process, but intentional team-building activities will enhance the outcome.

You and student leaders also need to consider what will need attention following the retreat. For example, how can the value of the workshop be extended for the next weeks and months? Goals, schedules, or plans need to finalized and distributed by the planner. Notes ought to be sent to the participants thanking them for

Exhibit 3.4. Teamwork Activity

> **Directions:** Distribute a copy of the sheet to each participant. Allow them time to identify at least one technique to increase teamwork for each symptom listed. Following completion, discuss the techniques that participants have identified.

What do you do when you do not see evidence of cohesiveness and productivity or when cohesiveness and productivity begin to show signs of decline?

Symptoms	*Techniques to Improve*
Lack of participation in meeting	
Personal distance	
Putting effort in the wrong places	
Letting others do the work	
Putting off the start of new projects	
Slow progress	
Decreasing interpersonal contact	
"Same old stuff" attitude	
Inaccurate, late work	
Lack of direction	

their involvement and interaction; these notes are a good way of extending the value of the workshop back to the campus.

We have already mentioned that planners need to choose a facilitator for the retreat. One good strategy is to use an individual from outside the organization as a facilitator. This person will need to have strong facilitator skills and possess a knowledge of the organization, and he or she should be a person who can challenge the organization to develop plans consistent with the purpose of the retreat. A person from outside the organization can be a different, expert voice, someone who can introduce new activities or processes to meet the retreat's goals.

Performance Planning.   The second stage in the supervisory cycle is performance planning. Performance planning includes writing position descriptions, determining and listing expectations, and setting goals.

Each of the executive and key leadership positions in the organization should have a position description. Exhibits 3.5 through 3.9 are examples of position descriptions for the president, vice president, secretary, treasurer, and adviser. You should participate in an open discussion of these position descriptions immediately following the appointment or election of students to these positions. This initial meeting should include a discussion of adding or deleting elements of the position descriptions for the time of appointment or election. The position descriptions should then be agreed on and signed, and all officers should receive copies. From time to time during the year, the position descriptions should be reviewed in individual and group settings.

Another aspect of performance planning is setting expectations. Expectations can be generated and agreed on by several different groups. The institution may have a list of expectations for the adviser, including attending organizational meetings, meeting weekly with the president of the organization, meeting weekly with the executive officers of the organization, attending adviser training sessions, attending conferences, attending programs and events organized by the organization as often as possible, and learning the traditions and history of the organization. Expectations of the adviser also can be generated by the organization's members. These expectations might include providing occasional meals, attending the various meetings, being available, serving as a resource, or acting as a liaison to the administration. In addition, you can generate a list of expectations for the organization's members that might include informing you of decisions that are made, providing open and honest feedback, balancing their academic work with their activities, not expecting you to attend all events

Exhibit 3.5. President Job Description

The following represent duties for which an organization president might be responsible:

- Preside at organization meetings
- Facilitate executive board meetings
- Represent the organization to the institution
- Meet weekly with the adviser
- Be aware of all money matters
- Assist all executive officers
- Serve as spokesperson for the executive board and organization
- Provide motivation for the organization
- Prepare for all meetings
- Coordinate campuswide programs
- Serve on various committees or task forces
- Prepare prior to all interviews
- Be open to all opinions and input
- Provide follow-up to organizational tasks
- Inform the executive board of other meeting information
- Organize executive board retreats
- Prepare for the annual banquet
- Coordinate the executive board transition

Exhibit 3.6. Vice President Job Description

The following represent duties for which an organization vice president might be responsible:

- Preside at organization meetings in the absence of the president
- Serve as Parliamentarian
- Direct constitutional updating and revision
- Facilitate elections
- Submit term reports
- Serve as liaison to committees
- Perform other duties as directed by the president

Exhibit 3.7. Treasurer Job Description

The following represent duties for which an organization treasurer might be responsible:

- Prepare the organizational budget
- Serve as chair of a finance committee
- Prepare purchase orders, requisition forms, or supply requests
- Audit books twice per term with adviser
- Maintain a financial history of the organization
- Maintain a working relationship with institutional accounting
- Inform the executive board of all financial department personnel matters
- Serve on various committees and task forces
- Coordinate solicitations
- Claim all stolen or lost equipment
- Maintain an inventory of all equipment and its condition
- Make quarterly reports of all receipts and disbursements
- Perform other duties as directed by the president

Exhibit 3.8. Secretary Job Description

The following represent duties for which an organization secretary might be responsible:

- Record and maintain minutes of all organization meetings
- Send minutes to all appropriate members and institutional staff
- Prepare an agenda with the president for all meetings
- Keep the organization informed
- Maintain attendance (roll call) at all meetings
- Maintain a calendar of events
- Serve as the organization's recognition coordinator
- Maintain a phone and e-mail directory of all members
- Maintain name tags and folders for all members
- Organize an end-of-year slide show
- Reserve meeting rooms for the term and year
- Advise on public relations
- Maintain the office
- Perform other duties as assigned by the president

Exhibit 3.9. Adviser Job Description

The following represent duties for which an organization adviser might be responsible:

- Meet weekly with the organization's president
- Meet weekly with the executive board
- Attend all organization meetings
- Give a report during the organization meeting
- Keep the executive board informed on institutional matters
- Maintain a relationship with institutional accounting
- Audit finances with the treasurer
- Attend and advise delegations during trips to conferences, business meetings, and so on
- Provide developmental activities to the executive board to assist in developing group cohesiveness
- Assist the organization with election concerns
- Respect and encourage all organizational functions
- Provide a background history and insight to the organization
- Maintain a history of the organization
- Hold a goal-setting meeting for the executive board
- Coordinate an executive board retreat annually
- Assist with risk management decisions

and activities, assisting with leadership development of the organization's members, or asking for help. The lists of expectations should be developed early in your year of duty with the students. These expectations should be discussed openly, agreed to, and reviewed periodically.

One other consideration in performance planning is goal setting. Goal setting can be completed for the organization by the president and executive board, with your assistance. Goal setting for the year is important for knowing what work will be required at various times of the year, what positions will need to be filled and the subsequent training involved, or what finances will be committed. Goal setting also can be accomplished for individual events, activities, and projects.

The process of setting goals involves some key ingredients. Goal statements must be measurable and realistic, and they must include a time period for attainment. Setting goals that the organization cannot attain can lead to frustration and a sense of under-achievement by the students. Each goal statement should be followed by a set of objectives and an action plan for achieving each objective. An example of a goal statement, a set of objectives, and action plans is shown in Exhibit 3.10.

Communication.   The third stage of supervision that includes transferable knowledge for an adviser is regular communication and feedback. Communication is both verbal and nonverbal.

The actual words in verbal communication carry only a portion of the intended message. "A psychologist devised this message: Of the total impact of a message, 7 percent is verbal (word choice), 38 percent is vocal (oral expression), and 55 percent is facial expression" (St. John, 1985, p. 40). Students' posture, gestures, facial expression, hand and foot positions, and dress carry nonverbal messages. St. John (1985) concludes: (1) if a person is kept waiting for a meeting, the communication is one of a negative, disrespectful attitude; (2) the arrangement of furniture should not create obstacles to communication; (3) the surroundings should

---

Exhibit 3.10. Sample Goal Statement

Goal: To increase sorority chapter membership by 20 percent within the first two months of next year's fall term

Objective: To create a publicity campaign informing students about the chapter

Action plan: To send chapter representatives to summer orientation programs to talk about chapter activities

Action plan: To have the membership chair meet with the student activities graphics office staff to develop a membership recruitment brochure by November 1st

Action plan: To have the chapter publicity director send weekly public service announcements to the campus newspapers between September 1st and December 1st

Objective: To develop an agreement with the on-campus housing office to release contracts of students wanting to live in the chapter house

Action plan: To have the chapter president secure copies of other campus agreements by September 1st

Action plan: To have the chapter president and membership chair meet with the director of housing by September 10th

Objective: To develop a database of all chapter alumnae

Action plan: To have the membership chair take old chapter rosters to the alumni office to access addresses by September 30th

Action plan: To have the membership chair meet with the chapter technology chair to develop a database program by October 1st

be attractive and well maintained; (4) the proximity of the speaker and listener should be relatively close to give a welcoming feeling; (5) a person's posture can convey several messages such as energy, interest, confidence, or approachability; (6) gestures convey attitudes (for example, open palms are welcoming, a clenched fist, threatening); (7) facial expressions are clear indicators of interpersonal attitudes: for example, lack of eye contact expresses disinterest, nodding the head expresses approval, shaking the head expresses disagreement, and peering over one's glasses expresses skepticism; (8) the use of one's hands and feet convey messages: for example, a foot tapping on the floor indicates impatience, and crossed arms are a barrier; (9) the use of silence can serve to emphasize a point or can be sensed as boredom; and (10) voice characteristics convey emotions and attitudes: for example, speaking loudly can indicate anger, speaking quickly may indicate impatience. You can work with students to help them understand these aspects of nonverbal communication by videotaping exchanges and showing them while offering feedback. You also can use the communications activity found in Exhibit 3.11 to emphasize the importance of nonverbal communication. You can use this activity with any number of participants if the room has adequate space.

You need to be knowledgeable about several written forms of communication, including memos and letters, agendas, minutes, and resolutions. Students need to document their decisions and planning; the memos and letters they write create a record that can be used for planning specific activities, documenting phone calls, planning the year's calendar, or providing copies to individuals to inform them of happenings. Exhibit 3.12 is an example of a memo sent by a student to a vice president for student affairs. Memos should be written on the organization's letterhead if it is available; computer-generated letterhead is now very easy to create. The memo should always identify who is to receive copies.

As the organizational leaders plan for their regularly scheduled meetings, the president, working with the secretary, will generate an agenda for the formal meeting. The agenda, the "map" that will be followed during the meeting, is agreed on by the organization using proper order and is facilitated by the president. Exhibit 3.13 is a sample organizational agenda. During the meeting, the secretary takes minutes of the general discussion and the decisions agreed on. These minutes should report the money spent, the individuals who introduced motions and those who seconded them, dates of activities, and any other pertinent information that would benefit the organization. Minutes need not be a word-for-word transcription of the meeting; a summary will suffice. An example of a set of organizational minutes is shown in Exhibit 3.14.

Exhibit 3.11. Nonverbal Communication Activity

Back-to-Back Communication

Directions: Everyone except the facilitator of this activity needs to find a partner and sit down back to back. One person will be given a small picture of a boat (the facilitator can draw and make copies of a picture of a sailboat on water, a fish in the water, a sun, and two or three birds flying) and the other person will be given a blank piece of paper and a pen or pencil. (Make sure all the "drawers" are facing the same direction so that they cannot see another pair's boat picture).

The person with the picture describes the picture to his or her partners using any descriptive wording except the following words: bird, sun, boat, sail, fish, and water. The person drawing cannot ask any clarifying questions. All the person can do is draw what he or she hears the partner describe. Once most people appear to have finished, take the new drawings and hang them on the wall.

The facilitator can repeat the activity with a different picture and have the partners reverse roles. This time the "drawer" can ask clarifying questions, but again the person describing the picture may not use the key words. When the activity is completed, hang these pictures on the wall.

The facilitator can process this activity using the following questions:

1. For "drawer": What clues did your partner give you that were helpful?

2. For describer: What frustrated you?

3. For describer: What did you want to do that might have made this easier?

4. Everyone had the same picture to describe, so what happened? What is responsible for the differences in the appearance of the final drawings?

5. Why is the ability to communicate effectively important, especially for students in an organization?

6. What did you do with your eyes during this activity?

7. Did you use any nonverbal communication?

8. What nonverbal actions would have made this activity easier?

Have the group select the drawing that best represents the original picture. Have the partners describe how they approached the activity.

Exhibit 3.12. Sample Memo

DATE: September 10, 1996

TO: Dr. Chris Smith
           Vice President for Student Affairs

FROM: Mark Stone, President
           Campus Debate Club

RE: Speaking at meeting

Dr. Smith, per our telephone conversation of September 8, 1996, I would like to formally invite you to speak at our October meeting. As we discussed, you would speak about your thoughts regarding leadership development and transferable skills.

Our meeting will be on Thursday, October 24, 1996, at 7:00 p.m. in the Student Union, room 282. We invite you to come at 6:30 p.m. to participate in a reception in the same location if you wish.

We look forward to your visit with us. Please contact me if there is anything I can do for you prior to the meeting.

cc: Wayne Parks, Chair, Department of Communication
     Mary Armstrong, Campus Debate Club Adviser
     File

Depending on the organization, the executive board will need to decide whether to use parliamentary procedure, an adaptation of it, or another approach to formatting the formal meeting. When an organization with a large representative group meets or when an organization needs to maneuver through a lengthy agenda, parliamentary procedure can assist the president in keeping order. Parliamentary procedure allows all members the opportunity to participate in discussion, debate, and decisions. Your understanding basic parliamentary procedure is essential, particularly if the organization actively uses it. *Robert's Rules of Order* (Robert, 1996) provides detailed information on all aspects of the rules of order. Exhibit 3.15 summarizes how different motions are handled.

Organizations possessing clear and defined purposes are willing to take a stand or position on a specific issue. Communicating these positions to the institutional community may be conducted verbally or by way of a memo. A more formal document for expressing the organization's position is a resolution, a sample of which appears in Exhibit 3.16.

Exhibit 3.13. Sample Agenda

Community Involvement Club
Rolling Brook College

Date

Call to order—president

Roll call—secretary

Approval of the minutes—president

Officer and adviser reports

    President

    Vice president

    Treasurer

    Secretary

    Adviser

Decision and discussion

    Second readings

    First readings

Issue forum

Committee, event, and project reports

Announcements and comments

Adjournment—president

Exhibit 3.14. Sample Minutes

Community Involvement Club
Rolling Brook College

Date

Call to order: 5:15 p.m.

Roll call: 65 in attendance

   15 absent

Officer and adviser reports

   President: sign up for spring honor roll if eligible; accepting applications for fall dance director.

   Vice president: received and read a letter from the university president.

   Treasurer: we presently have $6,000.00 in the checking account and $352.00 in the housing account.

   Secretary: sign-up for Adopt-a-Highway was passed around.

   Adviser: passed out scholarship application materials.

Decision and discussion

   Second readings: none

   First readings: the treasurer presented the fall budget of $6,352.00. John S. moved and Nancy D. seconded to approve the budget. Following minimal discussion, the budget passed 60–4-1.

Issue forum

   There were questions raised as to why the garbage trucks pick up trash so early in the morning. The adviser responded and explained the garbage pickup schedule.
Committee, event, and project reports

   Adopt-a-Highway: a sign-up sheet was passed around, and training has been scheduled for October 5, 1996, at 7:00 p.m. in the workshop.

   Fall dance: applications are available for the director position.

Announcements and comments

   Bill B.: thanked the body for all their good input

   Amanda P.: announced a birthday party

Adjournment: 6:25 P.M.

Exhibit 3.15. Chart for Handling Motions

Types of Motions	Interrupt Speaker	Second Required	Debatable	Amendable	Vote Required	Remarks	Example
MAIN MOTION	No	Yes	Yes	Yes	Majority	Introduces business or states a proposal for group action.	I move that the club sponsor a dance, Friday, November 7.
To take from table	No	Yes	No	No	Majority	The purpose is to bring up for debate motions that were tabled earlier.	I move the motion, namely, (state motion) be taken from the table.
To reconsider	No	Yes	Yes[a]	No	Majority	Motion to reconsider may be made only by a person who voted on the prevailing side. Must be made during meeting or at next meeting.	I voted with the prevailing side of the motion that (state motion), and move to reconsider the action taken. Or . . . move to have the motion reconsidered at the next meeting.
To rescind or repeal	No	Yes	Yes	Yes	Two-thirds or majority	The purpose is to rescind or repeal previous action. May be done with majority vote if prior notice is given.	I move that we rescind the motion (state motion), which was passed at the meeting of (date).
SUBSIDIARY[b] MOTIONS							
Postpone indefinitely	No	Yes	Yes	No	Majority	Used to test the strength of the main motion. If the motion carries, the main motion is lost.	I move the matter be postponed indefinitely.
Amend motion or substitute motion	No	Yes	Yes	Yes	Majority	Ways to amend: insert, add to, strike out, or strike out and insert. Substitute motion replaces main motion if passed.	I move to amend the motion by striking out the words "Friday, November 7" and inserting the words "Saturday, November 22." Or: I move the substitute motion namely, that the dance be on the "22nd of November."

Types of Motions	Interrupt Speaker	Second Required	Debatable	Amendable	Vote Required	Remarks	Example
Amend amendment	No	Yes	Yes	No	Majority	Pertains only to the part that has been included in amendment.	I move to amend the amendment by striking out the words "Saturday, November 22" and inserting the words "October 25."
Refer to committee	No	Yes	Yes	Yes	Majority	May be assigned to a standing committee or to a committee to be appointed or elected with instructions to investigate, recommend, or take action.	I move that we refer this matter to the social committee.
Postpone to a definite time	No	Yes	Yes	Yes	Majority	Purpose is to delay action to some specific time.	I move to postpone action on this matter until our next meeting.
Previous question leads to close of debate	No	Yes	No	No	Two-thirds	Applies to main motions only, except when others are specified. Purpose is to limit or stop debate.	I move the previous questions (the main motion).
Table	No	Yes	No	No	Majority	Purpose is to postpone for more pressing business until later in the meeting or until next meeting. Sec.: To take from table.	I move to table the motion until a future meeting.
PRIVILEGED MOTIONS[c]							
Orders of the day, or refer to the agenda	Yes	No	No	No	No vote	A demand that meeting conform to agenda.	I call for the orders of the day. Or: I move that we consider the topic on the agenda, namely . . . .

Types of Motions	Interrupt Speaker	Second Required	Debatable	Amendable	Vote Required	Remarks	Example
Question of privilege	Yes	No	No	No	No vote	Purpose is to bring up an urgent matter on rights of members, such as noise or disturbance during the meeting.	I rise to a question of privilege.
Recess	No[d]	Yes	Yes	Yes	Majority	Intermission for meals, counting ballots, and the like.	I move we have a ten-minute recess to count the ballots.
Adjourn	No[d]	Yes	No	No	Majority	Purpose is to terminate the meeting.	I move that we adjourn.
Set time for next meeting	No	Yes	No	Yes	Majority	When a meeting is needed but not yet scheduled.	I move to set the time for our next meeting for 7:00 p.m. tomorrow to continue the present discussion.
INCIDENTAL MOTIONS[e]							
To rise to a point of order	Yes	No	No	No	No vote	This means that the person feels that there has been a breach of parliamentary rules or decorum.	I rise to a point of order. (State point.) I believe that it is not within school policy to hold school-sponsored dances outside of the Village of Chagrin Falls.
To appeal from the decision of chair	Yes	Yes	Yes	No	Majority	Must be made immediately. Used when it is thought that the chair has made an incorrect decision.	I appeal from the decision of the chair. (State appeal.)
To suspend a rule	No	Yes	No	No	Two-thirds	An agreement to temporarily change the order of business. If there is no objection, the chairman may call for a vote.	I move to suspend the rules in order to allow the speaker his full thirty minutes.

Types of Motions	Interrupt Speaker	Second Required	Debatable	Amendable	Vote Required	Remarks	Example
Object to consideration of motion	Yes	No	No	No	Two-thirds (negotiable)	Applies to main motion only, and must be made before any debate.	I object to consideration of this motion.
Division of assembly	Yes	No	No	No	No vote	Verifies by hand, standing, or roll call vote the decision of the chair.	I call for a division of the house.
Parliamentary inquiry information	Yes	No	No	No	No vote	An inquiry or request is addressed to the chair, but if permission is granted, may be addressed to other members of the group.	I rise to a parliamentary inquiry. Or: I rise for information. (State question.) Or: May I have the chair's permission to ask a question? (State the question.)
Withdraw motion	No	No	No	No	No vote	Member who was making motion withdraws motion before discussion or, with general consent, before the vote.	I request permission to withdraw my motion, namely, (state the motion).
To close nominations	No	Yes	No	Yes	Two-thirds	The chairman may close nominations without a vote after giving the group the opportunity to make more nominations. I move the nominations cease.	

a When the motion is debatable.

b Subsidiary motions change in the same way as the main motion. They have precedence in the order in which they are listed. The further they are down the list, the higher their priority.

c Privileged motions have precedence over main motions and all subsidiary motions. The further they are down the list, the higher their priority.

d May interrupt in an emergency. Privileged when other business is before the house; otherwise, treat as a main motion.

e Incidental motions have equal rank. They have precedence or priority only over those motions to which they apply.

Source: Adapted with permission from University of Kansas, Organizations and Activities Center, 1996.

Exhibit 3.16. Sample Resolution

Student Body Resolution 96–105

TITLE: Resolution in Opposition of Proposed Ordinance 96–40

SPONSOR: Student Judiciary Committee

THE STUDENT SENATE OF THE UNIVERSITY OF FLORIDA DOES HEREBY RESOLVE:

WHEREAS, In Fall 1995 the Gainesville City Commission created an ad hoc committee to address issues involving student renters; and

WHEREAS, The Rentals in Residential Neighborhoods Ad Hoc Committee has been meeting to discuss such issues as violations of ordinances dealing with noise, trash, pets, parking, single-family neighborhood habitation, and landlord permits; and

WHEREAS, This committee made several recommendations to the Gainesville Code of Ordinances, namely amendments to the noise ordinance, landlord permit law, and front-yard parking; and

WHEREAS, The City Commission has already amended the noise ordinance (Ordinance No. 951346) to change the manner of measuring noise ordinance violations from a quantifiable standard to a "plainly audible" standard, and making it easier for a resident to violate the noise ordinance by penalizing an individual for violating the ordinance twice in one month rather than twice in one day; and

WHEREAS, The City Commission will consider an amendment to the city code dealing with front-yard parking which would unfairly target home renters, and allow enforcement of the new regulations only to renters and not to home owners; and

WHEREAS, The City Commission has passed on first reading proposed Ordinance 96–40, an amendment to the landlord permit ordinance which allows a landlord to evict a tenant for one violation of the city's noise ordinances, animal control ordinances, solid waste ordinances, or the provisions of section 30–57 concerning the number of unrelated persons living in a home; and

WHEREAS, The purpose of the ad hoc committee was to provide solutions to problem renters, and proposed Ordinance 96–40 is too severe in that it allows for the eviction of a first-time offender, which is contrary to the purpose of the ad hoc committee; and

WHEREAS, Proposed Ordinance 96–40 could allow a vindictive or corrupt landlord to legitimately evict a renter for one single violation of the city ordinances; and

WHEREAS, Proposed Ordinance 96–40 allows those individuals that file complaints against alleged violators of city ordinances to do so anonymously, which could allow for harassment of law-abiding renters; and

WHEREAS, The Student Government of both the University of Florida and Santa Fe Community College have offered to publish a pamphlet which would be distributed to all students informing students of the ordinances that are applicable to renters in residential neighborhoods; and

WHEREAS, In an effort to offer solutions to the tensions between home owners and student renters, the University of Florida Student Government has offered to establish a mediation service which would provide for intervention programs between neighbors before situations escalate to severe problems;

NOW. THEREFORE, BE IT RESOLVED by the University of Florida Student Senate, as the elected representatives of the 40,000 University of Florida Student Body, that it is staunchly opposed to the passage of proposed Ordinance 96–40, because this ordinance allows for the eviction of first-time offenders and allows for discrimination and harassment of student renters by allowing anonymous complaints;

BE IT FURTHER RESOLVED that the University of Florida Student Senate recognizes the problem that the Gainesville community is facing with problem renters, but a law which targets a few problem renters should not be passed when it could potentially adversely affect the enter renter population;

BE IT FURTHER RESOLVED that the University of Florida Student Senate supports the establishment of a mediation process which would attempt to resolve disputes before they escalate, and the University of Florida Student Senate supports open dialogue between members of the Gainesville and student community;

BE IT FURTHER RESOLVED that the University of Florida Student Senate insists the Gainesville City Commission not pass proposed Ordinance 96–40, or any other proposed anti-student ordinances.

Signature:

_____

Catalina Obesso,   Date
Student Senate President

Copies to:

University President
University Vice President
Student Body President
Student Body Vice President
Student Body Treasurer
Student Honor Court

Gainesville City Commission

Passed 7/22/96

SBR96–105

Organizations increasingly are relying on electronic communication: they use e-mail to notify members of meetings, activities, and changes in calendars; they use electronic voting in student senate meetings and ask for feedback on proposals; they maintain rosters and establish organization home pages to inform a wider population about their activities.

If an individual member establishes a home page or discussion list, the organization needs to address who will maintain it once the individual leaves. Maintenance of a home page is the responsibility of the organization.

Many organizations maintain discussion lists of individuals who share interests. Numerous discussion lists are available for Greek organizations, student governments, residence hall associations, and honors organizations, to mention a few. Members should use the technology available that will best assist them in communicating their needs, wishes, and desires.

Recognition.   Recognition is the fourth stage of the supervision flowchart that you can use in your work with students. As a faculty or staff member advising an organization, you will participate in many conferences with individual students. These students may express a wide range of emotions; you need a knowledge of student emotions, characteristics, and backgrounds to respond effectively in unexpected situations. Exhibit 3.17 will help you identify your responses to emotion.

Some situations require documenting the incident for your protection and for the protection of the institution. Written documentation should include the specific nature of the exchange and situation, the date and time, the individuals involved, and the outcome of the exchange. Chapter Eight provides detailed information on institutional responsibilities. Other situations may result in violations of the student code or institutional rules. These circumstances generally necessitate documentation and referral to the campus judicial office. You should have a working knowledge of the campus judicial process or know the person responsible for the campus judicial process.

Self-Assessment.   The fifth stage of the supervision cycle is self-assessment. If you meet frequently with students, you should ask them to complete a verbal or written self-assessment of how they are progressing in their position and their academics. This opportunity allows students to reflect on programs, their skills, their involvement in the organization, and their responsibilities. Students can break down their duties, academic progress, or goal achievement into reflective thoughts. This self-assessment can be

Exhibit 3.17. Emotion-Response Activity

As an adviser, how would you respond if a student were to express one of the following emotions? Fill in the appropriate response for each of the emotional expressions. This practice of identifying responses will assist you if an unexpected situation were to arise.

Emotional Expression   *Response*

Anger

Tears

Denial

Contradictions

Silence

Frustration

Screaming

Gestures

Threatening

formal, in which the student completes a form, or the student can simply take time to reflect. This process is important for student leaders to use with their executive boards, committee chairpersons, or project managers, and it serves as a check and balance to a process or project, slowing down the time line for a moment to ensure that all aspects of the project are being covered.

Evaluation.   The sixth and final stage of the supervision flowchart that can be valuable for you is formal evaluation. Some institutions require students to complete various evaluations, including the following: program evaluations such as the one found in Exhibit 3.18; performance appraisals of paid students in organizations; audits of records and accounts; and progress reports for various institutional office staff. Evaluations may come with rating scales, checklists, rankings, or open-ended responses, or may use a management-by-objectives approach. You should know what forms the students need to complete as part of the duties of their office or in order to fulfill institutional requirements.

A formal evaluation is an opportunity for you to provide feedback to the organization or to individual members. Your participation in the evaluation process should be understood early in your relationship with the organization so as not to come as a surprise to students. You may receive the evaluative audits of records or accounts as the institution representative, you may be required to sign off on performance appraisals of paid students, and you may receive copies of progress reports to be ensured that money is spent within institutional guidelines or that institutional liability concerns are being attended to. Again, it is important for you to understand the role and implications of your involvement in the evaluation process. The first step in any evaluation is for participants to understand that evaluation is beneficial to the organization and to the individuals involved.

Preparation is essential to effective evaluation. If the evaluation is conducted on paid personnel, typically a supervisory relationship is already in place, complete with personnel files to review or forms to use. Similarly, if the evaluation is of financial records or processes, information and records should already exist to properly document the evaluation. Aside from the accuracy of the information, the setting in which a formal evaluation of personnel takes place and the final evaluation (during which personnel sign forms and receive copies) are important parts of the evaluation process.

Some difficulties one may encounter in the evaluation process include poor records, personnel vacancies, instrumental flaws in the evaluation forms, poor organizational climate and morale, lack

Exhibit 3.18. Sample Program Report

_____

Student responsible for organizing the program   Hall

Program title or topic

Program date   Time   Location

Program presenter(s)

Type of program (circle all that apply):

      Educational   Community development

      Dining service   Faculty associate

Please give a brief description of the program:

Rate the effectiveness of the program:

   Ineffective   Effective

   1   2   3   4   5

Rate the effectiveness of the presenter:

   Ineffective   Effective

   1   2   3   4   5

What types of publicity and resources did you use?

What funding was used?

Did this program meet your expectations? Why or why not?

of an understanding of the benefits of evaluation, or evaluator errors. You should understand the potential challenges associated with evaluations and work closely with student leaders to reduce the likelihood of problems occurring. Chapter Ten covers evaluation issues in detail.

Teacher

As an organization adviser, you must be aware of two considerations as you assist students in their success and the success of their communities. First, the greatest influence on student success on a campus is the level of involvement that the student has with faculty. Second, the "lack of student community has stronger direct effects on student satisfaction with the overall college experience than any other environmental measure. Additionally, the lack of student community also produces negative indirect effects on satisfaction with faculty. . . ." (Astin, 1993, p. 352).

All advisers want students to succeed academically and socially and to be satisfied with their campus experiences in and out of the classroom. Astin (1993) maintains that it is not the number of hours teaching in class or advising students but the quality of the contact that is most critical. You should review your level of involvement with the student organization and its members in this context. You should examine the quality of your involvement in terms of meeting the needs and expectations of the students in the organization. You can perform this review shortly after the election of officers as expectations are identified for officers, through informal review sessions during the course of the year, or as part of a formal evaluation of the organization. Regardless of when the review is scheduled, discussions between you and the organization's president should cover the quality of the relationship between you, the executive board, and the members.

The development of student community can take place in a residence hall, classroom, or student organization. Clearly, residence hall staff and faculty work to establish the environment of the residence halls and classrooms. An organization's student leadership is responsible for establishing the community environment of the student organization. An inviting, inclusive organization that allows members to take ownership, give feedback, and become involved will be an organization with a strong community environment. You can play a key role in assisting the student leadership to develop strategies and goals that provide for the members' ownership, feedback, and involvement.

Advisers who also serve full-time as student affairs professionals in student activities, unions, student services, and so forth have developed and participated in numerous training sessions. These advisers are capable of facilitating training sessions, because for many of them, training is one of their job responsibilities. For advisers to student organizations who primarily serve as faculty from any discipline, their preparation has been to *teach*. In drawing the distinction between training and teaching, Fried (1989, p. 355) states that the "purpose of training is to help people learn skills to solve problems . . . training imposes a certain uniformity on the practice of a skill, and this uniformity is the basis on which skill development can be evaluated." About teaching, Fried states: "the purpose of teaching is quite the opposite—to broaden a person's understanding, to help the person examine a problem from several different points of view, and to place the problem in a cultural and historical context" (p. 355). Regardless of your field, you should keep these important differences in mind in your work with student organizations.

Leader

Students get involved in groups and organizations for a variety of reasons; one reason many students report is that they joined in order to develop their leadership abilities.

Leadership is one of the most studied topics in social science. Numerous publications, tapes, conferences, and presentations are available to the public on leadership development, organizational development, and leadership skills. Clearly, leadership ability can be interpreted broadly. No one theory or model incorporates all leadership skill and trait development.

Woodard (1994, pp. 96–97) believes that "faculty and student affairs practitioners need to work collaboratively to define and create opportunities for students to learn more about leadership and participate in activities that enhance leadership development. Leadership development should not be primarily focused on visible campus student leaders or centered in student government activities, rather, it should be seen as an opportunity to involve many students in activities both on and off campus." Woodard recommends guidelines for the planning of leadership development opportunities, including theory (exposing students to different organizational and leadership theories); values clarification (developing an understanding of the values needed to lead in society); skills development (developing such areas as social activism, conflict resolution, collaborative learning, decision making, judgment, and communication); societal issues (exposing students to major societal challenges); and experience (providing students with opportunities to try their leadership).

Hersey and Blanchard (1988) define leadership as an individual's attempt to influence. According to this definition, students in organizations can assume a leadership role whether they are members or executive officers. Assuming a student's leadership role is an attempt or potential to influence, the student is practicing what Hersey and Blanchard term as power.

You need to be aware of power bases as you work with students in leadership positions. When asked for their perception of the word *power,* most students refer to its negative connotation. You can help educate students to understand that there are several kinds of power bases. Students who possess a working knowledge of these bases will more likely change their negative perceptions of power and will be better able to work with their organization.

Etzioni (1961) draws a distinction between *personal power,* used when a person influences others by working through his or her followers, and *position power,* a person's ability to influence others by way of the position he or she holds. Hersey and Blanchard (1988) define seven different power bases. The first four are related to position power, the remaining three to personal power. The first power base is coercive power, or the perceived ability to provide sanctions. The second is connection power, or the perceived association with influential persons or organizations. The third is reward power, or the perceived ability to provide things that people would like to have. The fourth is legitimate power, or the perception that it is appropriate for the leader to make decisions due to title or position in the organization. The fifth is referent power, or the perceived attractiveness of interacting with another person. The sixth is information power, or the perceived access to or possession of useful information. The seventh power base is expert power, or the perception that the leader has relevant education, experience, and expertise. You can describe positive examples of these power bases to your students and facilitate good discussions on the uses and abuses of power.

Kouzes and Pozner (1987) identify five fundamental practices found in leaders of effective organizations. Applying these practices to student organizations, we can say that leaders (1) challenge the process by seeking ways to improve the organization; (2) inspire a shared vision by creating an image of what the organization can become; (3) enable others to act by involving students in activities and on committees and task forces; (4) model the way by setting standards and assisting other students through their problems and concerns; and (5) encourage the heart by recognizing members for their achievements and by motivating members to accomplish goals. Executive boards can use these five fundamental practices in their development of annual goals and team working practices, and in self-assessment of their performance.

Civic leadership connects people to each other, to the community, and to a shared vision. Civic leadership moves away from the traditional leader-follower approaches. "Current practices in the study of leadership are still very leader-centric; a movement toward each member's role in the leadership dynamic is more fruitful for highly relational civic communities" (Komives, 1994, p. 226). Students increasingly have added civic student organizations to the registered student organization rosters in an effort to fulfill their need to provide a common good to the greater community. Student organizations now offer alternative spring breaks (for example, building homes, cleaning rivers, and so on), cuddle clubs (offering cuddling for babies infected with HIV), or community volunteerism (such as working in soup kitchens, driving senior citizens, holding conversations with nursing home residents, and so on). You will need to understand that although the student leadership of these organizations may possess a different set of motives for their involvement, they require guidance and direction as any student organization would for success.

Follower

The characteristics of followers are important for you to understand in your work with student organization leaders. If the followers in an organization choose not to follow, the leadership of the organization must take the problem seriously.

Followers have expectations of their leaders. You can assist the student leadership in developing activities to identify follower expectations of them. Exhibit 3.19 is an activity that you can use after the election of the organization's officers. This activity allows the membership to identify expectations collectively and, with the assistance of a facilitator, discuss the expectations. Following the discussion, the members decide which expectations they accept as being realistic and measurable, taking into consideration the student leaders' limitations (because of classes, work, office hours, and so on).

From Hersey and Blanchard's definition of leadership (1988), "it follows that the leadership process is a function of the *leader,* the *follower,* and other *situational* variables—$L = f(l,f,s)$. It is important to note that this definition makes no mention of any particular type of organization . . . everyone attempts leadership at one time or another" (p. 86), regardless of what type of activity they are involved in. Working with the executive board, you can assist

Exhibit 3.19. Follower Expectations Activity

_____

Name of student leader

Our expectations of your communications to us:

Our expectations of your relationship to us:

Our expectations of your helping us with problems:

Our expectations of your providing us leadership development:

Our expectations of your politics in the organization:

Our expectations of your facilitating meetings:

Our expectations of _____:

Facilitator Process Questions

1. What was difficult about this activity?
2. For which category was it most difficult to generate expectations?
3. What limitations does [Name] have that would effect these expectations?
4. Let us discuss each category of expectations considering [Name]'s limitations in order to come to a decision about which expectations are realistic and measurable. The agreed-upon expectations will then be typed and distributed to the membership for review at a future time.

Exhibit 3.20. Identifying Motives

Directions: Tape three sheets of newsprint to the wall with sufficient space between the sheets that a group of five or six participants can stand in front of each sheet. The sheets should be labeled with one of the following as a heading.

1. List the things that motivate you
2. List ways that you would like to be recognized
3. List items that de-motivate you

Allow the participants ten to fifteen minutes to create a list on their sheet. Rotate the groups of participants from one sheet to the next, allowing them time to add to each list. Discuss the following questions:

1. Which items involve money?
2. Which items can our organization control?
3. Which items can we individually control?
4. Does our organization practice any unmotivational actions? Do our members?
5. Which items should our organization or membership spend time on?

organization members in the development of a basic understanding of leaders and followers.

Motivating Students

Understanding what motivates students may be your single most desirable skill. If it isn't evident to you already, you will soon find in your work with students that some of them have what appears to be an innate desire to become involved, work hard, and make a difference in the organization. Conversely, some students do not seem to be ambitious at all. Understanding the range of motivating factors will enable you to help individual students take on responsibilities and become involved.

"Motives are sometimes defined as needs, wants, drives, or impulses within the individual. Motives are directed toward goals, which may be conscious or subconscious. . . . Goals are often called incentives by psychologists" (Hersey and Blanchard, 1988, p. 19). As you would expect, different individuals will possess different motives for participating in an organization. Exhibit 3.20 describes an activity that you can work on with students to help them identify what motivates them; you can then begin to assist the students in preparing a plan to achieve these goals (or to acquire the motivating items).

Exhibit 3.21. Recognition Activities

- T-shirts: an excellent way to promote unity and community.
- Friendship plants: give one to a person who has helped.
- Magnificent marble: a person receives the marble and passes it on.
- Wishing well: a plastic bottle to which members add pennies and make a verbal wish as a good warmup exercise for a goal-setting program.
- Member of the _____: have the organization select a member of the day, week, month, or year.
- Notes: send a note recognizing a person's achievement.
- Dinner with execs: sponsor a dinner for members to eat with the executive officers of the organization.
- Letters to families: a powerful public relations tool to enhance the status of the organization by promoting to families that the member is important.
- Success jar: have members write down a success and drop it in a jar; read one at every meeting.
- Posi-squad: a button and certificate is given to a member of the organization who exhibits positive statements or positive behaviors.
- Energizer award: a battery given to the member who does the most during a week to energize the organization.
- Publicity releases: create publicity releases on members of the organization and send them to the local and hometown newspapers.
- Service pins: consider giving service pins to those members involved in the organization for a length of time, for special positions held, or for scholastic achievement.
- Key chains: give key chains with the organization's name or events on it to members of the organization or students at the institution.
- Medallions: present small medallions to members to praise them or thank them whenever a boost would be helpful.
- Certificates: presented to members for many different achievements, including scholarship, participation, appointment or election to leadership positions, program presenting, and so forth.
- Door decorations: place them on a member's door; decoration should include the person's name and position, and the organization's logo
- Buttons: these can advertise or recognize a number of things, including membership or special achievements.
- Campus TV or radio: use the campus TV or radio station to promote outstanding achievement by members.
- Adjourn in honor of _____: a simple recognition to allow graduating seniors to adjourn the last meeting of the year or adjourn a regular meeting in the name of a member in honor of his or her special achievement
- Personal ads: take out a personal ad in the campus paper to recognize a member for an outstanding achievement.

- Institutional signs: some institutions have entrance signs that can have special announcements placed on them in recognition of a member.
- Day in honor of _____: identify a day in the name of one of the members.
- Leader trees: plant trees on campus to honor student leaders.
- Proclamations: have the campus president or dean of students issue proclamations that recognize the achievements and involvement of outstanding members.
- President's lunch: have the institution president take an outstanding member to lunch once per month; this will also provide top administrators with exposure to the organization.
- Plaques and trophies: these make outstanding mementos of involvement and achievement.
- Paper clip award: present an oversized paper clip to the member who has kept the organization together and organized.
- Banner: create a banner to recognize key members; display the banner in a high-traffic location.
- Flowers: share a bouquet of flowers with members at special times of the year.
- Chalk the walks: using sidewalk chalk, create displays in high-traffic areas to draw attention to the achievements of members.
- Phone calls: have key administrators give a phone call to a member of the organization.
- Bookmarks: create bookmarks that highlight the achievements of members; place these bookmarks at main desks.
- Dedications: dedicate programs, activities, and events to outstanding individuals on campus.

Source: Adapted with permission from the National Residence Hall Honorary, 1996.

Student motivation can be divided into two major categories: extrinsic (recognition, money, and achievement) and intrinsic (desire, value, and approval). In the following sections, we look at the six subcategories of motives.

Extrinsic Motives

As just mentioned, three types of extrinsic motives for students are recognition, money, and achievement.

Recognition. In our experience, recognition is the subcategory advisers use most frequently to motivate students. Exhibit 3.21 describes some of the many activities to recognize students. In using recognition it is important to understand that no one item will be warmly received by all members. You must be sensitive to each student's motives.

Money   To pay or not to pay students is a question advisers, administrators, and students have struggled with for years. Many student organizations do not have to consider money as a reward for student leadership. Honor clubs, departmental organizations, special-interest clubs, and the like generally have positions of leadership for which the duties and responsibilities are limited in scope when compared to campus student governments, residence hall associations, or fraternity and sorority chapters.

The issue of paying student leaders is divisive; many institutions take the philosophical position that offices do not require a stipend. This line of thinking goes that students can manage their responsibilities and duties, and that by paying them the volunteer nature of their job is lost. Other institutions argue that major student leadership positions are given exemption from full-time class loads in recognition of the heavy responsibilities, time commitments, and pressures of their positions, and that because of these same factors, student leaders do not have the time to hold a part-time job to augment their finances. Paying the student is absolutely necessary for them to fulfill their duties. Magee (1994, pp. 30–31) states that "some schools have found it necessary and valuable to compensate student leaders for their time and efforts, whether that compensation is offered through academic credit or through a monetary stipend. However, when a volunteer receives a stipend, the rules of the game take on a new dimension. Justification for that stipend becomes necessary because most stipends are generated from student activities fees. Accountability and supervision of students receiving stipends become additional responsibilities for staff members."

Mitchell (1993) surveyed advisers of residence hall associations and developed a list of perceived advantages and disadvantages of paying students for leadership positions within residence hall associations. The perceived advantages were as follows: (1) possible higher motivation and commitment to the position, (2) appropriate recognition of the time and energy students place in the positions, (3) encouragement of students to participate who might not have, due to financial constraints, (4) greater accountability of the student in a particular position, and (5) stability in leadership if competing compensated positions are readily available for talented students. The perceived disadvantages were the following: (1) the opinion that remuneration is contrary to the spirit of volunteerism, (2) a narrowing of the roles between the student and adviser, (3) concerns about whether pay is a primary motivator for students instead of altruistic reasons, (4) problems in identifying resources to fund positions, and (5) issues about which roles would be compensated and possible inequities with unpaid roles.

Advisers, administrators, and students will need to resolve the issue of payment. If the decision to compensate is made, it can take several possible forms:

- *Reimbursement of conference costs.* Many student organizations travel to conferences, conventions, and meetings. The travel costs, registration, accommodations, and food may be paid by the institution or organization.
- *Summer jobs.* Institutions have provided summer employment to student leaders of organizations that meet during the academic year. Jobs can include working for dining services, doing research, holding student assistant positions, helping prepare athletic facilities, or serving on maintenance, custodial, or grounds crews.
- *Room and board.* Institutions provide a variety of compensation packages built on room and board stipends. Some provide a stipend covering all or a portion of the room or board expenses; others provide a single room in a residence hall at a double rate or provide a meal card at the on-campus dining facility.
- *Tuition or class credit.* An institution can defer the costs of tuition during the time a student leader is in office or can provide class credit for the leadership experience gained from the position.
- *Salaries or stipends.* One choice is to provide a stipend to executive board members. In residence hall associations, the stipend can range from $100 to $1,500 per term. For student government officers, the range can be from $100 per term to over $8,000 per year. Campus programming boards provide some executive officers $200 to $3,000 per year.
- *Miscellaneous.* Campuses can provide various student leaders stipends to cover parking, telephone expenses, mailing expenses, and travel per diems.

The salary and stipend rewards given to students can be viewed as reinforcers that "strengthen behavior in the sense that rewarded behaviors are likely to recur" (Beck, 1983, p. 171). Salary and stipend rewards can also be seen as incentives that lead to the anticipation of rewards (1983). Whether the salary or stipend is considered a reinforcer or an incentive, you, the administrator, and the students must work together to understand the nature of the student leader's motive and subsequently, the need to provide a salary or stipend.

Achievement. The need for achievement may be defined as a tendency "to overcome obstacles, to exercise power, to strive to do something difficult as well and as quickly as possible" (Murray, 1938, pp. 80–81). Students motivated by achievement are driven to take on increasing levels of responsibility and authority; they may be looking for additional power to be gained from a position; they exercise control and seek tasks that other students may not assume because of the difficulty of the tasks. When you recognize the achievement motivation in a student, you should work with the student leadership to assist in identifying positions of increasing responsibility, sense of autonomy, or authority. You must work closely with students motivated by achievement in order to avoid their advancing too quickly, losing motivation because of the attitudes of less driven students, becoming frustrated at the pace of a project, or failing to involve other students to achieve a task or project.

Intrinsic Motives

Three types of intrinsic motives for students are desire, value, and approval.

Desire.   As we would expect, students are interested in becoming involved in organizations and activities that will provide a desirable outcome; they do not look for organizations or activities that will lead to an aversive outcome. Students will consider a leadership position, a project, travel to a conference, or a presentation desirable if they understand it to be an outcome already known to be desirable. For example, students who had previously held the position might state that the position led to greater things or that travel to a conference helped them to grow and to develop their leadership skills. Similarly, if an outcome is already known to be aversive, students will be less likely to desire to attend or participate.

Value.   The student who perceives a value in participating in an organization, chairing a committee, or attending a conference will be motivated to become involved. You and student leaders can determine the value of various involvements by surveying the membership. Members may, for example, determine that the values received from chairing a committee are visibility on campus, increased communication and organizational skills, a better understanding of the organization, and a leadership role in the organization.

Approval.   Approval is a feeling that a student may perceive. Students may be motivated by earning a sense of approval from friends, family, or advisers. Approval may come in the form of a note, a pat on the back, public recognition, or a kind word of a job well done; you need to identify which students are motivated by approval and provide the appropriate recognition.

CHAPTER 4

Understanding Group Dynamics

Group dynamics "is the scientific study of behavior in groups to advance our knowledge about the nature of groups, group development, and the interrelations between groups and individuals, other groups, and larger entities" (Johnson and Johnson, 1991, p. 14). Group dynamics is a field that includes theory, research, and practice. As an adviser to a student organization, you work daily observing group dynamics and working with organizational leadership to solve problems, alleviate concerns, and remove obstacles to the organization or membership that are a function of group dynamics. It is important for you to understand "that all groups have a basic structure . . . and that groups change and develop over time, and you must comprehend the difference between effective and ineffective groups" (Johnson and Johnson, 1991, p. 15).

Groups move through stages of growth over time. "In work groups, social or political groups, sports teams, and classroom groups, a predictable pattern of group evolution emerges in which each stage has certain definite characteristics" (Napier and Gershenfeld, 1989, p. 470). Numerous theories, models, and studies exist regarding group dynamics. In this chapter we look at a number of theories and concepts of group development and dynamics, and in order to provide practical information, we have applied these ideas to the various roles advisers play within student organizations. We have included activities, exercises, and case studies for you to use in determining an organization's or executive board's stage of development, to help you identify whether the organization is effective or ineffective, and to design programs to meet an organization's need.

Group Effectiveness

Groups can function in either a productive or unproductive manner. Merely calling members together and expecting that the resulting group will be productive is unrealistic. Members must approach their group intentionally with a model of group effectiveness. An effective group performs "three core activities: (1) accomplishing its goals, (2) maintaining good working relationships among members, and (3) developing and adapting to changing conditions in ways that improve its effectiveness" (Johnson and Johnson, 1991, p. 21). Johnson and Johnson provide a nine-point model of group effectiveness.

1. Group goals must be clearly understood, be relevant to the needs of group members, highlight the positive interdependence of members, and evoke from every member a high level of commitment to their accomplishment.

2. Group members must communicate their ideas and feelings accurately and clearly.

3. Participation and leadership must be distributed among members.

4. Appropriate decision-making procedures must be flexible in order to match them with the needs of the situation.

5. Conflicts should be encouraged and managed constructively. (Controversies promote quality, creativity in decision making, involvement in the group's work, and commitment to implementing the group's decisions.)

6. Power and influence need to be approximately equal throughout the group.

7. Group cohesion needs to be high.

8. Problem-solving adequacy should be high.

9. The interpersonal effectiveness of members needs to be high.

Group Norms

Group norms are the rules of behavior that have been developed and accepted by the group. "Group norms regulate the performance of the group as an organized unit" (Napier and Gershenfeld, 1987, p. 114). When students join a group they may experience an initial period of anxiety. "The initial anxious feelings and thoughts are supplanted by firm, accepted ideas about personal security, safety, and membership status. Members come to feel comfortable in the group" (Napier and Gershenfeld, 1987, p. 115). Tuckman (1965) has referred to this process of growing comfortable in the group as *norming.*

Group norms may range from explicit, formal, behavioral expectations of members to implicit feelings and behaviors. Napier and Gershenfeld (1987) have identified three categories of norms that may regulate a group's performance:

- *Written rules.* Written rules may include a published set of standards or guidelines that is included in the organization's constitution. Student organizations may have judicial codes and written guidelines regarding membership, attendance, academic standards, committee involvement, appropriate dress, use of money, and access to offices.

- *Nonexplicit, informal norms.* These norms could be referred to as the silent norms. Blake and Mouton (1985) identify the silent norms as invisible group norms that can stifle the creativity of the organization. These unstated norms in a student organization can include, for example, who is exempt from having to attend meetings, who sits in a particular place during meetings, and who motions for approval of annual budget recommendations.

- *Norms beyond awareness.* Some norms operate without our conscious knowledge. These norms in a student organization might include "automatically raising the hand when one wants to be recognized; saying hello to those members who one is familiar with when entering the meeting; expecting a certain order at a meeting; an opening, the minutes, the treasurer's report, old business, then new business; expecting paid-up members to be notified of meetings" (Napier and Gershenfeld, 1987, p. 127). Exhibit 4.1 provides an activity for the leadership or members of an organization to use in identifying the organization's norms.

Theories of Group Development and Behavior

In this section we summarize several theories about how groups are formed and how people behave in them. We encourage you to refer to the original source material for additional ideas and details regarding these concepts. The first model is our favorite: it is understandable, teachable, and applicable to advisers and student organizations regardless of type, size, or tradition.

Exhibit 4.1. Organizational Norms

Directions: Have each member of the executive board identify the organization's norms for each of the following categories. When they are finished, allow time for the members to compare and discuss their lists. Discussion questions are provided.

Process Questions

1. Are the norms you identified written or implicit?
2. Do the norms you identified apply differently among the executive officers than they do among the members?
3. Do any of the identified norms restrict or enhance members' ability to function?
4. Which of the norms were the clearest to understand?
5. Which of the identified norms are associated with organizational tradition or history?

Meeting structure (who leads, what pattern is followed, who reports, who makes decisions, who moves approval, who decides on seating, and so on):

Position requirements (academic, judicial, experience, length of service, and so on):

Dress (type of dress for occasions, conference travel, meetings, and so on):

Communication (frequency, type, formality, and so on):

Tuckman's Model of Group Development

Tuckman (1965) reviewed approximately fifty studies on group development that were conducted in a wide range of group settings within different time periods. Following this review he categorized group development into four stages: forming, storming, norming, and performing. Tuckman and Jensen (1977) conducted a later review and added a fifth group developmental stage, adjourning. In the forming stage, members determine their place in the organization, go through a testing or orientation process, and are more independent. The organization in the storming stage has members who react negatively to the demands of whatever tasks need to be accomplished; conflicts arise as members resist influence, and there is a high level of emotion. In the norming stage, in-group feelings and cohesiveness develop, and members accept the rules of behavior and discover new ways to work together. In the performing stage, the group becomes quite functional in dealing with tasks and responsibilities. Members have worked through issues of membership and roles; they focus their efforts and achieve their goals. In the adjourning stage, the group brings finality to the process, tasks are closed, and members anticipate a change in relationships.

You may assist the executive board and members in the involvement, participation, or planning of a number of activities for the organization during each of the five stages. The following lists outline activities for you to use at each stage.

Forming

- Develop ice breakers to help the members become acquainted.
- Coordinate a retreat or workshop for the executive officers or the organization members.
- Review the organization's mission and purpose with the membership.
- Identify the expectations of members and executive officers.
- Work with executive officers to share organizational history and tradition.
- Provide information to the executives and members on institutional policies and procedures.
- Have individual meetings with the organization president.
- Discuss effective meeting management, planning programs, and team building with the executive officers.
- Provide support to the executive officers.

- Provide an initial "to do" list for executives to assist them in beginning their duties.

Storming

- Provide mediation resources when conflicts become difficult for the group to manage.
- Teach confrontation and communication skills to the executive officers and members.
- Hold a roundtable discussion on issues with which the organization and membership are involved.
- Review the mission statement, purpose, and expectations in order to redefine the organization's action plans.
- Conduct a group decision-making activity.
- Discuss and review the executive officer roles.
- Develop a "rebuilding" team activity.
- Remind everyone that the storming stage is a natural part of the formation of a group.

Norming

- Schedule a more in-depth team-building activity that includes greater self-disclosure.
- Have the members design T-shirts, pins, or some other emblem with which to identify themselves and the group.
- Assist the group in starting a new program that will create a tradition.
- Review and possibly establish new goals for the organization.
- Maintain executive board and member relationships so as to avoid reverting back to the storming stage.

Performing

- Ensure that the organization and membership have a task.
- Support the members and executive officers by giving feedback about what is going well and what can be improved upon for the next year.
- Step back and allow the organization to perform.

Adjourning

- Develop a closure activity to help members determine what they learned and benefited from during the year.
- Conduct an assessment or evaluation of the year.
- Develop transition reports for new executives.

- Ensure that a plan of recognition is in place for the close of the year.
- Coordinate a closing banquet with awards and other expressions of appreciation.
- Encourage the executive officers and members to assist the group for next year in training, orientation, or other responsibilities.
- Identify how the organization contributed to the history or tradition of the organization.
- Ensure that the minutes, reports, and correspondence are properly stored and maintained in an archive.
- Record the addresses and phone numbers of graduating and other departing members for future correspondence.
- Give the members gifts of appreciation for their involvement in the organization.

Sherif and Sherif's Concepts on Adviser Acceptance

Sherif and Sherif (1964) provide us with insight on how groups view advisers. They believe that in order to develop good rapport and gain acceptance by the group, advisers need to (1) ensure by word and deed that group members are aware of the adviser's lack of authority in situations where the group needs to be together; (2) appear in word and deed as a "bigger brother" or "bigger sister" who is interested in the members and wishes them well, and who may be helpful on occasion; (3) avoid any signs of dislike or disapproval of any member, on the one hand, or signs of favoritism on the other; (4) avoid suggesting or initiating activities for the group, unless such activities are deliberately planned as a part of the organization's calendar; (5) be helpful in activities initiated by group members without displaying skills that will put the adviser in competition for status with group members.

Sherif and Sherif found that the greatest difficulty advisers faced was in avoiding two extremes: on one hand, they should not appear too involved or too aggressive, lest they create the impression that they are trying to take control; on the other hand, they cannot appear too uninvolved or passive, or they will give the impression that they are not interested in the group. A good adviser can strike a balance between being too involved or controlling and too passive. Exhibit 4.2 is an activity you can use with your organization to gauge how the members view you on the continuum of involvement. Once completed, this activity provides a good basis for discussion with the executive board.

Intentionally Structured Groups

An Intentionally Structured Group (ISG) is an "intervention designed to promote specific goals; it has a planned structure or framework and a specified duration—usually relatively short" (Winston, Bonney, Miller, and Dagley, 1988, p. 6). Winston and his colleagues have found that as vehicles for enhancing student development, groups have a number of advantages over individuals:

1. Groups are economical.
2. Groups appear less threatening than an individual seeking an outcome.
3. Groups often have a synergic effect—that is, the members of the group gain more from the experience than they would have through individual interventions.
4. Groups often focus attention on developmental areas for which the stimulus for change is too diluted in the overall campus environment.
5. Students generally give positive evaluations of and report enjoying well-designed and implemented group experiences.
6. Groups are versatile; they can focus on a given population of students, an identified problem, or a developmental task.
7. Group settings can provide a "safe" place to try out new roles and to practice different ways of relating to others.
8. Well-designed, well-implemented groups make excellent use of the instructional strategies identified in several student development interventions.

An ISG will typically have five stages: (1) establishment, (2) exploration, (3) transition, (4) working, and (5) termination (Winston, Miller, Bonney, and Dagley, 1988). In the establishment stage, members begin to learn each other's name and background, establish ground rules, and identify group norms; members together form a group identity; and the leader identifies the goals. In the exploration stage, roles are assigned by the group, and a hierarchy is developed based upon role assignment by the group; members test the ground rules, begin to develop trust, assess the leader's competence, and recognize the value of participating. In the transition stage, some members may violate group norms to determine consequences, noncommitted members may leave, and members recognize the importance of specific group members' influence, the power of the group, and the leader's limitations. In the working

Exhibit 4.2. Adviser Involvement

Directions: Have every member of the organization complete this exercise. It is designed to gauge the members' perceptions of your level of involvement. Different activities and events can be changed to suit those of your organization. Please circle the number that best represents your impression of your adviser's level of involvement.

		Low involvement			High involvement		
1.	Attendance at weekly meetings Comments:	1 2 3		4	5	6	7
2.	Speaking during weekly meetings Comments:	1 2 3		4	5	6	7
3.	Attendance at monthly activities Comments:	1 2 3		4	5	6	7

		Low involvement				High involvement		
4.	Making decisions for the organization Comments:	1	2	3	4	5	6	7
5.	Serving as a resource during weekly meetings Comments:	1	2	3	4	5	6	7
6.	Available to meet individually with members Comments:	1	2	3	4	5	6	7
7.	Assisting in travel preparations for conferences Comments:	1	2	3	4	5	6	7
8.	Other:							

stage, achieving goals is a cooperative effort; members practice new behaviors, provide and receive feedback, take more risks, express concern over group progress, and communicate among themselves; the leader acts as a consultant. In the termination stage, members achieve goal-related closure, evaluate the total experience, project into the future, and say good-bye to one another (Winston, Bonney, Miller, and Dagley, 1988).

ISGs can be effective tools for a student organization. You may recognize situations for which an ISG may be the best approach for resolving a problem; ISGs can be used when the organization seeks to identify student concerns, to conduct a needs assessment, to evaluate the organization's effectiveness, to train or orient leaders, to evaluate organizational structures, or to develop community responsibility.

Feldman and Newcomb (1969) studied student peer group functions and influences. They found that peer groups

> help individuals make the transition from the dependent role in the family to full membership in the postcollege adult world; can either support or discourage acceptance of the academic goals of the college; can provide students occasions for practice and getting along with people whose backgrounds, interests, and values are different from their own; and can provide support for the status quo, or they can challenge old values, provide intellectual stimulation, and act as a sounding board for new points of view, present new information and new experiences to the student, help to clarify new self-definitions, suggest new career possibilities, and provide emotional support for students who are changing. [pp. 236–237]

Lifton's Group Member Roles

Lifton (1967) identified three types of member roles in groups attempting to identify, select, and solve problems. The categories of roles are group task, group growing and vitalizing, and antigroup.

The group task roles for members attempting to identify, select, and solve problems are as follows:

Initiator contributor. Offers new ideas or a change of ways.

Information seeker. Seeks clarification of suggestions.

Opinion seeker. Seeks clarification of group values.

Information giver. Offers facts or generalizations.

Opinion giver. States beliefs or opinions pertinent to suggestions.

Elaborator. Gives examples or develops meanings.

Coordinator. Pulls ideas and suggestions together.

Orienter. Defines position of the group with respect to goals.

Evaluator. May evaluate or question the group's function.

Energizer. Prods the group to action or decision.

Procedural technician. Performs tasks and manipulates objects.

Recorder. Writes everything down and serves as the group memory.

The group growing and vitalizing roles for members are the following:

Encourager. Praises, agrees with, and accepts others' ideas.

Harmonizer. Mediates intergroup conflicts.

Compromiser. Operates from within the group to "come halfway."

Gatekeeper and expediter. Encourages and facilitates participation.

Standard setter or ego ideal. Expresses standards for the group.

Group observer and commentator. Keeps records of group processes.

Follower. Goes along somewhat passively.

The antigroup roles for members are the following:

Aggressor. Deflates status of others.

Blocker. Negativistic, stubborn, and unreasonably unrealistic.

Recognition seeker. Tries to call attention to self.

Self-confessor. Uses group to express non-group-oriented feelings.

Playboy. Displays lack of involvement in group's work.

Dominator. Tries to assert authority to manipulate members.

Help-seeker. Tries to get a sympathy response from others.

Special-interest pleader. Attempts to grow a grassroots effort.

You can work with the organization's leadership to assist the students in identifying the members who might take on antigroup roles and list possible strategies should those roles become evident when the group is attempting to identify, diagnose, or solve problems. Exhibit 4.3 is a progressive case study illustrating several of the member roles described by Lifton (1967).

Carl Rogers's Group Model

Carl Rogers (1948) provided a comprehensive analysis of groups that remains up-to-date for student organization advisers. He

Exhibit 4.3. Group Member Role Case Study

Directions: You can use the following progressive case study with groups of students or the executive board. Pass out the initial case to the participants and allow them time to answer the two questions. When they have completed the questions, take ten to fifteen minutes to discuss their answers. Following discussion, give the participants the first update and again allow time to complete the questions; continue with the second and third updates in the same way. To finish the activity, allow the participants time to complete the final questions prior to discussion.

Initial Case

You are an adviser to a sorority. You have served as adviser for the past eight years. The sorority has developed a six-person committee to review and make recommendations regarding the sorority's organizational structure.

You attend the first meeting of the committee, and it appears to you that the committee is made up of two initiator contributors, one evaluator, one harmonizer, one aggressor, and one dominator.

1. What are your concerns as an adviser at this point in the situation?

2. What action do you take at this point in the situation?

Update One

Following the second meeting, the sorority executive board announces that the committee will be chaired by Cindy (the harmonizer). The committee has struggled for the past two meetings since no chairperson was identified.

1. What are your concerns as an adviser at this point in the situation?

2. What action do you take at this point in the situation?

Update Two

During the next meeting of the committee, all representatives are in character. The dominator is asserting herself, the aggressor is deflating the others' status, and so on. The committee chair, Cindy, is desperately trying to keep the group on track. Following the meeting (you were not in attendance), she calls you and wants to meet with you and the sorority president. During that meeting, she announces that she wants to step down as chair.

1. What are your concerns as an adviser at this point in the situation?

2. What action do you take at this point in the situation?

Update Three

Following a lengthy discussion, Cindy has decided to stay on as chair. Her plan is to start over with a team-building activity, a goal development activity, and a role identification activity.

1. What are your concerns as an adviser at this point in the situation?

2. What action do you take at this point in the situation?

Final Questions

1. Could the executive board have made a better decision about how it composed the committee?

2. How did the late announcement of the committee chair affect the committee's work?

3. How would this situation have been different if another member of the committee had been chair?

4. What other strategies could the chair have employed to keep the committee on task?

5. Have you experienced a similar situation?

identified seven basic phases to the group process: (1) emotional release, (2) gradual exploration of attitudes, (3) growing conscious awareness of denied elements, (4) a changed perception of the problem in an altered frame of reference, (5) a changed concept of the group and the self, (6) a new course of consciously controlled action better adapted to the underlying reality of the situation, and (7) a resulting improvement in social and interpersonal relationships (Rogers, 1948).

In his discussion of Rogers, Sampson (1993, p. 72) states that Rogers reminds advisers of "the importance of the affective as well as cognitive dimensions of the group experience. He [reminds] us that it is as important to recognize the process that goes on in groups as it is to focus on the content as one attempts to solve problems or tackle tasks."

Cartwright's Group Dynamics

Cartwright (1951) developed eight principles of group dynamics that can enhance behavior or attitude change among group members:

1. If the group is to be used effectively as a medium of change, those people who are to be changed and those who are to exert influence for change must have a strong sense of belonging to the same group.

2. The more attractive the group is to its members, the greater the influence the group can exert on its members.

3. In an attempt to change attitudes, values, or behavior, the more relevant these are to the basis of attraction to the group, the greater will be the influence the group can exert upon them.

4. The greater the prestige of a group member in the eyes of other members, the greater the influence he or she can exert.

5. Efforts to change individuals or subparts of a group will encounter strong resistance if the outcome of those efforts would be the individuals' or subparts' deviating from the norms of the group.

6. Strong pressure for changes in the group may be established by the organization's leadership, creating a shared perception by members of the need for change, thus making the source of pressure for change the organization's membership.

7. For a change to be realized, information relating to the need for changes, the plans for change, and the consequences of change must be shared with all relevant people in the group.

8. Changes in one part of a group produce strain in other parts, which can be reduced only by eliminating the change or by bringing about readjustment in the related parts.

Astin (1993) conducted a number of empirical studies on the influences of the peer group. He concludes: "the student's peer group is the single most potent source of influence on growth and development during the undergraduate years" (p. 398). He adds that "student's values, beliefs, and aspirations tend to change in the direction of the dominant values, beliefs, and aspirations of the peer groups" (p. 398). This evidence supports Cartwright's assertions.

The effective student organization leader and adviser will recognize the power of the group development, a process in which values, pressures, norms, and issues are at work. You and the leaders of your organization should observe group dynamics early to identify subtle meanings, hints of potential problem areas, and relationships that could cause difficulty for the organization's leadership.

Napier and Gershenfeld's Stages of Group Development

Napier and Gershenfeld (1987) analyzed more than twenty group development concepts and created a composite model of the stages of group development and the activities, events, and feelings associated with those stages. Napier and Gershenfeld acknowledge that a wide variety of groups exist and that those groups have individual differences; nonetheless, their composite, outlined in the following sections, identifies many of the common themes observed in groups.

The Beginning.   During this stage, member expectations are established prior to a group meeting. Individuals bring their skills, experiences, and knowledge to the formative stage of group development. It is important for members to accept each other, after which they focus on the development of group goals. Studying the members of a group at this stage, we might observe the following feelings or behavior (Napier and Gershenfeld, 1987, p. 471):

- Keeping feelings to oneself until the situation is known
- Being watchful
- Being pleasant, certainly not hostile
- Being confused as to what is expected of members
- Desiring structure and order to reduce personal pressure to perform
- Finding personal immediate needs to be of primary importance
- Waiting for the leader to establish goals . . . and responsibilities
- Looking more secure in the surroundings than people might feel

The beginning is a time for members' observing, determining their place in the group, and establishing goals and parameters. Members may feel uncomfortable until they have found their place; they have little trust but are optimistic about the group's purpose.

Movement Toward Confrontation.   The second stage begins when the initial discomfort passes and the searching for place is resolved. Leadership and power relationships begin to evolve among members during this stage. Members begin to feel comfortable voicing their opinions, resulting in subgroups taking sides. Arguments ensue as members attempt to test their power and influence. "Group members may feel dissatisfied, angry, frustrated, and sad because they perceive the discrepancy between the initial hopes and expectations and the reality of group life, between the task and the ability to accomplish the task" (Napier and Gershenfeld, 1987, p. 473).

Compromise and Harmony. During this stage group members move to resolve differences, and their behaviors are more acceptable. The group is able to informally assess how the members have worked together and how they might enhance further work together; they allow each other time to express opinions, and they are open to those opinions. Group members have been observed to be less efficient during this time of harmony. Decisions are difficult to make because there is an increase in passive resistance.

Reassessment. During this stage, the group revisits and possibly revises its goals. Group member roles, "decision-making procedures, and leadership and communication patterns are likely to come under close scrutiny as are the personal behaviors that facilitated or inhibited the group" (Napier and Gershenfeld, 1987, p. 474). Group members realize that efforts to achieve goals must be distributed to all members. With an understanding that all members must participate, communicate, and complete tasks, the group can better focus on determining its direction and on attaining goals. Group member trust and risk taking are increasing during this stage.

Resolution and Recycling. The group at this stage is very productive, highly efficient, and very positive. Members still may possess some feelings of conflict and distrust, but the productivity of the group has matured to a point that these are nonissues. A measure of the maturity of the group is not that tensions do not exist but how effectively the group deals with these issues through good lines of communication, openness to feedback, and secure positive relationships.

It is important to remember that not all groups move beyond subgroup influences, destructive communication, or high levels of tension and negative feelings. In many instances, however, the maturity of the group will prevail if the group's leadership provides direction. Exhibit 4.4 is a case study that an organization's student leadership can use to practice identifying potential problems and to discuss their observations. The group leaders will be able to draw on this practice and discussion throughout the year as their organization passes through its developmental stages.

Exhibit 4.4. Group Stage Case Study

Directions: You can use the following progressive case study with a student organization's executive board. Pass out the Initial case to the participants and allow them time to answer the two questions. When they have completed the questions, take ten to fifteen minutes to discuss their answers. Following discussion, give the participants the first update and again allow time to complete the questions; continue with the second and third updates in the same way. To finish the activity, allow the participants time to complete the final questions prior to discussion.

Initial Case

You are members of the executive board to the Racquetball Club, a registered student organization. The club has been on campus for the past twenty years. You are all new members of the executive board. The club started meeting six weeks ago, with weekly meetings. Your adviser is a state champion racquetball player and has advised the club for the past ten years. At the last meeting, several new novice-level members of the club spoke up, stating that they feel the club does not have time for them because they are only beginners and the club stresses state and regional tournament play.

1. At what Napier and Gershenfeld stage is your organization, and why?

2. What action do you take at this point in the situation?

Update One

The president of the executive board responds to the club members that she would like to form a committee to evaluate the club's emphasis on tournament play. The expert members of the club voice their displeasure, stating that the reason they joined the club was to participate in tournaments. They further state that if the emphasis on tournament play is decreased, they will leave the club and start a new club that meets their needs.

1. At what Napier and Gershenfeld stage is your organization now, and why?

2. What action do you take at this point in the situation?

Update Two

The president is able to effectively close the meeting without any members quitting. The president contacts a member of the club who is seen as a leader by the tournament players. This member agrees with the president that the novice-level members should not be forgotten, considering that the expert members were once at that level themselves, and agrees to chair the review committee. By speaking individually with members, the president is able to recruit an equal number of novice- and tournament-level members to serve on the review committee.

1. At what Napier and Gershenfeld stage is your organization, and why?

2. What action do you take at this point in the situation?

Update Three

The review committee meets over the course of the next two months, providing updates every two to three weeks. There are still a few tournament members who feel that with a new purpose (to include the novice-level members), they will not receive the funding they have enjoyed in the past. The review committee makes its final recommendation; the club votes to accept the new purpose of equally emphasizing novice-level members and tournament members. The vote carries, with three of the thirty members voting against the recommendation.

1. At what Napier and Gershenfeld stage is your organization, and why?

2. What action do you take at this point in the situation?

Final Questions

1. What was the role of the adviser throughout this situation?

2. How would this situation have been different if a different member of the club had chaired the review committee?

3. What future problems might the club face as a result of this situation?

4. What can the executive board and adviser do now to alleviate the potential future problems?

Glanz and Hayes's Model

Glanz and Hayes (1967) distinguish groups from other formal gatherings in the following ways: (1) the members must be in face-to-face contact with one another; (2) it must be possible for them to have a high degree of interaction; and (3) they must have some common goal for whose attainment they are willing to expend certain energies.

Glanz and Hayes believe that groups fall into one of three categories: those that attempt to accomplish a task, those that attempt to develop or change participants, or those that provide structure to learning situations. Glanz and Hayes remind "group observers of the importance of the distinction of the content and the process of groups. Content is the 'what' of a group discussion; the subject matter of the group deliberations or actions. Process is the 'how' of a group discussion or the way the content is handled or discussed by the group" (Sampson, 1993, p. 73). According to Glanz and Hayes's model, a group brought together to complete a task should be as small as possible in order not to diffuse the task among a large number of people.

CHAPTER 5

Providing Academic
and Career Assistance

Many students begin their college education confused and indecisive about choosing their major; they may be concerned about how their peers will view them and about finding their way around campus. Becoming involved in campus life is one of the best ways for students to deal with their concerns, and it is also the most important variable in determining student academic success (Astin, 1993). The first step in providing academic and career guidance is to understand the crucial role that involvement plays in a student's success.

As an adviser, you become students' confidant, informal academic counselor, career counselor, and reference. Understanding the basic functions of career and educational guidance will prepare you to work more effectively with the organization's members. You do not need to become an expert at career or academic counseling, nor should you attempt to replace the services of other campus offices. However, in many cases, you are the first institutional representative a student will approach with regard to career issues. Through your involvement with the student organization, you will develop relationships with students in which they feel comfortable seeking your advice about career and academic matters.

In this chapter we provide information on career development that you can use in your work with students. The student's career development process includes developing an involvement log; completing an occupational analysis; understanding how values, ethics, and moral development influence the decisions made in their career development process; completing a transferable skills exercise; writing cover letters and a résumé; networking; identifying job and nonjob factors in choosing a career; and interviewing. Our discussion of educational guidance includes selected academic issues and information on making proper referrals.

Career Development

Career development is a process. A student's career identity and the role that work will play in his or her life emerge gradually (Super, 1980). Students will explore their values to clarify such career-related decisions as their choice of major, choice of career, work experience, and so on.

Students also must work within specific guidelines and requirements imposed by the university as part of its registration process or placement services, and you need to be aware of these broad institutional policies. An institution may, for example, require that students declare majors upon matriculation or that students will be admitted to an academic department only on the condition that they have completed a certain number of credit hours. The aspects of career development that we discuss here can help you assist students as they encounter challenges during these turning points in their academic careers. (If you are an adviser who is not directly involved in the academic advising, teaching classes, or other academic aspect of the institution, a student's selection of a college and subsequent major are issues that you should refer to the responsible campus agency.)

Involvement Log

Students benefit from beginning an involvement log upon enrollment and maintaining it throughout their time on campus, as they become involved in numerous leadership positions and work opportunities, or receive honors and awards. By keeping track of these experiences as they occur, students will later be able to identify the key activities from the involvement log to use in their résumé or for interviews. The involvement log should be as complete as possible. Students also should begin to identify the supervisors, faculty, or student organization advisers they would want to have serve as references for job searches, internships, or scholarship applications. You can promote the use of an involvement log and pass out copies to organization members. Exhibit 5.1 provides an example of an involvement log.

Exhibit 5.1. Involvement Log

Directions: Create an involvement log by filling in the items that follow.

Full Name _____

Education: Include degree-major-minor, date, location.

Honor Societies (for example, Blue Key): Include activity, dates, leadership positions.

Residence Hall Involvement (for example, hall government): Include activity, dates, leadership positions.

Campuswide Groups (for example, summer orientation staff): Include activity, dates, leadership positions.

Greek Life (for example, Delta Delta Delta): Include activity, dates, leadership positions.

Spiritual Organizations (for example, Jewish Student Organization): Include activity, dates, leadership positions.

Service Organizations (for example, Habitat for Humanity): Include activity, dates, leadership positions.

Recreation Sports (for example, intramural football): Include activity, dates, leadership positions.

Departmental and Professional Organizations (for example, American Marketing Association): Include activity, dates, leadership positions.

Conferences and Workshops Attended (for example, Graduate Student and Faculty Forum): Include activity, dates, leadership positions.

Presentations and Publications: Include activity, dates.

Other Activities: Include activity, dates, leadership positions.

On-Campus, Off-Campus Employment: Include position or organization, description, dates.

Awards, Scholarships, Special Recognition: Include name and basis for award.

References: Include name, position, address, phone.

Occupational Analysis

For students to confirm their choice of academic major, work experience, or career, it is crucial that they find out enough information about the career or occupation to know whether it matches their skills, aspirations, and interests. Performing an occupational analysis is a simple approach to identifying the information and skills necessary for that specific career or occupation. You should encourage students to use the campus placement office to access information on various companies and occupations. Exhibit 5.2 illustrates an occupational analysis form.

Values, Ethics, and Moral Development

You can provide information that augments students' ability to make academic and career decisions by helping them develop an understanding of values, ethics, and moral development. In the following sections, we provide relatively simple definitions of these concepts as well as several models that can be applied to situations you might encounter with student organizations. The literature on values, ethics, and moral development is extensive; we encourage you to explore these writings for more complex approaches to these vitally important topics.

Values.   According to *The Merriam-Webster Dictionary* (1995, p. 575), a value is "something (as a principle or ideal) intrinsically valuable or desirable." One's values determine the worth that is placed on things. "Our values even influence the selection and formulation of the facts. There are no totally value-free observations People often agree on the facts and still disagree about the facts' meaning, because people use different values to evaluate them" (Brown, 1990, p. 36).

Following are two examples illustrating how differences in values among members can be quite dramatic even when there is agreement on a basic concept. The situations described would provide excellent opportunities for organization members to discuss differences in values.

> A group of student organization members who will be driving to a conference agree that they will need to rent two vans. Some students want two fifteen-passenger vans with a television and VCR because they believe there should be additional space for comfort and a VCR for entertainment. Other students disagree: they want to settle on two twelve-passenger vans with standard interiors because they believe that spending money on larger vans with a VCR is a waste of money.

Exhibit 5.2. Occupational Analysis

You will find much of the information necessary to complete this occupational analysis in the placement center library. Please make comments on as many of these items as possible.

Position, title, occupation, or career field:

Types of companies and organizations that would employ such occupations:

Opportunities for advancement in such a company:

Advantages in the position or occupation:

Disadvantages in the position or occupation:

Training programs available:

Salary range:

Geographical mobility—any restrictions:

Sources of challenge and support for this position or occupation:

Status of influence or position:

Scope of responsibilities in the position or occupation:

Problem solving responsibility in the position or occupation:

Competition for positions:

Stress of work environment:

Educational background or experience needed:

Physical abilities needed:

Merit rewards for results:

Source: Adapted with permission from Dunkel, Bray, and Wofford, 1989.

All the organization's members agree that an end-of-year banquet is a good idea. Some members want to have the meal on campus, using the institution's dining service. Others would like to go to a local restaurant buffet and use a private room, and still other members would like to go to the local hotel, rent a dining room, and have a sit-down catered meal.

"Whether values are taught formally in the curriculum or not, the attitude, conduct, and belief of students have always been influenced by their colleges. The specific organization of knowledge, . . . the manner in which faculty relate to the students, the role accorded to out-of-class experiences, . . . all reveal certain values of the college, and their expectations for values development in students" (Sandeen, 1985, p. 2). As an adviser, you have an opportunity to assist students as they make difficult, value-laden decisions for themselves and their organizations.

Ethics. Ethics is "the discipline dealing with good and evil and with moral duty" (*The Merriam-Webster Dictionary*, 1995, p. 177). Brown (1990, p. 16) asserts that "ethics assumes that people have the freedom and power to respond—that is, the freedom and power to consider different options, to analyze the options' strengths and weaknesses, and to choose one option over the others based on its merits." Guiding students' decisions are the right and wrong or good and bad actions that are the consequences of those decisions.

Karen Kitchener (1985) provides an excellent model for ethical decision making. She has adapted five principles that are relevant in dealing with the behavior of students. The first principle, *respecting autonomy*, includes the right of individuals to decide how to live their lives as long as their actions do not interfere with the welfare of others. The second principle is *doing no harm*. (Harm is further defined as either psychological or physical.) This principle encourages organizations to examine their policies and practices to ensure there is no long-term potential for doing harm. The third principle, *benefiting others*, includes the assertion that one should make decisions that have the potential for a positive effect on others. The fourth principle is *being just*, which incorporates the need for people to be fair and to treat others as they would like to be treated. The final principle is *being faithful*, which involves issues of loyalty, truthfulness, promise keeping, and respect.

These five principles can serve as a basis for student discussion in dealing with individual or organizational decisions. Similarly, using the following "ethics check" questions can sharpen the decision-making process and ensure that the organization is adhering to the five ethical principles.

Blanchard and Peale (1988) provide questions to help examine ethical decisions. The first question an individual or organization must ask is, Is the proposed action or decision legal? This includes the issue of whether or not the decision will violate civil law, the university code of conduct, or university policies. The second question is, Is the decision balanced? Balance means that the decision must be fair to all concerned in the short and long term and should promote a winning relationship. The third question is, How will the decision make me feel about myself? The decision should make one feel proud; one would feel good if it were released to the media and good if one's family knew about it.

These three straightforward questions allow students to understand the ramifications of their individual and organizational decisions more clearly. Exhibit 5.3 provides a progressive case study on ethical decision making.

Morals.   Morals are "of or relating to principles of right or wrong . . . conforming to a standard of right behavior" (*The Merriam-Webster Dictionary*, 1995, p. 338). We have found three models of moral development to be particularly useful to advisers; we will briefly describe each.

The first is Rest's Model (1983), which identifies four distinct activities that an individual must perform in order to engage in moral behavior. They may be summarized as (1) interpreting the situation, (2) deciding what is morally right, (3) choosing between moral values and other values, and (4) implementing a plan of action. This model provides a simple, understandable approach that students can apply to their individual and organizational decisions. Differences of opinion may emerge among the students as to what is morally right or even regarding their interpretation of a given situation. Facilitated discussion of these differences will benefit everyone.

The second model is Kohlberg's Six Stages of Moral Development (1984). In this model, stages of moral development describe what motivates individuals to make decisions about right and wrong action.

1. *Fear of punishment.* The person is motivated to obey not because he or she agrees with the rules but simply to avoid punishment.

2. *Seeking rewards.* The person is motivated to act if there is something to gain.

3. *Seeking approval.* Friendship and mutual understanding of one another's feelings, needs, and wants lead to cooperation.

Exhibit 5.3. Ethics Case Study

Directions: You can use this progressive case study yourself or with students. Pass out the initial case to the participants and allow them time to answer the question at the end. When they have completed the question, take ten to fifteen minutes to discuss their answers. Pass out the first update and discuss; continue with the second, third, and fourth updates in the same way.

Initial Case

You are a senior and sorority president at Southern Gulf University. The football team beat one of its major rivals last night and there were numerous parties following the game. A nineteen-year-old member of your sorority attended one of the parties. On Saturday afternoon, the day following the game, the nineteen-year-old files a report with the University Police Department claiming she was raped at the previous night's party.

The student stated that she drank a great deal and went looking for a bathroom. A young man took her to a bathroom, where she was grabbed by a second man and subsequently sexually assaulted by both. Because the light was out she could not recognize the men.

The next morning, her roommate convinced her to go to the police. The investigators found evidence of the party in a residence hall, and the hall director gave full support. The police identified one suspect, Wayne, who was discovered unconscious in the bathroom. Wayne has a reputation for being a ladies' man and enjoying parties.

Because the lights were out at the time of the assault, the student could not identify Wayne, and no arrests were made.

Three years before this case, you lived in a coeducational residence hall with Wayne. Wayne came back to you after the recent incident and told you that he could not remember anything from the evening. He stated that he didn't think he assaulted the woman, but he was so drunk he was not sure. He was certainly not going to share that information with the police.

What do you do with the information Wayne has given you?

Update One

It is one year later. Wayne is applying to law school and has asked you to be a character reference for him. What do you tell him?

Update Two

It is ten years later. Wayne is interviewing for a faculty position at the university where you work. You personally know the selection committee chair. Do you contact the chair? If so, what do you say?

Update Three

It is five years later. You are now the vice president for student affairs. Wayne is up for tenure, yet there is a rumor that he dates students. An assistant dean has made you aware of the rumors. What do you do at this point?

Update Four

It is three years later. Your daughter now attends the university; one day she comes home and tells you that she has met a wonderful man named Wayne who is an assistant professor at the university. Now what do you do?

4. *Obeying rules of societal order.* People follow the law and do their jobs knowing that others are doing the same.

5. *Concern with individual rights and social contracts.* Laws are in place and ensure basic rights; each person has a say in the decision-making process.

6. *Concern with consistent, comprehensive, and ethical principles.* No person deviates from cooperation because doing so would give some members an advantage at the expense of others.

The third model is Carol Gilligan's Theory of Moral Judgment (1982). According to Beabout and Wenneman (1994, pp. 39–40), Gilligan believes that Kohlberg's approach places "too much emphasis on moral rules, and not enough accent on relationships. . . . She claimed that Kohlberg's method of evaluating moral development emphasized rules and was therefore biased against females." Gilligan believes that the moral development of women is different than that of men. In her view, women focus on relationships, which includes caring and sensitivity, whereas men focus on judging, which includes rules, confrontation, and conflict resolution.

Exhibit 5.4 is a brief case study to assist students and advisers with questions of moral development.

Transferable Skills

You have an opportunity to assist students in identifying the skills they have acquired and refined through their involvement in organizational meetings, writing reports, traveling to conferences, participating in competitions, presenting programs, coordinating events, facilitating speakers, and so forth. These skills and traits can be discussed in résumés and interviews, and they may be transferable to the students' daily practice or in their career position following graduation (Dunkel, Bray, and Wofford, 1989).

Sidney Fine (1985) developed a definition and taxonomy of career skills. His first category includes adaptive skills, or self-management skills. We acquire skills in our early years from family, peers, and school; they relate to environments, and particularly to the requirements or demands for social conformity and continuity. An example of this might be managing oneself in one's relation to authority or punctuality.

The second category is functional skills, which are instrumental or transferable skills. We acquire these skills either as natural-born talents, through experience or education, or through specific

Exhibit 5.4. Moral Development Case Study

> **Directions:** You can work on this case study yourself or with students. Pass out the case study and allow participants time to read and individually answer the questions. Facilitate a group discussion of the responses.

Case Study

You are the adviser to the rugby club at Maple College. You have served as adviser for the past three years. The rugby club has been at Maple College for over twenty-five years and has a winning reputation.

Mark is the rugby club president. He is a sophomore majoring in journalism. At the beginning of the fall term, Mark is aggressive in his recruiting of new members, and once he recruits them, he wants to initiate them with the traditional night of heavy drinking and activities.

Paul is a senior and has been a member for the past three years. At the beginning of his fourth year, he has the idea that new members ought to participate in building a home for Habitat for Humanity.

Mike is a graduate student and has been a member for two years. As an undergraduate he had been a member of the rugby club at a large university. Mike states that when he was at the other institution, his rugby club was on probation for two years because of hazing and serving minors at alcohol functions. He does not want that to happen to the Maple College rugby club and presses the membership to become involved as security escorts at night as part of a program offered by the college police.

1. At what Kohlberg stages are Mark, Paul, and Mike? Why?

2. What will likely occur with the club if Mark has his way? If Paul has his way?

3. What is the role of the adviser in this situation?

4. How could Rest's Model be applied to this situation?

educational, vocational, or avocational training. Transferable or instrumental skills are related to people, data, and things in a generalizable or transferable fashion (for example, from one field, profession, occupation, or job to another). Examples of this type of skill are operating machinery and compiling or analyzing data.

The third category is specific or work-content skills, which relate to particular job conditions or vocabulary skills. These skills are acquired through reading, apprenticeship, technical training, institutes, or school, and are often acquired on the job. These skills relate to performing a job in a particular field, profession, or occupation, according to the specifications and conditions of a particular employer.

Exhibit 5.5 is an exercise to help students identify their transferable skills.

Cover Letters and Résumés

In the next two sections we discuss the cover letter and the résumé, and provide tips for students to help them in preparing each of these documents.

Cover Letter.   The cover letter is a student's response to a notice about a particular job or position, and it serves to introduce the student to the employer. The letter should highlight aspects of the student's work, education, or experience but not duplicate his or her résumé. The following tips will assist students in the preparation of a cover letter, and Exhibit 5.6 provides a sample.

- Always include a cover letter when sending a résumé.
- Each cover letter should be written for a particular position. Never send a form letter to replace a cover letter. Take the time to tailor an individual letter to each employer.
- Do not begin each line or paragraph with "I."
- Address the cover letter to an individual, preferably the individual who will make the hiring decisions. Students may have to do some homework to identify who that person is.
- Start the cover letter with information on how you learned of the vacancy and the title of the vacant position.
- Highlight information from your résumé that is relevant to the qualifications of the position.
- Highlight one or two achievements that indicate how you can meet the needs of the company to which the application is directed.

Exhibit 5.5. Transferable Skills Exercise

Directions: This exercise can be completed by one student or a group of students working individually. Students should be given ample time to review the following list of skills and traits. The list represents adaptive, functional, and work-content skills. Remind students to check only those skills they have used in their position. At the end of the exercise is a discussion on how to apply the findings.

Communication

_____ negotiating	_____ foreign language
_____ mediating	_____ reading
_____ public speaking	_____ writing minutes
_____ debating	_____ sign language
_____ mediating	_____ braille
_____ interviewing	_____ active listening
_____ arbitrating	_____ briefing
_____ creative writing	_____ technical writing
_____ business writing	_____ telephoning
_____ editing	_____ translating
_____ speech writing	_____ summarizing
_____ proofreading	_____ influencing
_____ persuading	_____ informing
_____ spelling	_____ lecturing

Physical

_____ motor coordination	_____ endurance
_____ strength	_____ agility
_____ speed	_____ competitiveness

Self-Management

_____ self-directing	_____ goal setting
_____ patient	_____ ambitious
_____ time management	_____ realistic
_____ prioritizing tasks	_____ follow-through
_____ dependable	_____ stress management
_____ calm	_____ self-disciplined
_____ mature	_____ handle variety of tasks

_____ assertive　　　　　　　　　　_____ traveling

_____ risk taking　　　　　　　　　　_____ modeling

_____ move into new environments　　_____ vision
　　　on your own

Researching and Data Collection

_____ record keeping　　　　　　　_____ technical reading

_____ memory for detail　　　　　　_____ observing

_____ organizing data　　　　　　　_____ note taking

_____ retrieving data　　　　　　　_____ analyzing quantitative data

_____ testing　　　　　　　　　　　_____ developing a budget

_____ investigation　　　　　　　　_____ information processing

_____ scientific writing　　　　　　_____ researching data

Mathematical and Scientific

_____ lab techniques　　　　　　　_____ use of lab equipment

_____ inventing　　　　　　　　　　_____ accuracy

_____ accounting　　　　　　　　　_____ finance

_____ administer a budget　　　　　_____ advanced math abilities

_____ detailed instructions　　　　_____ field work abilities

_____ memorization　　　　　　　　_____ conceptual thinking

_____ pragmatic　　　　　　　　　　_____ systematic

Creative

_____ imaginative　　　　　　　　　_____ composing

_____ illustrating　　　　　　　　　_____ musical ability

_____ interior decorating　　　　　_____ singing

_____ drawing　　　　　　　　　　　_____ performing

_____ painting　　　　　　　　　　　_____ dance

_____ sketching　　　　　　　　　　_____ showmanship

_____ landscaping　　　　　　　　　_____ creative visual displays

_____ photography　　　　　　　　　_____ culinary talent

_____ pantomime　　　　　　　　　　_____ computer freehand

Leadership

_____ directing　　　　　　　　　　_____ team building

_____ group facilitating　　　　　　_____ motivating

_____ supervising
_____ coaching
_____ policymaking
_____ parliamentary procedure
_____ delegating
_____ planning
_____ decision making
_____ business approach

_____ teaching
_____ mentoring
_____ chairing committees
_____ organizing
_____ promoting
_____ self-confidence
_____ programming
_____ developing procedures

Logic

_____ troubleshooting
_____ rational thinking
_____ forecasting
_____ quick thinking
_____ legal concepts

_____ problem solving
_____ diagnosing
_____ problem identification
_____ cause-effect relationships
_____ decision making

Programming

_____ hosting conferences
_____ productive
_____ social
_____ enterprising
_____ publicity
_____ financial planning
_____ evaluation
_____ foresight

_____ energetic
_____ educational
_____ resourceful
_____ solicitations
_____ designing projects
_____ assessment
_____ reports
_____ referrals

Interpersonal Relationships

_____ advising
_____ understanding
_____ sensitivity
_____ goal clarification
_____ training
_____ positive attitude
_____ counseling
_____ rapport
_____ personable
_____ networking
_____ personal growth

_____ patience
_____ liaison
_____ warmth
_____ empathetic
_____ serving others
_____ crisis intervention
_____ recruiting talent
_____ trust
_____ poised
_____ enthusiasm
_____ helpful

Review the skills and traits you have checked. Identify the twenty most applicable to your current position and record them below:

1.	11.
2.	12.
3.	13.
4.	14.
5.	15.
6.	16.
7.	17.
8.	18.
9.	19.
10.	20.

Review Sidney Fine's definition of skills. Identify which of your twenty are adaptive, functional, or work-content skills. List each of your twenty skills or traits under the appropriate column below:

Adaptive   *Functional*   *Specific or Work Content*

These twenty skills or traits will be most valuable to you in composing your résumé (mention the skills or traits in the description of your experiences), preparing for interviews (identify key skills or traits that were gained or enhanced through involvement in a specific position or organization), and in recruiting students to leadership positions (when seeking applications, identify the skills and traits gained or enhanced by involvement in the leadership position). You should review this list on an annual basis; make changes and revisions as you remain in your position or when you change positions.

Source: Adapted from Dunkel, Bray, and Wofford, 1989.

Exhibit 5.6. Sample Cover Letter

_____

Date

Name of person (hiring agent)

Name of company

Address

City, state, zip

Dear _____:

First paragraph: include where you heard of the position, why you are applying, and the title of the position.

Second (and third) paragraph: include your reasons for applying for the position. Identify one or two achievements to demonstrate your production and how you can meet the needs of the company.

Final paragraph: introduce an opportunity for an interview by providing information such as a phone number or an appointment date.

Sincerely,

Full Name

Encl: Résumé of [your name]

- Include any information that is not provided on the résumé, such as a change in telephone number during spring break.

- Keep the length of the cover letter to one page. Allow the résumé to provide the specific information on education, work experience, awards, and so forth.

- Sign the letter with black ink. If an employer wants to make additional copies, black ink reproduces much better than other colored inks.

- Print the cover letter on paper that is white, ivory, eggshell, gray, or some other conservative color. The paper should be of the same weight as the résumé (usually greater than twenty pounds) and should be of the same color.

Résumé. Munschauer (1986, p. 26) states that the "uses of a résumé are many. It might be used to convince an employer to interview you, perhaps as part of a prescreening program. Sometimes it is used as a follow-up to an interview to summarize and highlight your qualifications. It might be tailored to complement a letter of application for a particular job, or it might be designed to appeal to employers in a broad field—sales, for example—and used as an attachment for a letter to sales managers." A résumé can provide information to an employer that will reveal the following four qualities (Munschauer, 1986, p. 26): "(1) Industriousness and ambition through activities, employment, and achievements, (2) Cooperative attitude through participation in activities, clubs, and sports, (3) Interest in the work and enthusiasm for the employer's product or service through a positive job objective or statement of career interest . . ., and (4) An orderly and businesslike mind through a crisp, neat format which reflects a businesslike mind. A poorly typed and sloppily reproduced résumé triggers a dislike."

You should refer students to the campus placement center for consultation on the process of preparing a résumé. The following suggestions will also be of help, and Exhibit 5.7 provides a sample résumé.

- Provide your formal name, address, telephone number, and e-mail address. You must be available at all times. If there is a point during the term when your availability is different, include that information in your cover letter.

- Identify a clear, job-specific professional objective.

- Design your résumé to show the most important qualification first. Typically, this will be the education category. Include your grade-point average in the education category if it has received recognition.

Exhibit 5.7. Sample Résumé

John A. Smith

Local:	Permanent (after 5-5-98):
1921 South Main, Apt. 4	168-2nd Street
Bayview Heights, GA 23412	Ashton, IL 61006
(121) 355-1289	(815) 453-2221
John@bayview.edu	

Professional Objective: An entry-level position in sales management, with interest in computer trends analysis.

Education:	Bachelor of Science in Marketing	May, 1997
	Bayview Heights College	Bayview Heights, GA
	Major Grade-Point Average 3.85/4.0	

Work Experience: Financed 95 percent of college expenses through the following jobs

Salesperson	November 1996 to present
Front Marketing Specialist	Atlanta, GA

Responsible for inventory control, training of new employees, cash drawer accounting, and closing of the store.

Resident Assistant	August 1995 to May 1996
Bayview Heights College	Bayview Heights, GA

Responsible for developing social and educational programs, monitoring the discipline process, peer counseling, and crisis management for fifty men in a residence hall.

Leadership Experience:

President, American Marketing Association, Bayview Heights College Chapter, August 1996 to present. Facilitated weekly meetings, organized an annual marketing experiences seminar, recruited new members, and developed a computer analysis of alumni members.

Member, College Computer Graphics Club, November 1994 to present. Participated in several computer graphics development projects.

Member, Bayview Heights College Varsity Tennis Team, August 1994 to May 1995.

Special Interests: Using software and hardware on an IBM platform, tennis, traveling.

References: Available upon request.

- Develop an employment category that lists your work chronologically, with the most recent employment first. It is important to include all work experience in this category. Employers are interested in reading your work history whether or not all the positions apply to the position for which you have applied.

- Develop a leadership category to include student leadership positions and active memberships. Employers are interested in these experiences, because they indicate leadership, communication skills, organizational skills, and so on.

- Pay attention to how you highlight the headings. Boldface, underlining, capitalization, italics, and colons highlight words or headings. Do not combine several of these in the same heading, as that will both overaccentuate that heading and look unprofessional.

- Try to keep the length of the résumé to one page if you have a bachelor's degree. Understand the standards of the field to which you are applying. Some career fields allow for a lengthier résumé, whereas others dictate clearly that the résumé should be one page, with black ink on white paper.

- Provide a list of at least three references when requested. The references should be individuals who have served as supervisors from your work experience, advisers from your organizational experience, and faculty from your major course work. Include the complete address, telephone numbers, fax numbers, and e-mail addresses of the references.

- Print the résumé on paper that is white, ivory, eggshell, gray, or some other conservative color. The weight of the paper should be at least twenty pounds and be the same color as the cover letter.

Networking

Networking is the process of making personal and professional contacts for the primary purpose of advancing one's career. These personal contacts can provide a student information about what it is like to work in a particular job. Professional contacts can assist the student in opening doors to discuss job opportunities with an appropriate person or can provide information on the best way to apply, interview, or possibly negotiate for a job. Through networking, students also can gain firsthand knowledge of potential job opportunities that might not be made public (George Mason University, 1988). Exhibit 5.8 provides a list of possible personal and professional contacts for networking.

Job and Nonjob Factors

Students inevitably will ask you questions about the location of a job, how much money they will make, or what kind of weather exists in a certain part of the country. All these questions pertain to what we can call job and nonjob factors. It is important that students determine which values in their lives are of higher priority than others and which they might compromise in order to secure a specific job. For instance, if a student practices a specific religion and a job is offered in a part of the country where the closest house of worship is fifty miles away, is the student willing to compromise in order to work for that company? Exhibit 5.9 is an exercise to help students identify the job and nonjob factors they will want to take into account when considering a specific company or job.

Exhibit 5.8. Networking List

It is important to begin developing a networking list early in your student career. Your list can include many people you have known even though you did not realize they had networking potential.

First, contact people you know well to discuss your résumé and experiences. As you become comfortable discussing these experiences, broaden your network by making an appointment to meet with an individual in a company, or by talking on the telephone with a person you met at a conference.

Friends:

Family	Relatives
Doctors	Neighbors
Dentists	Faculty
Adviser	Classmates
Organization members	Spiritual
Sports	Alumni

Business:

Political	Recruiters
Former employers	Owners
Colleagues	Trainers
Personnel directors	Contributors
Sales	Administrators
Insurance	Attorneys

Exhibit 5.9. Job and Nonjob Factors

The job factors listed below are examples of what you might want to consider prior to selecting a job. Read through the list and then rank your five most important job factors.

Hours worked per week   Salary
Vacation time   Sick time
Travel   Type of supervisor
Work environment   Frequency of moves
Type of product   Training available
Opportunity for advancement   Type of coworkers
Opportunity for education   Flexibility of hours
Size of company   Technology available
Supplies provided   Break facilities
Clientele served   ADA compliant

Select your five most important:

1. _____

2. _____

3. _____

4. _____

5. _____

The nonjob factors listed below are examples of what you might want to consider prior to selecting a job. Read through the list and then rank your five most important nonjob factors.

Recreational opportunities   Climate
Schools and universities in area Cost of living
Cultural events   Opportunities for partner
Local taxes and fees   Spiritual opportunities
Volunteer opportunities   Size of community
Proximity to family   Proximity to friends
Distance to work   Crime
Condition of roads   Shopping opportunities
Phone and cable service

Select your five most important:

1. _____

2. _____

3. _____

4. _____

5. _____

Exhibit 5.10. Interviewing

The following are tips to help prospective employees have successful interviews.

Pre-Interview

- Start a file on the company that has the vacancy (include any correspondence, salary information, locations, and so on).
- Know your skills so that you can openly discuss them.
- Role-play the interview for practice.
- Know the interviewer's full name and write it down for quick reference.
- Avoid extremes in dress (check with the campus placement office for published material on what to wear during interviews).
- Bring paperwork to the interview (including extra copies of your résumé, application, portfolio, and so on).
- Be prepared to ask one or two standard questions (for example, What are the opportunities for professional development?).
- Use a good-quality portfolio to bring materials to the interview, and have a nice pen.
- Arrive about ten minutes prior to the interview; stop by the restroom and look in the mirror to ensure that your hair, clothes, and so forth are in order.

Interview

- Follow the interviewer's lead as to where to sit.
- Offer your hand and use a firm grip.
- Walk with good, upright posture.
- Smile and practice good eye contact with the interviewer.
- Use nonverbal communication when answering questions.
- Use a good, upright sitting posture to appear businesslike but not too rigid.
- Sit with your legs uncrossed, if possible.
- Be concise in your answers but not too brief.
- Give the interviewer an opportunity to ask several questions.
- Use some levity, if appropriate.
- Be enthusiastic about the company, the position, and the interview.
- Don't be afraid of a few moments of silence when you are collecting your thoughts.
- Do not fill silences with "ah" and "um."
- Take care not to overtly drop names—of employees working for the company, former employees, or other individuals.
- Concentrate on your strong points when answering questions.
- Be prepared to answer skill-set questions about goals that you set this past year, what skills you developed through your involvement in a specific leadership position, or situations in which you have had to solve a problem and follow up on it in writing.
- Prepare for the conclusion of the interview.
- Let the interviewer take the lead in the closing.

- Be prepared for the interviewer's asking you if there are any other questions or points that should be shared.
- Exit as gracefully as you entered.

Post-Interview

- Send thank-you notes immediately to the interviewer, support staff, and anyone else who assisted in the interview process.
- Call the appropriate person if other questions come up as a result of the interview.
- Send any additional information that might have been requested at the time of the interview.
- Follow up with any travel information or receipts that need to be submitted to the company.
- Analyze the interview to determine your strengths, areas that need improvement, and so forth.

Interviewing

The student and the hiring authority get to know one another during an interview, which is far more than the typical informal conversation. The student needs to complete certain activities prior to, during, and following the interview; Exhibit 5.10 summarizes some of these activities. Becoming familiar with them will be valuable to you in your work with students; you may also want to arrange a program in which students conduct mock interviews.

Educational Assistance _____

We stated in the Preface that this book does not provide information directly related to academic advising. We have also pointed out, however, that students will be asking you any number of questions related to academic concerns. You may be well prepared to respond to academically related questions if you are a member of the faculty, perform academic advising functions as a responsibility, or work in a campus department that provides related services such as registration or admissions. If you are not in one of these departments, you will want to refer students with academic questions to the appropriate campus resource. Regardless of your position, knowledge of some academic issues will help you respond to basic student questions. Advisers who are prepared to respond with information or a proper referral will enhance their relationship with the members of the student organization. Making a commitment to understand the details of this aspect of the campus will be a small investment that leads to great benefits both personally and professionally. The following list itemizes some of these academic issues.

Know critical academic dates: when students register for classes, the last day to add or drop, the last day to withdraw, when classes begin, when classes end, and when midterms and finals are scheduled.

Understand the process for withdrawing from a course or term for medical, psychological, or other reasons.

Identify the location of academic advisers or counselors on campus.

Know when a student must declare a major and what minimum grade-point average is required to enter a department, college, or degree program.

Know the cost of tuition.

Know where to refer students when they are having difficulty taking tests, taking notes, or studying for exams.

Know key exam dates including the GRE, MCAT, and LSAT.

Understand the application process and qualifications for admission to the graduate school.

Know where to send students if they have a grievance or want to petition for a grade change.

Understand the academic requirements for students to maintain an elected position in a student organization, such as carrying a full load of classes, maintaining a certain grade-point average, being accepted into a degree-granting program, and so forth. Also, know where a student can petition for an exemption from the requirements.

Know where to refer a student if he or she is having difficulty selecting a major (typically the campus academic advising center, the counseling center, or the career planning center) or wants to change a major.

A student's ability to manage an academic load and extracurricular involvement is determined by his or her time management skills. Inevitably, you will spend considerable time working individually with students as they struggle to manage their time. In some cases an adjustment to the student's daily routine is all that is necessary, whereas in other cases, dropping activities, reducing his or her work load, or limiting other involvements may be the only answer to alleviating scheduling problems. Exhibit 5.11 provides a time management analysis that you can use to assist students in identifying their activities and the amount of time involved.

Exhibit 5.11. Time Management Analysis

Directions: Have the student log all his or her activities for the course of one week on an Activity Log. The log should include time spent sleeping, getting ready in the morning, being in classes, going to and from classes, eating, watching television, and so on. All twenty-four hours of each day should be accounted for.

Following the student's completion of the log, meet with him or her to analyze the information in order to plan accordingly.

1. Analyze the present situation by asking the student to respond to the following questions:

   How are you presently using your time?

   What are your time-wasting activities?

   For which activities do you have control of the amount of time you spend?

2. Have the student establish priorities for a given week.

3. Have the student set goals for the amount of time for each activity.

4. Have the student schedule the week according to the priorities set.

5. Have the student experience the week and record any modification to the schedule.

6. Meet with the student to analyze the modification and develop another week's schedule.

CHAPTER 6

Representing Group and Institutional Interests

By definition, student organizations function within institutions of higher education. These organizations exist within a framework designed for them by the policies and procedures adopted by the college or university. Policies are established by administrators or faculty, or by the students themselves, either through their governmental organizations or their constitution and by-laws.

The leadership of student organizations changes almost every year: there is a new president, a new treasurer; new members join, former members and leaders drop out for various reasons. As a consequence, the new leaders and members may have a very limited sense of the history of the organization, and they may not know how to accomplish their objectives within the framework of the institution. In these situations, you play a key role, because as an adviser you are likely to have a better sense of the history of the organization and how the institution operates than have any of the student leaders. Although there are always exceptions, it is possible that you will serve in your role for several years, especially those who are advisers as a result of their assignment in the university. Included in this group are the Greek adviser, the union board adviser, the residence hall association adviser, and so on. You will thus provide a framework to your student leaders and organization members for such matters as how to accomplish administrative tasks on campus and what activities the organization can expect to participate in during the course of the academic year. In short, you serve as a bridge from one year to the next for the organization, reminding leaders about administrative procedures, keeping members apprised of campus policies, and serving as a point of contact for faculty and administrators in special situations.

In this chapter, we first briefly describe many of the common activities that student organizations will participate in as full members of the university community. Not all organizations will participate in all of these activities, but many organizations will participate in most of them. Second, we discuss a wide variety of policies and practices that influence how organizations function on campus. We provide suggestions about how you can work with the organization to navigate its way through administrative requirements. To be sure, every college is organized in a different way, but most colleges will have many of these policies and practices, and we think it is important that the adviser know about them and how to deal with them. (You would also be well served to visit with staff in the office of student activities for additional advice on policies unique to your campus.) At the end of the chapter are several case vignettes that deal with topics introduced in this chapter. We think it may be useful for you to read the cases and develop answers to the issues described in them.

Community Participation

In recent years, much has been written about college campuses as communities (Boyer 1987; Kuh, 1991). This literature emphasizes how important it is for all members of an institution to share common goals and values, a sense of history, symbols, and so on (Kuh, Schuh, and Whitt, 1991), and the lack of student community has been shown to have a negative effect on students (Astin, 1993). Student organizations contribute significantly to the sense of community that is shared on campus, and as members of the community, organizations must fulfill certain obligations and expectations.

New Student Recruitment

Student organizations can play an important role in recruiting new students to the college. Members and leaders can be available on "prospective student days" to visit with prospective students and their parents. Prospects want to know about the life of the campus and what is available for them outside the classroom. Extracurricular involvement has a salutary effect on students (Pascarella and Terenzini, 1991), and new students can be encouraged to join various student organizations.

You need to be aware of the calendar of the university and to know when these special days are scheduled. Student organizations can be a part of the recruitment process by developing displays, giving presentations to parents and students, handing out brochures, and providing general information about the campus. In some cases they will host breakfasts or luncheons, organize receptions, and provide valuable support to the office of student recruitment. You can ensure that the organization's leaders are part of broad-based efforts to recruit new students and that the organization's representatives know how to present themselves and their organization effectively and persuasively to prospects.

Service Learning

"Higher education is being called on to renew its historic commitment to service" (Jacoby, 1996, p. 3). Students give of their time in all kinds of ways to advance their institution—for example, by tutoring each other, escorting each other across campus at night, and helping clean up after disasters. In this section we will use the term *volunteer* as a shorthand synonym for participating in service learning, although participating in service learning experiences and volunteering are not the same (see Jacoby, 1996).

One of the ways that groups in need of assistance secure volunteers is to approach various student organizations both to provide information about the volunteer activity and to seek people to serve as volunteers. "Many institutions of higher education have become active members of their local communities in a variety of ways, with both sharing their human, educational, technical, and fiscal resources" (Gugerty and Swezey, 1996, p. 92). Whether members are volunteering for ongoing activities (Scheuermann, 1996) or participating in one-time or short-term activities (McCarthy, 1996), organizations can play a crucial role in encouraging their members to participate. Some organizations, such as the Volunteers in Action (VIA) program at the University of Vermont, are formed with the primary purpose of providing service. Another approach to community service is that taken by Michigan State's residence halls orientation week program, which incorporates volunteer service (Scheuermann, 1996). Organizations can compete with one another by counting the number of volunteers who participate in certain activities, or by keeping track of the number of hours contributed by members as volunteers.

You can encourage volunteering by emphasizing its value to students: what students learn from volunteering can be applied directly to some aspects of their course work, and volunteering experiences help students become more well rounded, contributing citizens of their communities. When the volunteering experience is over, you can work with students by asking them such questions as, What did you learn from this experience? In what ways are you likely to volunteer in the future? What else would you like to learn from serving as a volunteer?

Advisory Boards and Committees

Many students are asked to serve on various institutional advisory boards and committees. For some of these positions, students will serve on an ex officio basis, meaning that the office they hold automatically entitles them to serve on a specific board, whereas in other cases they are appointed to the assignments by an officer of the student body or a specific organization. Let us look at some of these positions.

Departmental Assignments.   Among the departmental assignments that may be available to students are promotion committees, search committees, and curriculum committees. Not all colleges will include students on these committees, but some of these assignments can be found on most campuses.

How is a student appointed to these committees? One of the most likely ways is for a student leader of a departmental club to be asked by the departmental chair to serve, perhaps as a result of a recommendation by the club's adviser. Another possibility is for the student to be appointed by the organization's president in consultation with the adviser. Occasionally volunteers simply are sought for committee service. The point is that the student organization will likely play a key role in this process, and you are likely to play a complementary role as well.

College Assignments.   *College* in this case means a degree-granting unit within a university. As is the case with departmental assignments, students may serve on college search committees (including the search committee that fills the dean's slot), promotion committees, and curriculum committees, again depending on traditions, campus policies, and the culture of the specific college.

Hosting special guests of the college, organizing interdisciplinary symposia, and planning special events for the summer are some of the special activities that take place in the life of the college. Regardless of the activity, students often are sought for their perspective as well as their help in accomplishing various tasks associated with hosting the event.

The students appointed to these committees are likely to be leaders in the college, and obviously, departmental clubs or other organizations in the college, such as the Model United Nations, and organizations that cut across several academic disciplines, provide an excellent "leadership pool" from which to choose student appointees.

Institutional Assignments.   Students also serve on institutional boards and committees. These bodies tend to be much more wide ranging than those at the departmental or college level. Besides the boards and committees that may be found on the academic side of the institution, students may also be members of the alumni association board, the athletic committee, the traffic ticket appeals board, or the parking committee. Many student affairs units will have an advisory board of one kind or another, and students can play important roles on these boards, perhaps even serving as chair.

Appointments to these boards may come from the president of the student body, who often has a major role in the life of the college simply because he or she makes appointments to these campus boards and committees. Other appointments result from an office or role that a student plays on campus. For example, the president of the residence hall association is a likely candidate to serve on the campus advisory board to the housing and residence life office.

Your role in these campus appointments is consultative only. The student body president or other experienced student leader is very likely to have ideas about whom to appoint to these various committees, many of which will evolve from the campus political process. You should be available to the student making the appointment, but it is unlikely that the student will seek much advise unless problems with confirmation arise.

Policies and Procedures

In this section we describe a number of policies and procedures that are essential to conducting business on campus, and your role in each.

Probably one of your primary questions regards why there are so many policies and regulations related to student organizations. These regulations exist so that all student organizations have a reasonable opportunity to conduct their business and accomplish their objectives. In addition, health and safety need to be ensured. Colleges and universities are complex enterprises, and for this reason, many organizations of the university are not aware of what the other organizations are doing, or they all want to do the same thing at the same time. Thus, for example, if many organizations want to reserve the most desirable meeting rooms on Tuesday night, some mechanism needs to be in place to ensure that rooms are not double booked.

Developing the Constitution

Most campuses require that student organizations have a constitution. You need to know whether the campus requires the organization to provide a copy of its constitution; if filing is required, you also need to know where and how often the organization should do so. Your group will also need to review its operating by-laws at least annually and to bring them up to date as needed. Help on technical questions related to constitution development is usually available at the student activities office, and we discuss the development of organizational constitutions elsewhere in this book.

Many institutions require a clause in the constitution stating that the organization will not discriminate in its membership policies and practices. This clause may be controversial in some instances; you can play a helpful role in explaining the purpose of such a clause and why it makes solid educational sense to have the statement included in your organization's constitution.

Registering the Organization

An organization frequently, or perhaps annually, has to file certain documents with the student activities office so that it can be registered on campus. Registration documents normally include a constitution, a list of officers that includes their addresses and telephone numbers, and the name of the adviser. Other material may need to be filed depending on the requirements of your campus.

In return for being registered, an organization is eligible for certain institutional benefits. Among these may be the use of space on campus for free or for a reduced charge, eligibility for funding from the student government association, and certain privileges related to fundraising on campus.

You need to make sure that students understand the value of having their organization registered on campus and to gently remind them of the deadlines they must meet to be registered.

Advertising

Student organizations commonly have to comply with specific regulations dealing with where advertising may be posted or flyers distributed. For example, the campus may not allow the use of banners for publicizing events, or it may not permit the posting of signs or flyers on the sides of buildings, or the taping of such flyers to the sidewalks on campus. The campus may require that organizations receive permission to set up tasks or booths on campus malls. Special permission may be needed for a non–residence hall organization to distribute flyers in a residence hall lobby, and it is highly unlikely that nonresidents can go door to door to notify residents of an event. Greek houses are considered private on most campuses, and nonmembers may not enter a house without having specific permission to do so.

You should be aware of these various campus policies related to advertising and to publicizing events; information about them is usually available in the student activities office. When students get together to discuss how to publicize events, you can point out that the campus has a policy governing such activity and let the students know where they can find a copy of the policy if it is not already in the organization's files.

Reserving Space

As already mentioned, registered student organizations are allowed to use campus space for meetings, lectures, and social events. To prevent rooms from being double booked, to provide for adequate security, and to ensure that buildings are unlocked, organizations normally are required to reserve their space through a scheduling office. Clubs and special-interest organizations may not have a home, unlike residence hall groups or Greek letter organizations. The student union is consequently the likely place for their events to be held on campus. The organization will need to reserve space through the scheduling office to make sure that the space is available at the time it desires.

As is the case with other policies, you should have a working knowledge of the campus space reservation policy. A copy of this policy should be in the organization's files. If the student leaders appear to be unaware of the policy, you can provide them with this information.

Registering Events

It is very common for campuses to have policies that require student organizations to register events they are sponsoring with the organization's governing body (the IRC for example). For Greek letter organizations and residence hall groups, registering events may be part of the by-laws of the governing organization. For other organizations, events must be registered with the office of student activities.

You should be knowledgeable about the campus's event registration policy and should notify your students if the policy applies to the events they are planning. For example, such a policy might not apply if the event is held off-campus. The last thing an organization needs is the threat of cancellation hovering over an event that the organization has failed to register.

Working with Food Service

One last policy is worth pointing out under the general category of reserving space and advertising meetings, namely, the campus policy related to the food service. Institutions often have an agreement with a food service vendor (either a private company or a campus food service operated by institutional employees) that gives the vendor exclusive rights to sell food on campus. This is done for two reasons. First, such an agreement helps to ensure the health and safety of those who consume the food. Food service purveyors need to work in clean kitchens, and those who are involved in food preparation normally are required to have a food handlers' permit or other certification. From a risk management perspective, having a professional responsible for preparing food is a means by which the institution can protect itself from various problems resulting from the improper handling of food. Second, the institution may receive as a commission a percentage of the receipts from food sales. The institution will not collect the commission if the students provide the food themselves.

Consequently, you will need to remind students who are planning an on-campus event with food that the campus policy will need to be checked, and if an exclusive arrangement to provide food has been granted to an operator, the students may not be able to provide the food unless the food is purchased or ordered through the on-campus vendor. The students can confer with the food service operator to determine whether any relief from the regulation can be provided. Another option is to hold the event off-campus.

Collecting and Disbursing Funds

Many campuses require student organizations to use a campus banking system for collecting and disbursing funds. Although it is not the same as a federally chartered financial institution, the campus bank allows student organizations to deposit funds and write checks (or request that checks against its account be drawn) to pay bills as instructed by the organization. In some cases, student organizations may not be able to receive funds from the student government or funds collected by the institution (such as activity fees appropriated for residence hall units as part of room and board fees) unless the campus banking system is used.

You should be knowledgeable about the campus banking system, if one exists, and should strongly encourage students not to establish off-campus bank accounts. Aside from the issue of campus policy, the transition in student leaders from one year to the next makes it very difficult to maintain the continuity of off-campus accounts. In addition, it is very likely that off-campus financial institutions have no knowledge about campus spending policies and will thus routinely process checks for the purchase of alcoholic beverages or for other purposes that are not in keeping with campus policies. Further information is available from the campus controller, the bursar, or from whatever office that deals with accounts receivable and payable. We discuss fiscal issues further in Chapter Seven.

Receiving Student Government Funding

Registered student organizations may be eligible for financial support from the campus student government. This money often is available through the activity fees that students pay as part of their tuition and fee bill. Exactly what kinds of funding are available to student groups will depend on the statutes of the campus student government, but among the expenses that may be covered are such items as printing and postage, advertising, travel expenses related to conference attendance, and fees associated with inviting speakers to the campus.

The process that groups must follow to apply for such support will vary from campus to campus. Generally, however, they will need to make a case that the funds are being spent wisely and in line with student government statutes. Student governments likely will ask the group to demonstrate how the student body will benefit from the expenditure, and the organization will need to present a plan detailing how members of the student body will become aware of the event. Some campuses will not fund expenditures for food or travel.

You can be very helpful in this kind of activity by reminding students that such funding is available and by helping the leaders develop a funding proposal. Many organizations, particularly those that have modest membership rolls and no direct funding (such as room and board fees for residence hall groups) will find this kind of funding to be extremely helpful in underwriting their costs for the academic year. Some campus student governments will accept requests for this kind of funding on a routine basis throughout the year, whereas in other cases, organizations need to submit proposals by a specific deadline. A call to the activities office will be helpful in identifying the deadlines, if any, for the academic year.

Raising Funds

Most campuses will want all fundraising activities, especially those related to seeking gifts from institutional benefactors, to be coordinated with its fundraising arm, commonly known as the college foundation or endowment association. This activity typically falls under the supervision of the advancement office. (We discuss this topic elsewhere in the book.) Institutions want to ensure that donors are not asked for multiple gifts in a given time, and if a college is cultivating a donor for a large gift, it will want to make sure that a small gift to a student organization does not short-circuit the process.

Once again, you need to be aware of the institution's approach to fundraising. In some cases the students can go right ahead and ask for a gift, but you or the student leaders can make a call to the fundraising office to head off potential problems.

Traveling

In Chapter Eight we discuss several issues related to the legal aspects of travel, but from a procedural point of view, student groups will need to take certain steps to be able to travel. Travel, especially that involving overnight trips out of state, requires planning and administrative work so that the trip can be funded and the costs of the trip provided for appropriately. Clearly, if students want to travel to another campus, pay for it on their own, and not go as institutional representatives, there is almost nothing the institution can do to stop them (even if it makes a tremendous effort to do so). But if the students want some campus support (for example, funding for the trip), they will need to work their way through the administrative maze. In addition, if the students want to attend a conference as the representatives of the college, they will need to do some planning before the trip.

Students will need to file forms, signed by the people on campus required to do so, well in advance of the trip. Estimated costs may be part of the information included in the forms. Some colleges require that individuals stay in lodging arranged by a travel agent under contract to the institution; other lodging may not be approved. If the trip involves using a common carrier, an institutional travel agent may need to make the reservations. Reservations made by the students may not be reimbursed.

If institutional vehicles are to be used for transportation, students will need to reserve them well in advance of the trip. Some campuses issue the caveat that should an emergency arise, the vehicles could be reassigned at the last moment. In Chapter Eight are some suggestions related to how to handle the safe assignment of drivers. Simply reserving the vehicles does not mean that the trip will go smoothly. Careful driving and caution will help ensure the safety of all the travelers.

Creating a World Wide Web Page

Institutions are finding the World Wide Web to be an important medium for providing information about programs and student organizations, one that can also be an integral part of the total educational experience of the campus. Student organizations may be asked to provide material for the institution's Web page, or they may ask to do this activity on their own.

Problems can arise, however, when groups create Web pages. What happens if students put material on their page that the institution does not want? An organization's Web page may have links to the Web pages of individual students. What if those pages include material the institution finds undesirable? What if students sell advertising on their Web page to businesses that the institution will not allow to advertise on campus, such as a liquor distributor? These questions and others are bound to arise.

Institutions of higher education are developing mechanisms to determine what their Web pages are going to include and how to construct theses pages. Usually a person, an administrative unit, or a committee serves as the gatekeeper to the institution's page. This resource can be very helpful in answering basic questions about the Web page. Less clear is exactly how to limit what is placed on the Web through the various links students can create. It is plausible that at some point in the not-too-distant future, every student will have a page, with links to other pages. The implication is obvious: as the number of linked pages increases, it will be virtually impossible to determine who will be able to access what through the college's Web page. Courts have handed down decisions in favor of not limiting what can be published on the Web. The institution may be able to limit what is on its "official" Web page, but moving beyond that may not be practical or legal. This area of law and technology will continue to evolve in the coming years, and we advise that you stay in contact with legal counsel as the courts hand down their decisions.

You can be helpful in showing students how to access their institution's Web page and in clarifying what policies they have to follow in order to contribute to it. Depending on your level of expertise, you can also explain to students how to prepare material for the Web. The Web has marvelous potential, and you can help shape the vision of how the institution's Web page will evolve, especially as this vision relates to student organizations.

Case Vignettes

We provide the following vignettes to give you an idea of the variety of situations involving policies and procedures that you may encounter as an adviser.

Group Trip

You are the adviser to a campus organization with fifty members. This is a special-interest organization with fairly modest resources. The leaders have found out that a similar organization exists on a campus in the next state, 225 miles from your campus. They want to travel to the other campus and discuss common issues. They have contacted the leaders of the other organization and report that the other campus is glad to host your group.

What policies would you need to review with the leaders before they make the trip?

End-of-Year Party

You are the adviser to a major organization on your campus. This organization has a large number of members and a strong alumni group. Funds are ample, and whenever the group has a financial problem, it can call up an alum who will gladly write a check. The group is planning a large end-of-year party off-campus.

What policies would you need to review with the leaders before they hold the party?

Starting a Club

Early in the academic year, a group of students in your department approach you in your office. They share a common interest in your discipline and would like to start a club. They are all underclass students and really are not active campus leaders. They would like to have you serve as their organization's adviser.

What steps might you take in advising the students about how to start an organization on campus? What policies would they need to review before they can start the club?

Student Representation

The senior academic officer of the college has just announced that a joint task force consisting of representatives of the academic senate and the office of academic affairs will conduct a review of requirements for certain academic degrees. The senior academic officer thinks that students ought to be represented on the committee but is unsure of precisely how to identify these students.

What would you recommend?

CHAPTER 7

Financial Management and Budgeting

One of your most important responsibilities as an adviser is to assist the organization in managing its financial matters. This activity can be quite simple, or it can involve handling hundreds of thousands of dollars each year in receipts and expenditures. Although you will not serve as the organization's treasurer, it is likely that you will work closely with the treasurer on financial matters. You may be asked to co-sign check requests, review purchase orders, and advise the organization's executive officers on financial matters.

This chapter is designed to provide you with basic information about financial management. We discuss various approaches to budgeting, introduce two common methods of accounting, describe how a typical budgeting process works, provide information about balance sheets, identify several fiscal controls that are available to you, and provide information about fundraising. We again provide case vignettes at the end of the chapter. Clearly, much more could be written about financial management and budgeting than could ever be contained in this chapter. An excellent resource is the institution's principal financial manager, often called a bursar or controller. You should contact this person as additional questions arise.

Budgets

Most organization budgets are basic from a conceptual point of view. This part of the chapter describes several common ways that budgets are configured, but it does not discuss such budgeting approaches as Program Planning Budgeting Systems (PPBS), program budgeting, performance budgeting, or formula budgeting, all of which have extremely limited applications to student organizations.

Line Item Budgets

Line item budgets are considered the simplest way to organize a budget. A line can represent a sum of individual expenditures, or individual expenditures can be broken down even further. For example, a line for personnel services could be broken down even further by listing each position (Douglas, 1991). Operating expenses can be aggregated or divided into categories such as stationery, office supplies, or equipment repair.

Line items tend to be quite precise in title and are easy to understand. Moreover, line item budgets are simple to develop, and they provide a good picture of what has been done in the past. Another advantage of this approach to budgeting is that budget managers can review a line item budget and make adjustments for the future quite easily (Schuh, 1995).

Incremental Budgets

Incremental budgets also are quite easy to follow, because they build on one another sequentially. With this type of budget, those responsible for developing a budget from one year to the next will apply a certain formula to the existing budget and use that as the basis for the next year's budget. For example, the inflation rate for certain operating supplies might be 3 percent. An increase of 3 percent is thus applied to each item in the supplies category to provide a new budgeted amount for the next fiscal year.

Incremental budgets are not difficult to develop, and they complement line item budgets. Normally, budgets for student organizations are fairly basic, so a combination of line item and incremental budgeting will be an adequate approach to budget organization and planning.

Zero-Based Budgeting

Zero-based budgets (ZBB) make the assumption that a budget is best developed when the organization starts its process by reducing all expenses and revenues to zero. Every proposed item to be included in the budget is reviewed for its worthiness and accuracy and is included or discarded on the basis of this scrutiny.

Woodard (1993) concludes that ZBB is quite attractive but very cumbersome. To build a complicated budget from scratch each year requires a tremendous amount of time and paperwork (Schuh, 1990). This approach might have a special appeal to a student organization, however, particularly if a new group of officers decides to take the organization in a different direction. Similarly, it could be used if certain major events are eliminated from the organization's program (such as an awards banquet), which would result in a different financial scenario in the future.

Cost Center Budgets

In working with a very complicated budget, such as that of the student government of a large residence complex, it might make sense to organize a budget using principles from cost center budgeting. Using this approach, the activities of various subunits are linked for budgeting proposes, so that each of these units stands alone as a "cost center." Each of these units is supposed to generate enough revenue to support its activities. An example would be a convenience market located in a residence complex and operated by the student government of the residence hall. The convenience market has to acquire items and pay overhead and salaries out of the funds it generates through sales. The convenience store, then, could be treated as a cost center. It derives revenues from its sales and must cover its expenses exclusively out of its revenues. A less complex example would be an annual awards dinner. If the organization chooses to treat its dinner as a cost center, the income from banquet tickets and other revenues (ads in the banquet program, for example) would be all the resources available to support the total cost of the event, including such items as food, rental of the hall, flowers, audio-visual equipment rental, and awards.

Cost center budgeting works very well with ancillary activities such those identified in the previous paragraph. It is unlikely that most student organizations will be so complicated that having cost centers will make much sense, although conceptually some activities might be thought of as cost centers. The typical student organization will not need to use cost center budgets for routine operations.

Revenues and Expenses _____

The following is a brief discussion of the sources of revenue and the common expenses of student organizations. Exhibit 7.1 illustrates a sample budget that includes many of the categories discussed here.

Revenues

Student organizations are fairly limited in terms of the sources they can use to generate revenues. Among the most common methods are charging their members dues or activity fees, charging individuals a fee to participate in a specific program, and holding fundraisers.

Dues and activity fees are self-explanatory. In the case of a club, for example, the organization may elect to assess each member an annual or periodic fee (such as by academic term) to remain in good standing and receive the benefits of membership. Setting the amount can be difficult: on the one hand, the organization needs to generate sufficient revenue to operate; on the other, if the fee is too high, people may choose not to join. Normally, the executive officers determine the amount to be charged, and the membership votes to accept it.

Activity fees also may be charged by such organizations as residence hall units or Greek letter organizations. These fees may be included in a room and board charge or may be assessed separately. The elected officers decide on the fee, and students must pay the fee to remain in the housing unit. The amount may range from just a few dollars per term to a more substantial amount in the case of a fraternity or sorority.

At times organizations will charge students a specific fee to support a social event, such as a dance or dinner, or to take a trip. In this case the organizers of the event determine the cost of the event, project the number of participants, and arrive at a per-person fee. These kinds of events might be budgeted as cost centers (as described in the section on cost center budgeting).

Fundraisers are those activities, such as a car wash or bake sale, that are designed expressly to supplement the organization's revenue. We discuss fundraising in greater detail later in this chapter.

As we touched on elsewhere, one other likely source of revenue, particularly for clubs, is funding from the student government allocation process. On many campuses, the student government receives funds from activity fees that all students pay; the government in turn allocates some of the money to student organizations through a defined process: it accepts applications on

Exhibit 7.1. Sample Budget

	Previous Year	Current Year
Revenue		
Dues and activity fees	_____	_____
Student government allocation	_____	_____
Services rendered	_____	_____
Commissions from machines	_____	_____
Sales	_____	_____
Fundraisers	_____	_____
Program receipts	_____	_____
Other receipts	_____	_____
Prior year carried forward	_____	_____
TOTAL REVENUE	_____	_____
Expenses		
Personnel services	_____	_____
Salaries	_____	_____
Hourly wages	_____	_____
Fringe benefits	_____	_____
Workers compensation	_____	_____
Social Security	_____	_____
Insurance	_____	_____
Operating expenses	_____	_____
Telephone line charge	_____	_____
Long distance	_____	_____
Other communications	_____	_____
Office supplies	_____	_____
Printing	_____	_____
Postage	_____	_____
Equipment rental	_____	_____
Equipment repair	_____	_____
Program expenses (Develop budget for each program)		
Newsletter	_____	_____
Speakers	_____	_____
Travel	_____	_____
Outstanding debt	_____	_____
Miscellaneous expenses	_____	_____
Capital		
List by item	_____	_____
Contingency	_____	_____
TOTAL EXPENSES	_____	_____
BALANCE	_____	_____

certain dates and holds formal hearings. This process should not be overlooked as a source of funding for student organizations.

Some organizations may be able to generate other funding through such campus work projects as directing traffic or parking cars at major events, receiving commissions from vending machines, cleaning the stadium after an athletic event, or renting equipment such as refrigerators and microwave ovens for the residence halls. These sources will vary from campus to campus, but they have the potential to provide substantial sources of funds.

Expenses

Expenses vary dramatically from organization to organization. In the case of a club, expenses might not be much more than printing and mailing, in addition to those incurred by perhaps one major event per semester. Other, more complex organizations can have very complicated budgets.

If the organization has any employees, it will incur expenses that can be characterized as "personnel services." These costs include salaries, wages, and fringe benefits. Fringe benefits very well may be determined by the college, and they include Social Security contributions, disability insurance, and worker's compensation. The student organization treasurer should check with the college's human resources office to determine exactly what fringe benefits must be paid.

Most organizations are also likely to have various operating expenses: telephone line and long-distance charges, and office supplies, printing, and postage costs. The range of operating expenses again will depend on the organization's complexity.

Program costs might be budgeted separately. By program costs we mean special events or activities that are not part of the routine expenses of the organization. Dances, film series, speakers, and convocations are examples of programs. In some cases these events might be funded entirely out of fees charged to participants, without support from the organization. This funding decision is as much a political decision as a financial one, and it should be made by the officers in consultation with the membership.

If the organization's members plan on taking trips, they will incur travel expenses, including transportation costs, lodging and meal charges, and perhaps registration fees for a conference. Travel, which can be quite expensive, can perhaps be budgeted as a separate item.

Two other items also may be identified as expense categories, namely, capital items and prior year debt. The definition of what constitutes a capital item will vary from college to college, but generally, items with a value over a certain amount (perhaps any-where from $100 to $500) that are not consumable (unlike paper or staples) are considered to be capital items. Organizations without offices generally will not be purchasing capital items, which could include computers or copy machines. But a Greek letter organization, a student government association, or a residence hall association very easily could buy substantial numbers of capital items.

In order to buy capital items, student organizations may at times borrow money. The lender could be the institution itself or perhaps the student government association or the residence hall association. To pay back the lender, the organization will have to budget funds, thus creating the prior-year debt category in the budget. This category is not all that common, as most organizations do not purchase substantial numbers of capital items, nor do they incur long-term debt.

Finally, there is a budget category for expenses that cannot be anticipated, which is referred to as contingency. A modest amount can be budgeted for contingencies, perhaps not more than 5 percent. The contingency allows for flexibility in funding an activity or project that could not be planned when the budget was developed.

The Budget Planning Process

"As a process, a budget allows for the participation of constituents and consensus building with regard to levels of funding by program, revenue source, and standards of accountability" (Woodard, 1993, p. 245). The budgeting process will vary substantially from one organization to another, mostly as a function of the level of sophistication of the organization's financial structure. An organization that collects modest dues and charges small fees for social events will have a very simple budget planning process. A residence hall association or Greek letter organization that has many members and is managing substantial ancillary operations will have a more complex budgeting process. In this section we discuss a budget planning process that applies to most organizations; please remember that naturally the budget details and complexity can vary widely from organization to organization. Much of our discussion is based on the ideas of Hennessy and Lorenz (1987).

The place to start in budget preparation is determining the extent of the program the organization intends to develop for the budgeting year. Program, in this case, refers to what the organization plans to do—take a trip, have a dinner, publish a newsletter, hire a part-time secretary, show three movies, and so on.

Committee chairs, executive officers, and even group members will make proposals for the activities that might be considered during the organization's fiscal year. These proposals are presented to the budget committee, which might be a separate group chaired by the treasurer or other organization member in the case of a large organization, or the executive committee in the case of a smaller group.

Programs require money, and to a great extent they drive the budget. Once the program is sketched out, the organization needs to estimate the amount of money it will require to underwrite the program and to determine the necessary sources of revenue. As mentioned earlier, revenues can include dues, fees for participation in certain events, special fundraisers, and gifts.

The budget, including projected revenues and expenditures, is then presented to the executive group for initial review. Changes to the budget may be made based on the recommendations of the officers. Revisions could include changes in the amount of dues charged, the number of special events held, or the amount of money that can be raised through special events. Assuming that the revised budget is approved, it is then presented to the organization's members for adoption. In the case of large, complex organizations, this step might be taken for informational purposes only. For smaller groups, such as a special-interest club, a vote of the members to adopt the budget is in order.

The adopted budget then becomes the organization's financial road map for the year. It can be changed if circumstances dictate, but that would require a vote according to the process prescribed in the organization's constitution or by-laws. It is common for organizations to make adjustments to their budget during the fiscal year. For example, the membership may be greater than anticipated, and the dues revenue realized will be a larger amount than was planned. Or a piece of equipment breaks and has to be repaired or replaced.

The treasurer prepares periodic reports related to the budget and presents them to the executive officers and members. We discuss this process later in the chapter.

Accounting Methods

You are likely to encounter one of two accounting methods, cash accounting and accrual accounting. Cash accounting is the approach that most individuals take when balancing their checkbooks. That is, every check they write is entered as an expense. Each time they make a deposit into the account, that amount is entered as well. Once per month they balance their checkbook and hope there is some money left in their account. "Revenue, expenses and balance sheet items are recorded when cash is paid or earned" (Finney, cited in Schuh, 1995, p. 468). In short, every transaction is recorded as the activity takes place.

Accrual accounting is different than cash accounting in that income and expenses are recorded when the commitment to receive or expend funds is made. Using this approach, when a student is billed for books, the bookstore records the income. When a purchase order for food items is processed, the food service commits its resources to paying for the items, even though the supplies have not been received and a check has not been sent to pay for them. Accrual accounting operates under the assumption that all billed funds will be received and that all obligations of the organization will be met. (Unfortunately, at times debts are not paid, requiring an expense category for bad debts.)

Auxiliary units such as housing or food service often use an accrual accounting approach. Cash accounting will serve most student organizations well. However, it is important to remember that the person authorized to keep the organization's books must know when commitments are made. One of the most common problems that can occur is that members of the organization make financial commitments for the organization that cannot be met. For example, a committee orders hundreds of dollars worth of fresh flowers as centerpieces for banquet tables when only seventy-five dollars was budgeted for decorations. When the flowers are delivered, the vendor expects to be paid. This unfortunate example illustrates what can happen when too many people get involved in making financial commitments for the organization.

Operating Statements and Balance Sheets

Two tools that provide information about the fiscal health of the organization are operating statements and balance sheets.

Operating Statements

Operating statements are produced on a periodic basis (preferably monthly but possibly quarterly) by the organization's treasurer. Assuming that such statements are developed monthly, the report would include all transactions that have occurred since the previous statement was produced one month before. and expenses are recorded, and a balance is reported at the end of the statement. The monthly statement also is reconciled with the year-to-date activity of the organization so that a clear picture of the organization's financial position can be established. A review of the statement will indicate the income of the organization, its expenses, and the organization's cash balance.

Sophisticated operating statements will report the amount of money the organization has projected it will receive for the fiscal year and the percentage of income that has been received to date; similarly, they report expenses. This level of detail may be a bit too much to expect of a student organization, but the more complicated the organization's finances, the more important it is to take advantage of fiscal tools such as well-conceived operating statements.

Balance Sheets

For the purposes of this explanation, the balance sheet is viewed much like an individual's statement of net worth. This sheet, which is produced quarterly at most, provides a thorough analysis of the assets and liabilities of the organization. It reports the cash position of the organization along with any other assets that the organization might have, minus its liabilities.

Examples of assets other than cash include certificates of deposit or other investments the organization might hold, as well as any other physical assets such as equipment or inventory. Most organizations have limited assets other than a checking account or the equivalent, and perhaps some money on deposit.

Liabilities include any long-term debts owed to other student organizations or the institution, and other funds owed to outside sources. Let us look at an example of a long-term liability. Suppose that the student government decided to rent refrigerators to residence hall students. If a $50,000 loan, to be paid back in $10,000 annual installments, had been underwritten to purchase the original inventory, a liability is recorded on the balance sheet. The $10,000 is an annual expense that is listed on the monthly operating statement. The overall debt of $50,000 appears on the balance sheet of the organization and is reduced each time a payment is made. The value of the refrigerators appears as a physical asset on the balance sheet of the organization, less any depreciation or other reduction in the value of the items (such as theft of or damage to the items).

Most student organizations have very limited assets or liabilities. Consequently, their balance sheets looks very much like their year-end operating statements. Regardless of the complexity of the operating statement or balance sheet, it is very useful for you to

Exhibit 7.2. Sample Balance Sheet

Date: _____

	Amount
Assets	
Cash on hand	_____
Accounts receivable	_____
Savings accounts (by number) _____	_____
_____	_____
Equipment (fair market value)	_____
_____	_____
_____	_____
Other property	_____
_____	_____
_____	_____
TOTAL ASSETS	_____
Liabilities	_____
Accounts Payable	_____
Long-term debts	_____
_____	_____
_____	_____
TOTAL LIABILITIES	_____
NET Value of organization	_____

pay careful attention to each month's activities. Any apparent irregularities should be discussed immediately so that problems do not go unresolved. A sample balance sheet is shown in Exhibit 7.2.

Fiscal Controls

Now that we have gone through the process of developing balance sheets and operating statements, one of the issues that need some attention is that of fiscal controls. How do you ensure that the organization's money is received and spent without irregularities? Several techniques help avoid problems.

Program Budgets

We believe that one of the classic mistakes organizations can make is to plan events and activities that require the expenditure of funds without having first developed a budget. A budget in this case is nothing more than a plan for how funds will be spent and how revenues will be generated to pay for the expenses. Any program or activity that expects to generate revenue and pay expenses should have a budget that is published for the officers and members to review, and that is passed through the appropriate process in a regular business meeting. The person or persons who are charged with managing the budget should provide periodic reports as to the progress made on program planning and how expenses are being managed. Are revenues in line with the budgeted projections? What about expenses? Have any anomalies been encountered? These questions and others should be reviewed regularly by the leadership, and if adjustments need to be made, the membership should have a chance to react.

Some program budgets are very simple. A reception is held for a campus speaker in a residence hall lounge, and the expenses consist of punch and cookies. A book is given to a speaker as a gift for conducting a workshop for sorority leaders. Other activities, which involve income in addition to expenditures, can be more complex. We have provided a sample budget for a Mardi Gras activity that includes substantial income and expenses (Exhibit 7.3). An organization that badly manages its program expenses can face early bankruptcy. We therefore recommend that you pay close attention when members propose programs and that you work closely with the leadership to make sure that budgets are executed in the spirit with which they are conceived.

Banking

One of the questions you will encounter is whether or not to use the campus banking service as opposed to a commercial banking facility. Campus banks are not banks in the traditional sense; they are an arm of the institution's business office and are not chartered financial institutions. Campus banking services generally will provide limited services to customers: receiving deposits, preparing periodic statements, and writing checks on receipt of an appropriate form requesting such. These services are often provided without charge to the student organization.

Commercial banks can provide a checking account for a student organization as well as deposit funds. They are open for longer hours and, if one has an ATM card, can provide twenty-four-

Exhibit 7.3. Sample Program Budget

	1996 Budgeted	1996 Actual	1996 (Over) Under	1997 Budgeted
Expense Items				
Food	400.00	345.18	54.82	430.00
Decorations	180.00	184.02	4.02	100.00
Carnival materials	280.00	262.04	17.96	300.00
Publicity	100.00	35.18	64.82	50.00
Entertainment	150.00	150.00	0.00	250.00
Printing	50.00	40.25	9.75	50.00
Transportation	75.00	87.10	(12.10)	90.00
Contingency	150.00	75.00	75.00	75.00
Total	1,385.00	1,178.77	206.23	1,345.00
Income Items				
Program ads	100.00	125.00	25.00	125.00
Admissions	1,100.00	995.00	(105.00)	1,050.00
Gifts	50.00	105.00	65.00	100.00
Transfer from operating account	135.00	0.00	0.00	70.00
Total	1,385.00	1,225.00	15.00	1,345.00
Net surplus (loss)	0.00	46.23	191.23	0.00

hour service. Customarily, banks levy a monthly service charge. The charge may not be acceptable to a nonprofit organization.

Each form of banking service has certain advantages and disadvantages. Commercial banks can act faster and provide more services than campus banks, and are more flexible. These advantages, however, do not come without cost. Campus "banks" are more used to dealing with the special situations that arise with student organizations. Frequently, however, they take more time to process checks and will not write checks counter to institutional policy (such as for the purchase of alcoholic beverages).

Our general recommendation is that student organizations should use the campus "bank." As mentioned in Chapter Six, in some cases the campus banking facility *must* be used in order for an organization to be registered or recognized on campus. In one study (Hudson and Hudson, 1993), 90 percent of the reporting institutions indicated that residence hall association funds were kept in the campus equivalent of a bank. And whenever possible, the adviser should co-sign check requests for the reasons enumerated in the next sections.

Cash

To put it simply: avoid using cash if it all possible. Receipts should be collected in the form of checks made out to the organization rather than in cash. Dues, fees, and other receivables should be collected by check. Using this method provides a record for the issuer of the check in the form of the canceled check, thereby eliminating the need for receipts. More important, the check is negotiable only to the extent that it can be deposited in the organization's account. It is much more difficult to keep track of cash, and, unfortunately, cash has a way of disappearing.

The organization's obligations should also be paid by check. Cash payments by officers, for example, will require reimbursement, which can be a bit messy. The person paying with cash on behalf of the organization will have to produce a receipt in order to be reimbursed. People lose receipts, and treasurers do not like having to keep a file of receipts, so the best way to handle all financial obligations is to pay them by check.

Co-Signing Checks

Eliminating the use of cash will not solve all the organization's financial problems. Checks over a certain amount should require a second signature. This approach will ensure, first, that significant expenditures are reviewed to make sure they are appropriate, and second, that the checks are being drawn to the right person or organization. Little could be worse for an organization in a financial sense than a misunderstanding arising over a large expenditure that was for the wrong item or that was drafted to the wrong payee. Failing to follow this procedure could be devastating for the organization and its members.

Periodic Reports

Periodic reports, as mentioned earlier in this chapter, should be produced by the treasurer to be reviewed by the leadership of the organization, you, and, as appropriate, the members. At a minimum, operating statements should be produced every quarter, although every month would be far more desirable. Balance sheets should be produced at least once each quarter, preferably at the end of the quarter. These materials are very useful to the leadership in determining if the budget for the organization is being managed as it was proposed. If there are substantial variances from the budgeted plan, they should be pointed out by the treasurer to the executive committee as soon as the problems are identified. You should spend extra time with the treasurer if problems arise that could potentially affect the organization's financial health. Financial problems rarely solve themselves; they should be addressed as early as possible in the fiscal year.

Audits

Most organizations undergo a change in leadership at least once a year. Consequently, student organizations frequently are in a state of transition, and the dilemma of who exactly is responsible for which tasks can lead to real problems. Student leaders come and go, but the fiscal records of the organization must be maintained from one year to the next. Accordingly, we recommend that an audit of the organization's financial records be conducted each time there is a change in the executive leadership (meaning the president, the treasurer, or both). The internal audit department of the institution can conduct the audit for major student organizations. For organizations with a more limited scope, a student majoring in accounting, finance, or a similar discipline could be invited to conduct the audit. Conducting an audit will serve as a good experience for the student and will be a valuable service for the organization.

Most audits are very simple. The auditor checks receipts against deposits, and expenditures against the disbursement records of the organization. If the auditor identifies a problem, it is more likely the result of an honest mistake than a major conspiracy to defraud the organization of funds. It is best that the audit be conducted as a matter of routine procedure rather than as a result of a disaster. You can be very helpful in insisting that the audit be conducted.

Taxes

We tread gingerly into the area of taxes because of the complexity of state and federal tax codes as well as various Social Security regulations. It is possible that a student organization may have to pay sales taxes on items sold (such as T-shirts or food for fundraisers), withhold income taxes and FICA contributions from employees (and make contributions on their behalf), pay worker's compensation insurance, and mail W-2 forms to employees. If the organization is formed as a corporation, it will have to file annual reports with the Internal Revenue Service, and if the organization holds real property, it may have to pay real estate taxes on that property. This last item might apply to Greek letter houses, for example. In addition, some states require that other property, such as motor vehicles, be subject to annual taxes. On the other hand, depending on the organization's relationship with its institution, it might be exempt from having to pay sales tax on items purchased. To make this discussion even more complex, an organization requires a tax ID number to establish a checking account, have investments as simple as a passbook savings account, or conduct other financial business.

Obviously the general subject of taxes is very complicated. Your role is not to serve as a tax consultant. Rather, you should know that the organization may have tax obligations and should urge the student leaders to file the necessary documents with the appropriate authorities in order to ensure that the requirements of state and federal law are met. Your institution's chief financial officer (vice president or vice chancellor for finance or business affairs) can provide information about these filings. Most student organizations do not have such complicated financial transactions that they will encounter tax problems. In fact, we suspect that most clubs or similar organizations have no tax obligations whatsoever because their finances are very simple and can be handled through a campus banking agency, as was described earlier.

Fundraising

Fundraising seems simple, but it is not. If it were, most institutions would experience record-breaking success in their advancement activities every year. Fundraising is hard work, with many disappointments along the way. Moreover, some institutions have very tight regulations governing fundraising activities on campus. Funds cannot be raised at any time, place, or manner convenient to students.

Exhibit 7.4 is a list of a few examples of fundraisers. Please remember that all of these fundraisers may not be appropriate for every campus, as regulations vary widely from college to college. Some activities may not even be legal in certain states.

In spite of the complexity of fundraising issues, there are some general elements that you should be aware of, if for no reason other than to help you advise the organization when problems arise.

Exhibit 7.4. Fundraisers

Income derived from services provided
Vending machines
Pinball, pool tables, video games
Facility rentals
Jewelry cleaning
Lawn mowing
Leaf raking
Typing or data entry

Income derived from sales or rental
Refrigerators
Lofts
Carpets
Buttons
Exam support baskets
T-shirts or sweatshirts
Telephones
Holiday cards or stationery
Pom-poms
Balloons
College or organization mugs and cups
Stamps
Candy or ice cream
Calendars or desk blotters

Other ideas
Raffles
Car wash, car wash "bash"
Flower sales related to a holiday
Bake sales
Stuffing newspaper inserts
Recycling
Selling dry erase phone boards
Sports tournaments
Food booths at various events
Casino nights
Cable television advertising sales
Auctions
Rent-a-person (for a specific period)
Santa grams, Valentine grams
Garage sales
Jail and bail, jail-a-thon
Starving artist festival
Tuition raffle
Book exchange

Legality

Although we discuss legal issues in Chapter Eight, let us say here that you need to remind the officers of your organization that fundraisers must be legal. Raffles, casino nights, lotteries, and other fundraisers related to games of chance may not be legal in your state. Moreover, such activities may violate the spirit of the institution. The legality of a fundraiser should be checked either with the campus police chief or the institution's legal counsel. The last thing anyone wants is for a fundraiser to be broken up by the local police as a result of a violation of gaming laws.

Food Sales

The second area of concern relates to the sale of food. Selling doughnuts or other pastries can make a quick profit for a student organization, but the campus may have granted exclusive rights to a commercial company to sell food items on campus. You should recommend that the officers check with the food contractor as to whether or not a proposed activity violates the agreement with the institution. Officers need to do this checking whether the campus has a commercial food contractor or operates its own food service.

It is also important to note that food must be handled appropriately, meaning that hot foods need to be kept hot and cold foods cold. Food handlers may need to undergo a health exam and have a permit from the local department of public health. These factors must be taken into consideration before having a spaghetti dinner, ice cream social, or other event that involves food sales.

Conflict with Campus Fundraising Plans

Another area of concern is that the organization must not find itself in conflict with long-range campus plans concerning fundraising. Most institutions are very careful in cultivating potential donors to the university. Should a student organization receive a modest gift from a potential benefactor, this act may obviate the potential donor's making a major gift to the institution. Thus, careful coordination with the fundraising office is in order. Students may not think about fundraising in the same way your institution does; you can make sure that your group's plans do not get in the way of those of the institution.

Corporate Fundraising

Dumhart and Schoen (1993) provide information about the use of corporate fundraisers for large campaigns. Private companies offer opportunities for student organizations to generate revenue; several of these companies sell or rent products such as refrigerators, welcome baskets, and lapel pins, with a percentage of the sales going to the student organization. Obviously, there are advantages and drawbacks to forming a partnership with a corporate fundraiser. Our best advice is that before your group adopts this approach, your officers should discuss the idea thoroughly with the campus fundraising staff. The student organization has to be careful that it does not commit itself to a major project that it cannot complete.

Case Vignettes

We provide the following vignettes to give you an idea of the variety of situations involving financial matters that you may encounter as an adviser.

Off-Campus Account

You have just become the adviser of a student club in your academic department. The club is quite popular in that it attracts many members and has an excellent reputation among students in the department. You have had a series of meetings to get acquainted with the officers, and in your conversation with the treasurer you have learned that although some of the club's money is deposited in an institution account with the bursar's office, most of the funds are in an off-campus bank account. The treasurer explained that this is done so that the "hassles" of the institution do not get in the way of spending money.

How might you respond to this situation?

Dues Hike

As the adviser to a student organization, you have been concerned about the direction of the group since a very acrimonious election was held a month ago. The election was decided by just a handful of votes. Only two weeks remain in the spring term before exams are held and students go home for the summer. You get wind of a plan the newly elected officers are proposing to adopt over the summer that would raise the dues of every member by 25 percent next fall. Although the leaders are officially able to do this under the constitution, you wonder what the effects will be of such a substantial increase without consultation with the members.

How do you proceed?

Conference

Your fairly modest club has decided that it wants to host a weekend conference for similar clubs from other colleges throughout the region. Your officers and members have lots of energy but little experience in organizing this kind of event. The treasurer freely admits that she is unsure how to handle her end of the conference, and has scheduled a meeting with you tomorrow about budgeting for this event and handling the funds that are generated by it. Several meals and receptions will be part of the program; the group also needs to plan interest sessions and host a plenary session speaker. In short, the budgetary implications of the event are enormous.

What will you recommend to the treasurer?

Sloppy Reports

The quarterly reports of your organization often are submitted late by the treasurer, and they usually contain many inaccuracies. You are concerned that the leaders and members of the group really do not know the complete financial picture of the organization. You realize that the work of the treasurer is crucial to the success of the organization.

What will be your next steps in dealing with this problem?

CHAPTER 8

Keeping Up with Legal Issues

There may be no aspect of contemporary collegiate life that is more challenging than the legal environment in which institutions of higher education operate. As Barr (1988a, p. xv) observes, "Within the last three decades, there also has been a major increase in the influence of the law on the campus. No longer are institutions of higher education isolated from the larger society and the law. Therefore, responsible administration requires that professionals understand the legal implications of both their actions and their inactions."

We have not prepared this chapter to scare you away from your assignment. Rather, we agree with Barr that advisers have a responsibility to conduct their practice with a rudimentary understanding of the law so that they can advise student organizations appropriately. We also want to make it crystal clear that neither of us is an attorney; we are long-time advisers to student organizations who have learned about legal issues through our experiences, and we are avid readers of court decisions involving student groups and their advisers. We want to emphasize that the advice we provide in this chapter will neither make you an expert on the law nor serve as a substitute for campus legal counsel. We do believe, however, that we can offer suggestions for practice that are consistent with basic principles of the law as it applies to student organizations so that you can point out potential problems to the members of the organization you advise.

In this chapter, we look at several fundamental distinctions between public and private institutions and at students' constitutional right to organize. Then we move into issues related to managing risk, which is a major problem for many student organizations. Finally, we discuss several special legal issues that apply to student organizations, including dealing with alcoholic beverages and transportation.

We also want to offer a word about working with legal counsel. Attorneys whose primary focus is to provide advice to faculty and staff about a myriad of issues are available on many campuses. However, these legal counselors can provide assistance only if you contact them. As Gehring (1987, p. 116) pointed out, "The office of institutional counsel can be a valuable asset to you, but only if you use it."

On the other hand, some decisions will be the group's to make. Legal counsel can provide advice to you on the ramifications of a certain course of action, but in the end, the choice will be yours, both group and adviser, to decide. For example, should the members of an organization drive fifty miles to attend a speech of an acclaimed world leader if weather forecasters have predicted a sleet storm? Legally they can. What happens if the storm causes unsafe conditions during the trip, and an accident results? Counsel can provide various legal scenarios if an accident occurs, but the organization has to decide whether or not to make the journey, and in many cases (such as in this example) the appropriate course of action is not clear-cut.

Distinctions Between Public and Private Institutions

The difference between public and private institutions is profound in the eyes of the law, although over time the lines between public and private colleges have become a bit blurred. Kaplin and Lee (1995, p. 46) offer the following distinction between public and private institutions: "public institutions and their officers are fully subject to the constraints of the federal Constitution, whereas private institutions and their officers are not. Because the federal Constitution was designed to limit only the exercise of government power, it does not prohibit private individuals or corporations from impinging on such freedoms as free speech, equal protection, and due process."

This distinction means that private institutions have more latitude to deal with students and their organizations than have public institutions. "Private institutions may prevent, limit, or refuse to authorize the peaceful assembly of any group, including student organizations" (Barr, 1996, p. 133). This latitude does not imply, however, that private institutions have complete freedom to deal with students and their organizations on a capricious basis. For as Correnti (1988, pp. 25–26) has observed, "a self-monitoring influence has evolved within private institutions. They are now taking care to define their relationship with students and to deal with them in fair and equitable ways." Barr (1996, p. 133) states: "Both private and public institutions must follow their own published rules; such rules should be reasonably specific, neither too vague nor too broad."

One of the ways that private institutions frame their relationship with students is through contract theory, which holds that the student and the institution engage in a contract that will govern their basic relationship. This relationship is spelled out in various documents, such as the catalog or student handbook that private institutions publish on a regular basis. Presumably private colleges follow Barr's admonition, meaning that the rules are specific enough so that a reasonable person will not have difficulty interpreting what is meant by them.

Right to Organize

Under the U.S. Constitution, students at public institutions have a right to form organizations. Gehring (1987, p. 119) describes this right in the following way: "The First Amendment to the United States Constitution provides the legal basis for the establishment and conduct of student groups on campus. The Amendment states that: Congress shall make no law respecting an establishment of religion, or prohibiting the free exercise thereof; or abridging the freedom of speech, or of the press; or the right of people peaceably to assemble, and to petition to Government for a redress of grievances." Consequently, students at state institutions may form clubs, interest groups, teams, and other organizations as they wish.

On the other hand, private colleges do not have to allow students to form organizations. Buchanan (1988) points out that the Fourteenth Amendment was adopted to apply to public officials but that the distinction between public and private colleges continues to be litigated. In the strictest sense, a private college may determine that having student organizations is not in the best interest of the college, and consequently may not allow such activity. But what happens if the college accepts federal funds to build a special building, and the students, all of whom received federal financial aid, want to form an organization and meet in that building? Lawsuits are made of such circumstances. As a practical matter, the educational benefits of students forming organizations are complementary with what most colleges desire from such experiences, and students are therefore allowed to organize. Several exceptions are notable, among them *Gay Rights Coalition of Georgetown University Law Center* v. *Georgetown University* (reported by Kaplin and Lee, 1995).

This does not mean, however, that student groups can do whatever they want, wherever they want, whenever they want. Kaplin and Lee (1995) cite *Healy* v. *James* as a leading case in this area of law. They conclude that three principles affect student organizations on campus. First, student organizations seeking recognition may be required to adhere to specific campus regulations requiring that their activities be peaceful. Second, administrators may deny recognition of student organizations that have been disruptive. Third, the institution may deny recognition of organizations that advocate violating the law.

In administrative practice, *Healy* v. *James* often is cited as providing the tools to administrators to regulate the time, place, and manner in which organizations go about their business on campus. "The Healy court held that universities retain the power to protect their legitimate educational interests by requiring student organizations seeking recognition to affirm a willingness to abide by university regulations and state and federal laws" (Barrow and Martin, 1996, p. 67). *Healy* also has been interpreted to mean that the general routine of colleges and universities may not be disrupted by students, such as by their taking over a classroom or making so much noise in a library that patrons cannot read.

From your perspective as an organization's adviser, it will suffice simply to know that students have a right to organize and that institutions can require them to follow a registration or recognition process to use campus facilities and services. "The terms *registration* and *recognition* are often used interchangeably," which will not cause a problem as long as the relationship between the institution and the organization is defined (Maloney, 1988, p. 287). Maloney points out, however, that groups that represent the institution or that are officially sponsored by the institution, such as sports clubs or the debate team, could be subject to more control by the college or university.

The burden of applying regulations fairly and without prejudice falls on the institution. As Kaplin and Lee (1995, p. 519) conclude, "Administrators should apply the rules evenhandedly, carefully avoiding selective applications to particular groups whose philosophy or activities are repugnant to the institution. . . . Denial of funding by a public institution to a group because of the views its members espouse is a clear violation of constitutional free speech protections, even if the denial comes from a student government committee rather than from an institutional official."

Federal and State Laws

It should go without saying that student organizations must comply with state and federal laws. Some students, however, operate under the assumption that because they are students they are exempted from state and federal laws. Obviously they enjoy no such immunity. One area of particular importance relates to the possession and use of alcoholic beverages. Although plenty of evidence is available for us to conclude that alcohol abuse is widespread on some campuses (Smith, 1989) and tolerated to a certain extent by some elements of the campus community (Wechsler, Kuh, and Davenport, 1996), law enforcement agencies do not view underage drinking in the same (at times lenient) way. Underage drinkers of alcoholic beverages run the risk of arrest; those providing the alcoholic beverages also may be liable to arrest and prosecution.

As we have stated elsewhere, most institutions have a variety of rules and regulations designed to influence the behavior of student organizations; some of the more common regulations prohibit the use of alcoholic beverages on campus and require that student organizations be registered to use space on campus. Some require adherence to policies regarding the display of posters in campus buildings. Many campuses prohibit organizations from hazing new members (some state laws also prohibit this activity).

Even though campus regulations do not carry the force of law, you are obligated to urge the student officers and members in the strongest terms possible to follow the letter and spirit of the regulations. You will not want to work with students who wiggle in and out of trouble because they have breached campus regulations on a chronic basis, nor do you want to expose yourself to the penalties of the legal system by condoning the violation of laws. Accordingly, we urge you to explain the law to students and emphatically point out the risks they run when they do violate laws or campus regulations. Organizations that are chronic violators of the law, in particular, should cause you to pause and reflect on whether being associated with them is in your best interest.

Managing Risk

Our discussion of managing risk should start with defining a tort. "A tort is generally defined as a civil wrong other than the breach of a contract for which the courts will provide a remedy in the form of damages" (Gehring, 1987, p. 137). In the case of advising, the most common tort is negligence. "Negligence demands that a duty of care be breached; and, as a result, an injury occurs. The duty or standard of care may be breached by an act of omission or commission" (Gehring, 1987, p. 161). Whipple (1996, citing Fenske and Johnson, 1990) points out that "tort law has most often been applied in negligent [sic] cases relating to personal injuries sustained while attending an activity sponsored by student group or the institution, while transiting university property, or while on a class field trip. Higher education institutions have a duty to protect their students and other invited guests from known or reasonable foreseeable dangers" (p. 326).

Although the risk of lawsuits centering on negligence is obvious, and you are not immune from being sued, nevertheless certain elements must be present for litigation to be successful for the plaintiff or claimant. Barr (1988b) identifies three elements that must be present in a negligence claim: (1) the defendant owed a duty of care to the claimant, (2) the defendant breached that duty, and (3) the breach of duty was the proximate cause of the injury. The applicable general standard in this situation is that you must behave like a "reasonable person," that is, behave the way a reasonable person would in a similar situation. The standard does not call for extraordinary insight, prescience, or some other quality that an average person normally would not apply to similar circumstances.

College students tend to see themselves as being invulnerable to accidents and injuries, and they may plan events without carefully reflecting on the risks involved. Thus it falls to you to apply the "reasonable person" standard to student events, reviewing activities with officers and other members who are planning programs and making sure that risks have been identified and minimized.

In practical terms, the "reasonable person" standard means that normal precautions should be taken to prevent problems from occurring that a reasonable person would anticipate. You are not expected to foresee that falling space junk will hit a car and cause an accident resulting in injuries to the passengers. On the other hand, "having the college touch football champions scrimmage with the Super Bowl champions would make no sense" (Schuh and Ogle, 1993, p. 113), because this activity would involve a great deal of risk, considering the physical size of the players and their level of skill. A reasonable person would not schedule such an event.

Job Descriptions

One of the best ways to manage the risks associated with being an organization's adviser is to ensure that this appointment is part of your official assignment at the university. In some cases being the organization's adviser makes perfect sense because being an adviser would follow naturally from your normal work assignment. For example, when a member of the student activities staff advises the union board, that is part of the person's work at the college. But suppose a faculty member from the botany department advises the parachuting club? Is advising the parachuting club part of the faculty member's work at the university, or is it simply a volunteer assignment that has no connection with the person's employment on campus?

We cannot overstate the importance of the advising role's being defined as part of your formal work at the university. If advising a student organization is not seen as part of your role on campus, then such resources as legal counsel or the university's insurance policy may not be available. It works to your advantage to make sure that the assignment is within the scope of your employment at the institution.

As a practical matter, most organizations will not be involved in high-risk behavior that could result in tremendous exposure to negligence. Departmental clubs, for example, generally are engaged in fairly benign activities. They have meetings, host speakers, hold banquets, and so on. On the other hand, many campuses have organizations that engage in high-risk activities, such as spelunking, skydiving, and water skiing, that can result in injuries. Moreover, some clubs take trips by car or van. As a matter of self-protection, advisers to all organizations should have confirmation that advising is part of their institutional assignment. It would be a painful lesson if you were to learn after the fact that university legal counsel and other resources such as insurance would not be available to provide a defense against a negligence claim.

Event Planning

Although things can go wrong even when events are well planned, your keeping the "reasonable person" standard in mind and trying to anticipate problems and provide solutions in advance make excellence sense. Three basic principles apply in event planning that will help minimize risk.

Industry Standards. Industry standards should be followed if they are available. For example, whenever equipment is to be used in an event, your group should follow the instructions provided by the manufacturer on how to use the equipment. In addition, governing bodies, such as the National Intramural–Recreational Sports Association, are sources of information on how to provide for the safety of participants in various activities. Many sporting events require certain kinds of equipment. Fast-pitch softball, for example, should not be played unless catchers wear face masks. Camping equipment ought to be checked by knowledgeable, well-trained staff before being used on a trip. If people supervising various elements of an event are required to have a certain level of skill, they should be trained in accordance with the industry standards. If an organization is having a swimming event, for example, the lifeguards should be trained to meet Red Cross standards. Similarly, officers who are hired to provide security at an event need to have appropriate training. Industry standards should never be compromised.

Transportation.   Student organizations may want to take field trips that require transportation off-campus. These trips may be to a local attraction, but in other cases they can involve trips of considerable distance. The use of private automobiles with student drivers has the potential for tremendous problems.

Clearly, the safest way to travel is to use a common carrier, meaning commercial transportation. When a common carrier is used, the risk associated with the trip is in effect partially transferred to that carrier. This approach assumes that the carrier is licensed to do business, does not have a history of accidents, and has not experienced any other problems. The use of a common carrier is always preferable to having members provide the transportation. Common carriers, unfortunately, are likely to be more expensive than private transportation, so the only practical way to take the trip may be to use student drivers. Alternate precautions will need to be taken to ensure a safe trip.

You certainly cannot ensure that problems will not arise during a trip, but your group should take several steps in advance of the trip to make sure that reasonable precautions are in place. Among these are the following:

- All drivers should have valid operating licenses.
- No drivers should have a history of speeding tickets, reckless driving, driving while intoxicated, or any other problems that would lead one to conclude that they are not prudent operators of vehicles. In short, all drivers should have a clean record.
- All drivers and vehicles should be insured.
- All vehicles should be in good operating condition.
- No vehicles should be operated in a fashion that is not consistent with how the vehicle was designed, for example,

overloaded with passengers and luggage, or with passengers riding in the open bed of a truck.

- No driver should be at the wheel for an extended period of time. Drivers should be rotated to avoid fatigue.

- No person should be allowed to drive after consuming alcoholic beverages.

You need to ask very pointed questions about the safety of the vehicles and the drivers' records. If any questions arise, the trip should be postponed until the problems can be addressed.

At times it may make more sense to use institutional vehicles rather than the members' vehicles. Again, this may require additional expense, but presumably vehicles kept in the institution's motor pool undergo routine maintenance and have excellent vehicle service records. If your group does use institutional vehicles, it will have to follow the institution's regulations regarding the use of such vehicles. For example, there may be issues related to insurance and to operator training. Obviously, your group must plan in advance if it intends to use institutional vehicles. We recommend that you call the motor pool administrator to avoid last-minute problems that could cause the trip to be canceled.

As the types of students who attend our colleges continue to diversify (see Kuh, 1990; Ramirez, 1993), several additional implications arise related to travel. What happens if organization members want to bring their children on a trip because long-term child care is difficult to arrange? May the nonstudent spouse of an organization member come on the trip? May a student who is a minor come on the trip? These scenarios and others illustrate thorny problems for groups, leaders, and advisers. Who will care for the child when the student is attending a session of a conference? Supposing that the college proscribes alcoholic beverages, may spouses drink if they are of age? What if the child suffers an accident and needs medical care? You and your group's leadership should consult with legal counsel on how to proceed.

Substitute Events.   Some kinds of activities—such as tugs of war, weight-lifting contests, and eating and drinking competitions—are inherently risky, and if it is possible, your group should plan substitute events. If an event is planned in which there is some risk, then your group should take steps to ensure that the risk is minimized. Miyamoto (1988, p. 176) emphasizes this point by recommending that "institutions should have procedures detailing the safety measures that organizers of an extracurricular activity must take given the nature of a particular event. Equally important, institutions should have a duty to take the necessary measures to reasonably ensure compliance with those regulations."

Waivers

One common way organizations attempt to minimize risk is by asking participants to sign waiver forms crafted so as to absolve the organization (and its leaders) from any responsibility for injury that may result from participating in the activity. The assumption underlying the use of waivers is that by having students waive their right to hold anyone responsible for their injuries, the institution (and the adviser and officers) will be held harmless from whatever occurs. In fact, these types of waivers do not carry that force with them.

Waivers have a more useful purpose: they can serve as documentation that the participant is aware of the risks involved in participating in certain kinds of activities. Richmond (1990, p. 329) states: "What a written release may do, and its real value, is demonstrate that the plaintiff assumes the obvious or ordinary risks incident to the activities in question." For example, if a student organization plans to go mountain climbing, and some of the students have not engaged in this kind of activity before, having them sign a form acknowledging their understanding of the risk would be useful. What would be even more useful would be to have them participate in a training program conducted by an expert so they could master the rudimentary skills necessary to participate in the outing.

To summarize, waivers are useful in documenting that participants understand the risks associated with participating in any event, but they do not provide an impenetrable barrier against legal action if a person is injured while participating in an event conducted by the organization. (Having signed a waiver may discourage a person from pursuing legal action, however.) Exhibit 8.1 is a sample informed consent form that you can copy onto the appropriate letterhead.

Insurance

Another way of minimizing risk is to purchase insurance, including health and accident insurance as well as liability insurance. There are two ways of using liability insurance. One approach is to make sure that you are covered under the institution's blanket liability insurance. Many institutions have a liability policy that protects employees against judgments against them in the course of their work; the insurance provides monetary compensation in

Exhibit 8.1. Informed Consent Form

_____

_____ is planning _____
               (Name of organization)   (Type of activity)

Date(s) of activity: _____

Location of activity: _____

Person in charge of activity: _____

Telephone number of person in charge: _____

Other people in charge of activity: _____

Departure information: _____

Return information: _____

Participants will need to bring: _____

_____

Transportation will be provided by: _____

Cost of the activity: _____

Special skills needed to be mastered by participants: _____

_____

_____

These skills can be learned by participating in the following: _____

_____

_____

Any special medical conditions of the participant: _____

_____

Person to contact in case of emergency: _____

_____
              (Address)   (Telephone number)

I understand that I assume risk in participating in this event. I have completed the learning activities identified above. I certify that I am in good health and will comply with all organizational and institutional regulations while participating in this activity.

_____
              (Signature)   (Date)

the case of an adverse judgment against the employee. As stated earlier, for insurance purposes it is imperative that you be defined as an institutional employee engaged in an assignment related to your work; you cannot be seen as performing this function as a volunteer.

The second method of securing liability insurance coverage is for you to purchase a private policy. Often, professional associations offer this kind of insurance for a fairly modest premium. Some advisers carry liability insurance even if their institution provides coverage as just described. The ultimate decision on purchasing personal liability insurance is yours to make. Our general view is that an adviser without some form of coverage is taking a big risk; a policy providing several million dollars in liability coverage would be very prudent.

Your organization should also consider requiring health and accident insurance for student participants in various events. The institution may have a health and accident insurance policy that can be made available to students on an event-by-event basis. If available, students (or the organization on their behalf) pay a modest premium in exchange for basic health and accident insurance. The value of this coverage is well worth the cost if a student suffers an injury in the course of the event and requires medical attention. If this kind of policy is available, the institution's office of risk management can describe the coverage in more detail.

Special Issues

For us to provide you with appropriate background on legal matters, we also need to address five special legal issues. These regard handling money; following the copyright law, especially as it applies to the use of videocassettes; hazing; the possession and use of alcoholic beverages; and serving people with disabilities.

Money

Chapter Seven is devoted to financial management, but we should also look at the legal context that governs how funds are handled. Maloney (1988) points to two aspects of handling money. First, more than one person should be responsible for financial transactions. Second, "an organization must follow federal, state local and university guidelines" (p. 304). He points out that a group's exemption from paying federal income taxes does not necessarily mean that the group does not have to collect sales taxes.

You do not serve as the organization's treasurer, but you should be keeping a careful eye on the legal aspects of how the organization handles its funds. Obviously, the organization must avoid expending funds in violation of state law or contrary to institutional regulations. Even the slightest hint of an irregularity demands an intervention on your part, through a direct discussion with the organization's officers, a call to the institution's student activities office, or a conference with the chief financial officer of the institution.

Copyright Laws

The copyright law of 1990 (Copyright Remedy Clarification Act of 1990, cited by Burgoyne, 1992) has special applications to student groups. Faculty commonly think of copyright laws in the context of their photocopying sections of books and using the resulting material in class, for research, or in any other way. Organizations are more vulnerable, however, to violating the copyright law as it applies to the use of videocassettes or music. The fair use doctrine is applied to determine whether or not a violation of the copyright law has occurred. The fair use doctrine comprises four elements: (1) the purpose and character of the use of the material, including whether such use is of a commercial nature or is for nonprofit educational purposes; (2) the nature of the copyrighted work; (3) the amount of the work that was used in relation to the copyrighted work as a whole; and (4) the effect of its use upon the potential market (Kaplin and Lee, 1995).

Renting a videocassette and showing it at a club meeting, a residence hall lounge, or a fraternity house may seem like a harmless, inexpensive form of entertainment. The problem with this scenario, unfortunately, is that it constitutes a public showing of a videocassette, which is illegal, assuming the material included in the video is copyrighted and those exhibiting the video have not purchased a special license. Without an agreement with the copyright holder, no one can show videocassettes in a public forum even if no fees or ticket sales are involved. So, unless your organization secures a special license, it will have to seek alternative forms of entertainment or risk exposure to legal penalties.

Similarly, the use of music is governed by copyright laws. Generally speaking, students cannot make copies of music performances and sell them as a fundraiser without violating the law (Janes, 1988). When the organization starts moving into any area involving music copyright, a conversation between you, the organization's leaders, and legal counsel is in order.

Hazing

The Fraternity Insurance Purchasing Group (1994, p. 1) defines hazing as "Any action taken or situation created, intentionally, whether on or off fraternity premises, to produce mental or physical discomfort, embarrassment, harassment, or ridicule." Hazing has become less common on contemporary college campuses than may have been the case years ago. Nonetheless, it has been known to be a part of the ritual of certain organizations and clubs. Consequently, it is important to point out that many states have passed laws that make hazing illegal. Many campuses also have policies that make hazing a violation of institutional regulations. Gehring's observation (1987, p. 132) about hazing provides an excellent summary of the consequences of such activity. "Advisors and students should be aware that, if found guilty, students who engage in hazing others where an injury results could be dismissed from school, fined, imprisoned and be assessed damages."

Alcoholic Beverages

The illegal possession and use of alcoholic beverages on college campuses is a real problem. Wechsler, Kuh, and Davenport (1996) point out that a wide variety of problems result when substance abuse occurs on campus. Greek letter organizations are particularly vulnerable to problems of substance abuse because of the nature of their culture (Kuh and Arnold, 1993), but other groups are not immune from such problems.

The concept of social-host liability has direct implications for you and the student organization you advise. "An increasing number of states also have social liability which holds a gratuitous provider of alcohol liable to third persons injured by an intoxicated guest. Usually, this liability is triggered when a host serves an underage consumer or a person already intoxicated" (Gehring, 1991, p. 404). "In addition to suing the person who caused the injury, the dramshop and social-host liability theories hold that the injured person may also sue the provider of the alcoholic beverages for negligence" (Gehring, 1993, p. 279). In other words, an organization and its adviser may be held responsible for what happens as a result of the misuse of alcoholic beverages by a participant in the organization's event.

One case involving alcoholic beverages and an automobile accident is particularly worthy of comment. In *Bradshaw* v. *Rawlings*, the organization's adviser played a key role in the case. At the college's sophomore class picnic, beer was furnished, and the adviser co-signed the check that was used to purchase the beer

(Kaplin and Lee, 1995). After the picnic, a student who had become intoxicated at the picnic drove a car that was involved in an accident resulting in another student becoming a quadriplegic. The jury found on behalf of the injured student and rendered a judgment in excess of $1 million against the college.

Even though the college ultimately won the case on appeal by successfully arguing that it did not have a duty to care, little comfort can be taken in the ruling. Poor judgment was exercised in furnishing the beer at the picnic, and under no circumstances should an intoxicated person have been behind the wheel of a motor vehicle. Similar tragedies involving alcoholic beverages have led to other cases, although again the institutions prevailed in a legal sense. In *Baldwin* v. *Zoradi* a student was injured by an intoxicated student who was involved in a drag racing contest. The intoxicated driver had been drinking in a residence hall room on campus. In *Beach* v. *University of Utah* an intoxicated student, who had been drinking in full view of the faculty adviser, fell off a cliff. In both cases the courts found for the university (Kaplin and Lee, 1995).

The institutions argued their cases following the same line of thinking as that in *Bradshaw,* namely, that they have no duty to supervise student behavior. Whether institutions have no such duty in a legal sense is almost beside the point. With more careful supervision, nobody would have been hurt.

Ultimately, the institutions won their cases, and the advisers did not have to pay monetary damages. But the personal anguish, time, and effort expended to prevail in court are a substantial price to pay. It thus bears repeating that although their winning in court sustains the actions taken by the advisers, a far better way to approach problems related to liability is to try to avoid the problems in the first place. The best risk management technique regarding alcohol is that it should not be available at student events. If it must be served, at a minimum you should make efforts to ensure that

- Underage people are not served.
- Anyone operating a motor vehicle is not served.
- A limit is placed on the amount of alcohol any single person can consume.
- Nonalcoholic beverages are available.
- Food is served.
- Alcoholic beverages are not served for at least an hour before the activity concludes.

Another strategy that you might want to encourage the organization to employ is to use a commercial vendor (such as a restaurant or club) for events involving alcoholic beverages. Let professional bartenders decide when people have had enough to drink. Participants should also use designated drivers or commercial transportation so that they can get home safely.

Using these strategies will not guarantee that alcoholic beverages won't cause problems—too much can go wrong when college students and alcohol mix—but at least you can provide yourself and the members of your organization with a margin of safety.

People with Disabilities

Section 504 of the Rehabilitation Act of 1973 states: "No otherwise qualified individual with a disability in the United States . . . shall, solely by reason of his [or her] disability, be excluded from the participation in, be denied the benefits of, or be subjected to discrimination under any program or activity receiving federal financial assistance" (cited by Kaplin and Lee, 1995, p. 822). This law prohibits excluding students from participating in campus organizations and activities. If activities require special accommodations for students with disabilities, those accommodations must be provided. For example, a student who has a hearing impairment may require an interpreter. Meetings and activities must be held in buildings accessible to students who use wheelchairs.

Most campuses have made tremendous progress in making programs and activities accessible, but other issues arise. What happens when the group travels to a conference? What if, because of the unusual circumstances of the trip, a student requires an attendant? Who pays for an interpreter? If the group is traveling by van, must the vehicle be accessible? These questions can lead to difficult and potentially expensive solutions. Again, take advantage of campus legal counsel; the director of campus services for students with disabilities will also be helpful. Contact these resources for their advice when your group is planning activities that will require special accommodations for students or advisers with disabilities.

Case Vignettes

We provide the following vignettes to give you an idea of the variety of situations involving legal issues that you may encounter as an adviser.

Lakeshore Bash

Your student group always ends the year with a picnic at the lakefront home of one of your most loyal alumnae. She turns the home over to the group and allows the students to have complete run of the home as well as the use of the dock and sailboat she owns. This year the students want to plan for a particularly memorable event, but they know they cannot use the organization's funds to buy beer. Instead, they propose to take up a collection of the people at the event and run over to the local convenience store to pick up as much beer as they can afford. They are looking to you for advice.

How would you respond?

Out-of-Town Party

Your organization is planning a midyear semiformal event at a town approximately fifty miles from campus. The leaders plan on providing bus transportation to and from the event, but some of the members do not like the idea of taking a bus with their escorts. Some of the members are proposing that members can either take the bus or drive their own cars to the event.

What do you think of this plan? What actions will you take?

X-Rated Fundraiser

Your organization is undergoing difficult financial times. A conference that the organization hosted lost quite a bit of money, and the organization needs to make some money fast. One of the members proposes that the group sponsor an X-rated film festival. The local district attorney has made it clear that he will arrest people involved in showing X-rated movies, citing a local ordinance as justification for his position. Before the ordinance was passed, X-rated film festivals made a great deal of money, and the members are convinced this is a good way to raise money. They think the district attorney is bluffing.

What do you think of the proposal? What might you do to respond to it? What will you advise the members?

Secret Ritual

For years, membership in your organization has been confirmed by a secret ritual, in addition to a formal ceremony. As the new adviser you have no knowledge of the ritual. You notice that the week before the initiation ceremony many of the students wishing to join seem to be awfully tired, and they wear the same clothes day after day. This situation concerns you, but you are unsure about what you should do.

What might you do to respond to this situation?

CHAPTER 9

Dealing with Conflicts and Other Problems

At various times you will have to assist the organization or individual members with conflicts and other problems. "Successful leaders have come to understand that conflict is not only inevitable in student organizations, but it is also beneficial and healthy, if properly managed. Conflict can stimulate new ideas, clarify elements of an issue, increase task motivation, and lead to better solutions because of increased understanding of opposing perspectives" (Franck, 1983, p. 2). It may be difficult, however, for a student or adviser to perceive the benefit of conflict while committee members are yelling at one another, when a member is in tears, or when one executive officer is left out of social functions by the other officers.

Conflict and problems may be caused by any number of factors, roles, or situations. In some situations, the conflict may be inherent to the structure of the particular student organization. In other situations, conflict may arise from members' and executive officers' inability to communicate, or may be due to members' wanting the organization to get involved in something other than its stated purpose. In this chapter, we categorize the sources of conflict and other problems as organizational structure, politics, funding issues, assumption of power, tradition and culture, communication, personalities, and differing purposes. For each category, we clarify terms and provide examples, and suggest solutions through activities and different approaches.

Organizational Structure _____

The organizational structure of a student group may lead to problems. In this section, we look at the adviser's level of authority in relation to the organization, the structure of the executive board, the apportionment of representatives, the members' constituency, and the size of the voting membership.

Authority Level of the Adviser

An organization's president may want to deal directly with a departmental chair or director rather than a graduate student assigned as the organization's adviser. Students may perceive that the graduate student adviser does not possess the authority to make decisions for the department regarding budgets, travel, or policies and procedures. An organization that includes in its purpose attention to divisional or campuswide matters would be best served by an adviser who is placed higher in an academic or student affairs department. Osteen and Tucker (forthcoming) have determined that one of the ingredients leading to success in residence hall associations is the authority level of the adviser. Because residence hall associations work on a systemwide basis, they believe the adviser should be a senior staff member from the central office. This authority level is one of the key ingredients found at the thirteen institutions that were determined to have the most successful residence hall associations in the country (Komives and Tucker, 1993).

Structure of the Executive Board

In some organizations, the officers of the executive board report to the organization's president. Presidents are seen to possess an administration, and they commonly refer to the executive board as "their administration." The relationships among board members and personality of the executive board may be directed or dictated by the president. The organization's members may approach only the president because they recognize that decisions are made by that person. This executive board structure may distance the executive officers from the organization's membership. An organization president who is concerned about potential conflicts and problems with the executive board structure can use a few strategies. First, the president might empower the executive board with specific duties and with decision-making authority that works with individuals in the organization's membership. Second, when members give reports during meetings regarding committee work or projects, they should stand and face the membership rather than the president or executive board, so as to give the impression that they are representing the organization. Third, the president should refrain from using such expressions as "my administration," "my executive board," or "I have decided," and should use the more inclusionary "we" or "the executive board."

Apportionment of Voting Members

For most student organizations, a number of members will attend the weekly meetings, and if any business is to be conducted, a simple show of hands is the deciding factor. For many larger organizations, however, such as student governments, the structure of the organization and voting privileges are apportioned. For example, each college on the campus might be given one voting seat, or each zip code may be allocated a specific number of voting seats. Apportionment is an intentional way of structuring an organization, but it can lead to conflict. To minimize conflicts or problems, how the apportionment is determined should be decided with proper and equitable involvement by all constituencies; otherwise some students may feel as if their voices were not heard. Second, if apportionment is structured by specific colleges or zip codes, it is important for the organization's leadership to ensure that the number of students represented in each bloc is equitable lest a constituency receive a disproportionate number of voting seats. Third, the organization should evaluate the apportionment plan on an annual basis. This evaluation will ensure that as colleges and zip codes change, representation will be adjusted accordingly.

Constituency Served by Voting Members

This issue may be closely related to the apportionment of the student organization, and again is more likely to occur in a large student organization rather than in a special-interest, military, or sports organization. These organizations adopt purposes that typically do not involve serving constituencies with radically different views because they share a common, nonpolitical constituency. However, in the case of student governments and residence hall associations, specific constituencies may attempt to secure a majority of the voting rights of the organization. Student government constituencies may be aligned with Greek letter organizations, specific academic units, or a particular political persuasion. Residence hall association constituencies may be aligned as individual residence halls or as underclass students against upperclass students.

One strategy used by organizations to reduce the likelihood of a constituency's gaining majority voting rights is to include a set of voting guidelines in the organization's constitution that eliminate majority constituency voting. These guidelines would establish a percentage of voting members from each constituency not to exceed 50 percent. For example, a residence hall association could be represented by a percentage of members from individual underclass and upperclass halls, at-large seats, and alumni seats, none of which make up a majority of the voting representatives. For some organizations, this is entirely possible, because the purpose of the organization dissuades members from politicizing their group through constituency management. For student governments, this basic organizational concept is the framework for party control in the organization and is included in the purpose of the organization. You need to recognize the constituencies represented in your organization to foresee the conflicts and problems that might arise among constituencies possessing differing purposes, goals, or objectives.

Size of the Voting Membership

For many organizations, the number of the voting members is never a problem, because the dozen members who attend the weekly or monthly meeting know each other or may have been involved with each other for a number of months. For student governments, residence hall associations, Greek letter, or some special-interest organizations, however, the size of the voting membership can be a problem. When a student government holds a vote for student body executive officer positions, many campuses allow the entire student body to vote. For some campuses, setting up a room in the student union with several voting tables is all that is necessary on the day of voting. For large campuses, a successful strategy has been to hire the city or county elections officials to staff multiple voting sites over the course of one or more days. The student government then pays the city or county a fee for administering the process.

Similar conflicts or problems may arise in Greek letter and some special-interest organizations that have memberships or representatives in excess of one hundred students. These student organizations similarly employ a voting process that allows only the members of the house or organizational representatives an opportunity to vote. This process restricts the voting to students who have worked with and know the strengths and weaknesses of those running for election. It also eliminates the potential expense or possible involvement of an individual voting or running for office who possess little knowledge or experience in the organization.

Organizations continue to develop new technological applications to improve the efficiency and accuracy of how they conduct business. Institutions are using database management to allow students on-line voting over the Internet and telephone. Although these systems increase the convenience for students, they also open new opportunities for abuse. You will want to monitor these systems closely and call on technology experts to help you understand the system and anticipate potential problems.

Politics

How the members of a student organization choose to work with each other and with other organizations may be best described as politics. *Politics* is a collective term that for some student organizations serves as the basis of their purpose. For other organizations to function properly over an extended period of time, they must conscientiously refrain from practicing politics in any form. A student organization's involvement in politics may lead to conflict and problems.

Politics can be closely compared to power. (Chapter Three discusses the seven different power bases.) When students take advantage of their position, their knowledge, their connections to other influential persons, or their ability to provide rewards, they are practicing a form of politics. When students begin to coalesce with similar views toward a specific agenda, they are practicing a lobbying or bloc voting approach. As these groups of students become more organized and intentional in their approaches, they begin to form parties. Some student organizations follow a party doctrine to give purpose to their organization. During campus elections for seats in a student government senate, these organizations may form a ticket of students from their organization to run collectively as a party. This party develops statements or planks that all members support. Students voting for individual senators may vote for the individual person or may vote all party members in to senate seats.

Throughout these processes the potential exists for conflict and problems; for example, students may feel pressured to vote for a specific person or party, legislation may fail to pass in a student senate because of bloc voting, or budget allocations may be hindered by various pressures or favors needing attention. Most student organizations will never be involved in these types of politics: their interest in political involvement is nonpartisan, or the organization takes a politically neutral stance. The few organizations that are involved in these political practices do so because of their interest in political processes, the legislative system, or campaign issues.

If you are an adviser to one of these types of organizations, you can assist in decreasing the likelihood of misuse of practices by ensuring that policies, guidelines, and proper financial practices are followed. Some additional strategies include meeting with the students involved in the student government executive and legislative branches jointly to discuss the use and misuse of their positions. Forming a student and faculty oversight committee is also a good strategy to prevent an organization or election process from getting involved in politics that create conflict or problems. The organization also can use the campus judicial system as an option when the student code of conduct has been violated.

Funding Issues

Although we discuss general financial matters at length in Chapter Seven, there are a number of funding issues that can lead to conflict and problems that go beyond the general level. In this section we discuss lack of funding, record management, use of funds, budget preparedness, and external influences.

Lack of Funding

Student organizations never seem to have enough funds to accomplish everything they would like. Komives and Tucker (1993) found that multiple-source funding was a common theme in organizations' success. Unfortunately, most student organizations receive funding from only one source: fundraising.

The major problem arising from a shortage of funds is that the time spent raising funds is time taken away from the enjoyment of fulfilling the organization's purpose. The members of a sailing club, for example, who must spend considerable time raising money through car washes, bake sales, or sponsorships, may find they have little time to practice sailing. Students can become quite frustrated.

Chapter Seven identifies sources of funds that student organizations might pursue. As the group's adviser, you can also stress that fundraising events themselves can provide positive experiences for the members other than just raising money. These events, if handled properly, can provide an opportunity for members to work on a project together, which creates teamwork and a sense of group purpose. Fundraisers also allow the students to get away from campus and have fun relaxing from the pressures of schoolwork, or to assist the community in a common venture. Through creatively planned fundraising events, students can focus their attention away from their frustration over the lack of funds.

Financial Record Management

Students elected or appointed to positions responsible for the financial records have an important responsibility. Conflict and problems arise when the student responsible for the record keeping, typically an organization's treasurer, auditor, or accountant, gets behind in his or her duties. For many student organizations, record keeping may simply be maintaining a checkbook. For larger student organizations, with several students working on financial matters, record keeping may involve a number of different agencies and full-time employees handling several accounts. Regardless of the complexity of the duty, it is important to maintain financial records in a timely fashion. Audit criticisms, returned checks, bounced checks, lost bank statements, or cash lying around can create problems both devastating for the organization and tremendously time-consuming to clear up. Chapter Seven discusses how audits, record keeping, and presentation of records can be best accomplished.

Use of Funds

Private and public institutions allow students to make decisions on the expenditure of funds, as regulated by the policies and procedures of the institution and the laws of the state. Occasionally, executive boards or individual members of student organizations make questionable decisions about how to spend their funds. Some student organizations have purchased vehicles and laptop computers for an individual's use; members have taken personal trips; and one student government even purchased one thousand pink plastic flamingos. In most of these extreme examples the oversight was not in place to cancel these purchases through such techniques as two-party signatures on checks or institutional staff involvement.

The types of conflict and other problems resulting from how funds are used can vary. Negative public reaction to the use of funds to purchase items for personal use is very difficult to overcome. In some instances, when use of funds appears to be out of control, all accounts are frozen while an audit takes place, staff involvement becomes a necessary step in the use of students funds, or an organization such as a student government may be forced to disband while an assessment and reorganization take place. Advisers who take the time to learn about the student organization's financial practices can assist the organization and its members in developing a sound system of fund use.

One good practice for a student organization is to conduct readings regarding the expenditure of funds, held over the course of two consecutive organizational meetings. An expense reading requires the expense to be proposed, debated, and voted on during a meeting. By using two meetings to discuss the information, members can take the information to their respective constituencies for feedback prior to the second reading. Also, both readings will be recorded in the organization's minutes. By involving membership in spending decisions, these practices help reduce the likelihood that funds will be misused.

Budget Development

The student responsible for preparing and presenting the budget may face conflicts and problems. The duty of the financial officer who prepares the budget is to secure the best information possible using both past and current figures. When a budget is presented to the membership for approval, it is important for the financial officer to be prepared to answer questions regarding how much money was spent on a specific line the previous term; how the amount in each line item was determined; who was involved in providing information for the budget; which items are new and were not included in the past; whether the organization has enough revenues to meet its expenses; what the source of the revenues is; or what difficulties the financial officer foresees in the budget for the given term. The membership can ask many questions related to the budget presentation. A good strategy to employ prior to presenting a budget is to have the financial officer prepare and present the budget to you and the organization's executive board. You and the board then can anticipate the questions that the membership is likely to ask. This "preview" gives the financial officer an opportunity to respond and to secure additional information or make additional copies of appropriate documents to support his or her answers. The more carefully the financial officer prepares the budget, the better able he or she is to make the presentation and to respond to questions from the organization's membership.

External Influences

Individuals representing various companies and agencies will approach a student organization's executive board or financial officer with proposals. On the surface these proposals may look like good arrangements for making additional money for the organization. Student organizations and advisers must take care in the relationship they establish with outside vendors, fundraisers, or individuals.

A number of reputable companies provide fundraising ideas, strategies, and services for student organizations. These companies have had success with institutions for many years by providing a percentage return to the organization for the sale of carpets, refrigerators, pennants, mugs, key chains, welcome baskets, and so forth. One factor to consider is that on some campuses, student government–funded organizations are not allowed to conduct fundraising. (Chapter Seven discusses the use of external vendors as a fundraising option.) Many problems can arise from contracts, guarantees, and formal arrangements that student organizations enter into to raise funds. The institutional general counsel's office is a good resource when a company or individual approaches an organization regarding these ventures.

Role Confusion

Student organizations have frequent turnover in executive board, committee, and task force members. In addition to this turnover, whenever students are elected, appointed, or assigned responsibilities, they assume a position with new responsibilities and duties. Member and leader turnover may result in role confusion and subsequent conflicts and problems.

As student organization executive boards are elected, several conflicts or problems might arise. The president of the organization may be elected from the membership or may, by constitutional designation, be required to have prior service on the executive board. Similarly, executive board members may have had to satisfy other qualifications in order to be elected. Conflict can arise if, following election, the executive board did not meet to identify and clarify their specific responsibilities and the duties of various board members. You can assist this process by ensuring that the executive board meets to discuss and agree on its responsibilities. Chapter Three discusses officer duties and the position descriptions of the officers in greater detail.

Role confusion can also interfere with the assumption of power and decision-making authority. For example, the financial officer may understand that decisions regarding finances are the responsibility of the financial officer, yet the president, assuming the role of leader of the organization, might believe that any decision regardless of the financial implications should be made by the president. Or the organization secretary, who is responsible for reserving meeting space, does so without the consent of the president, who wants to be involved in all operational decisions. Both examples highlight the need to discuss roles and responsibilities as soon after an election as possible.

Role confusion can also ensue for people serving as advisers, because they "are charged with maintaining fiscal responsibility, yet are also indoctrinated into the philosophy of allowing students to do their own programming. Often these two roles conflict as when students wish to sponsor a program requiring a considerable financial commitment, and it is unclear whether students can make the programming decision or the adviser can make the budget-conscious decision" (Franck, 1983, p. 2). As we have stated elsewhere, it is essential that you and the executive board hold a meeting to clarify and agree to everyone's roles as promptly as possible following the election.

Because students are involved in committees, task forces, and groups other than the executive board, it is important that these students receive a committee charge from the appropriate executive board member. A committee charge identifies the purpose of the committee, the role of committee members, a time line the committee should follow to fulfill its purpose, and how the committee should present the information it has worked on. Exhibit 9.1 provides an example of a committee charge. You too may have a role in assisting the executive board to determine or draft the committee charge. Large student organizations may require a separate, designated adviser to work with a committee, task force, or special project.

Tradition and Culture

Students join organizations for various reasons, one of which is their interest in the role an organization plays in campus traditions. There are many student organization traditions that are positive or service oriented. Greek letter organizations possess long-standing traditions of tapping members into chapters or using Greek letters and shields to reflect the history of the organization. Recognition and honorary organizations are steeped in tradition, as such organization names as Mortarboard or Cicerones would suggest. Sports organizations such as rugby clubs maintain traditions in the practice of their sport traced back to its European ancestry. Despite all the positive traditions and cultures attached to many student organizations, the potential for conflict or problems still exists. A tradition that is not in line with the educational mission of the

Exhibit 9.1. Committee Charge Example

Committee: Executive Board Organizational Review

Chair: Tom Benton

Members: Shawn Smith, Yvonne Titus, Samantha Simon, Ben Richards

Time line: To begin meeting immediately upon receipt of the committee charge. Committee meeting frequency is determined by committee members. Final report due at end of present term.

Purpose: To review the present organizational structure of the executive board. To provide a written report to the president outlining recommendations for organizational change and the rationale for the recommendations. To identify the steps taken and the individuals who provided information to the committee in considering recommendations.

Member role: To participate actively in committee discussion. To represent the constituency that appointed the member. To take information to the bimonthly organizational meetings for feedback.

President	Date

---

institution, or a practice that violates the student code of conduct or state and federal laws are two categories of traditions that you can work to avoid.

Educational Mission

When students stereotype an organization or a person who is a member of an organization, they engage in an activity that is not inclusive or accepting of that person or organization. Lack of inclusion or acceptance generally runs against the educational mission of an institution. You can work with student organizations by discussing stereotypes and the negative views associated with them. You can also assist in bringing members of different organizations together to speak on their purposes and programs. This meeting generally provides information that is beneficial to all the student organizations in attendance. For example, if members of an organization are stereotyping members of a computer club as being "techies" or "nerds," the adviser of the organization can work to bring his or her members to a meeting with members of the computer club. What may well be discovered is that the two groups can join together in a fundraiser using the club's expertise with computers and the other organization's expertise with publicity. Bringing two organizations together can be mutually beneficial and can work to eradicate stereotypes.

You also need to be aware of the membership cliques that form as members find commonalities. Classes of students entering the organization will have a tendency to form a clique of students with similar academic interests. Cliques can be exclusive and open to stereotyping, or they may begin to organize as separate, smaller entities in order to bloc vote during meetings. Together with student leaders, you can work to identify these problems early, associating returning members with new members early in the year or designing programs to combine the talents and skills of returning and new members. These efforts will provide benefits as the year progresses by encouraging open communication, fostering retention of new members, and involving members in programs.

Code or Law Violations

Traditions that violate the campus code of student conduct or state and federal laws clearly are problematic. Traditions such as hazing are associated with a number of organizations. As discussed from the legal viewpoint in Chapter Eight, hazing activities in Greek letter organizations are defined as:

> any action taken or situation created intentionally, whether on or off fraternity premises, to produce mental or physical discomfort, embarrassment, harassment, or ridicule. Such activities may include but are not limited to the following: use of alcohol; paddling in any form; creation of excessive fatigue; physical and psychological shocks; quests, treasure hunts, scavenger hunts, road trips, or any other such activities carried on outside or inside the confines of the chapter house; wearing of public apparel that is conspicuous and not normally in good taste; engaging in public stunts and buffoonery; morally degrading or humiliating games and activities; and any other activities that are not consistent with fraternal law, ritual, or policy or with the regulations and policies of the educational institution. [National Interfraternity Conference, 1991, p. I-34]

In the effort to eliminate these practices, campuses and governing bodies of fraternities are actively pursuing chapters that continue to practice hazing. If you discover any signs that your group is planning these types of activities, you should discuss it with organizational leadership immediately. You should remind student leaders that in a number of states hazing is illegal. In addition, you can develop programs that educate your organization's members about the types of activities that are considered hazing and the rationale for prohibiting hazing activities in an educational setting.

Another degrading activity that many student organizations practice is commonly referred to as an auction, during which individuals are auctioned to the highest bidder. The person may be auctioned as a date, to provide a package of gifts or services to the winning bidder, or because they are the best dressed. This type of fundraiser is particularly demeaning to African American students, who commonly view this activity as a continuation of the tradition of the sale of slaves. You can work with your student organization, first, to discuss why the name of the function is inappropriate, and you can work with other students who can in turn communicate information in a peer fashion to help members understand that the activity is demeaning. Second, you can work with the students to reconceive and rename the activity as perhaps a rental of services rather than as an auction. Your actively involving students in these discussions is crucial to students' understanding the problems with this type of activity.

Communication

Communication is the factor most likely to cause conflict and other problems in a student organization. Chapter Three discusses ways of enhancing various forms of communication on several different levels, and includes examples of agendas, minutes, and resolutions. In this section we discuss the communication conflicts and problems that you may encounter.

Communication can be intertwined with politics, funding issues, organizational structure, and any of the other factors that can cause conflict or problems in an organization. Because communication involves nonverbal, verbal, or written messages, it involves all facets of the student organization. Refer to Exhibit 9.2 for a case study on the potential conflicts and problems associated with communications.

Nonverbal Communication

A number of problems may result from the nonverbal communication and messages sent by you, the executive board, or members.

Exhibit 9.2. Communication Case Study

Directions: You can use the following progressive case study with groups of five or six students or advisers. Pass out the initial case to the participants and allow them time to answer the two questions. When they have completed the questions, take ten to fifteen minutes to discuss their answers. Following discussion, hand out the first update and again allow time to complete the questions that follow; continue with the second and third updates in the same way. To finish, allow the participants time to complete the final questions prior to discussion.

Initial Case

You are an adviser to a Greek letter organization. You have served as adviser for the past six years; you possess a good knowledge of the organization's history and procedures, and are familiar with the members. It is the middle of the fall term, and the organization meets on a weekly basis.

Your executive board is composed of three new members to the board and two who had served in varying positions on the board the previous year. At last night's meeting, the president did not recognize two members who wanted to speak.

1. What are your questions at this point in the situation?

2. What action do you take in the situation?

Update One

You have just met with the president to inquire as to why she did not recognize the two speakers. She tells you that several members approached her prior to the meeting and told her the two members would question why she has not sent a letter to the dean of students requesting an investigation of an alleged hazing activity the two members had witnessed.

1. What are your questions at this point in the situation?

2. What action do you take in the situation?

Update Two

The president reluctantly tells you that she was also present at the hazing activity but did not participate. She further explains that the activity caused no harm to anyone and was not meant to be seen by the two members.

1. What are your questions at this point in the situation?

2. What action do you take in the situation?

Update Three

You have not told anyone else about your conversation with the president. You have encouraged her to send the letter to the dean of students. During the next meeting, the president allows the two members to speak. They ask the president why the letter was not sent. The president states that she has taken care of the situation and that the situation did not warrant a full investigation. One of the two members reports that she has information that a sexual assault took place as a result of the hazing activity, and asks the president whether she was aware of that information.

1. What are your questions at this point in the situation?

2. What action do you take at this point in the situation?

Final Questions

1. What department, or agencies, or people should have been involved in this situation?

2. What kind of follow-up is necessary in this situation?

3. What other strategies could you have employed in this situation?

While a student organization meeting is in session, the individuals who are not currently speaking send strong messages to one another through their nonverbal communication.

Advisers.   Some student organizations have their adviser sit at the front table with the executive board. Other advisers sit in a front row of the body, and still others sit on the far end of the back row. Where you sit during the meeting will communicate whether you are an active or passive participant. We recommend that you sit in the front row on the side, where members can see you, recognize that you are paying attention during the meeting, and still understand that you are not an active participant in all meeting matters.

Executive Boards.   In larger organizations, the executive board may be seated at a front table; other groups have more informal meetings where the executive board and members are seated in a circle. Regardless of the level of formality, it is imperative that while a member is speaking, the executive board is attentive to the individual. Executive board officers who roll their eyes, shake their heads, or sigh in disgust send strong messages to every other individual in the room, each of whom will interpret the messages differently. You can work with executive board members to increase their understanding of the role of nonverbal communication, not only in meetings but also during individual conversations executive board officers have with members.

Members.   Some signals that individual members send during a formal meeting—by getting up to chat with other members, reading newspapers, wearing radios with headsets, or holding sidebar conversations—detract from the decorum of the meeting and send a message of being uninterested or of lacking respect for the speaker. The executive board can work with you to conduct a program for members on nonverbal communication and the messages it sends.

How members give their reports during meetings is also important, particularly for large formal meetings of student organizations. Members or chairs of committees who stand up and deliver the report to the executive board are sending the message that the report is exclusively for the executive board. To communicate the message that reports are for all the members of the student organization, the member or committee chair should stand in front of the room and turn to give the report to the members of the organization. This reporting procedure takes the emphasis away from the executive board and places it on the members.

Verbal Communication

You should take care as an institutional representative to provide appropriate information to the membership of a student organization Information used in the context of your regular staff or faculty duties may be confidential or subject to reaction from legal counsel prior to public consumption. Protected information regarding discipline, personnel, academic records, and so forth should be used only in the course of your job, not as part of your advising role.

When you choose to speak during the organization's meeting, you should always take care to avoid siding with one view of the membership. Your role in communicating information is to clarify institutional policies and procedures, to assist the organization's understanding of fiscal responsibility, to provide information on the history of the organization's involvements, and so forth. When you side with a particular subgroup's view, you risk polarizing the membership.

Executive board officers should receive proper training in effectively maintaining the decorum of meetings. Using proper procedure, executive officers can avoid an individual member's using all the available time or getting so emotionally involved as to disrupt the meeting. The organization's president can limit the length of debate, limit the number of times a member can speak about an issue, call a member out of order, or speak to the member following the meeting.

Written Communication

The written materials produced by members of a student organization convey a number of different messages. First, when executive officers produce correspondence, it should be organized and professional. It should not be handwritten on a sheet of notebook paper. The correspondence becomes a part of the history and files of the organization and should be treated professionally.

Similarly, sending copies of the correspondence to other individuals requires attention. When someone in the organization sends a memorandum to the director of the student union and copies are sent to the dean, the vice president for student affairs, and the president of the institution, the memo becomes much more important than a simple file copy. The author of the memo wants the other individuals to be aware of the contents of the memo, to take action, or to ensure that appropriate action is taken. You can assist the authors of correspondence in understanding the implications of copying memoranda to various institutional or state personnel. Occasions will no doubt arise when a student organization will want to send copies of memos or other documents to key administrators, but the authors should understand the potential impact of these communications.

Personalities

The personalities of an organization's members, executive officers, and adviser can lead to potential conflict or problems. Understanding individuals' psychological or personality type will allow you not only to assist the student organization through difficult times but also to reinforce the team building of the executive board and membership. One of the most widely used and accepted personality indicators is the Myers-Briggs Type Indicator (MBTI). Because of space restrictions, we will provide only a brief overview of the MBTI.

"C.G. Jung developed one of the most comprehensive of current theories to explain human personality" (Lawrence, 1995, p. 7). Whereas some people saw behavior as random, Jung saw behavior as patterned. The lifelong work of Isabel Briggs Myers "to carry Carl Jung's theory of type . . . into practical applications" (Lawrence, 1995, p. 6) resulted in the Myers-Briggs Type Indicator (MBTI), which Myers developed with her mother, Katherine Briggs.

The personality types identified in the MBTI are categorized by four dimensions: extroversion or introversion, sensing or intuition, thinking or feeling, and judgment or perception. Student organization members can take the MBTI and have the instrument scored to determine individual preferred types. Each individual would possess an identified preferred type in each of the four categories. Understanding the relationships between members who possess one of sixteen different combinations of traits will allow the members to recognize each other's motivations and actions. "If teachers and others in the helping professions were to learn just one thing about psychological types, the thing most important to understand is the power of the dominant process. . . . The most essential thing to know about the motivations of types is that thinking dominant types do their best work when pursuing logical order; feeling types do their best work when their heart is in it; sensing types do their best work when their practical skills are needed and valued; and intuitive types do their best work when pursuing an inspiration" (Lawrence, 1995, p. 16).

We suggest that you have the executive board and the organization's membership take the MBTI. A certified interpreter of the MBTI should present and facilitate a discussion on the MBTI. We find that the MBTI is a very teachable, understandable, and practical tool in developing understanding of personalities among the executive officers and membership of a student organization.

Differing Purposes

The challenges associated with differing purposes can arise at two levels—the organizational and the individual.

Organizational Level

The purpose statement of the student organization is included in the group's constitution. The student leadership should work with you to regularly review and interpret the purpose statement. The purpose statement guides the organization as it makes decisions, sets goals for the year, and becomes involved in campus matters. When an organization strays from its stated purpose, the potential for conflict and problems increases.

Problems for an organization may result when it becomes involved in an area where another student organization already works or performs a function; when it takes a political stand or supports a candidate even though the purpose dictates political neutrality; or when it fails to provide the basic programs, services, or funds called for by the purpose. In these circumstances you can work with the executive board to assist the organization in clarifying the purpose by holding a roundtable discussion or open forum. If the membership determines that the purpose needs modification, then the organization's constitution should provide the proper steps to modify the purpose.

Individual Level

Individuals involved in a student organization may possess differing attitudes toward its purposes. For example, one or two members of a student organization may strongly believe that the organization should move in a different direction because of religious, political, or philosophical views. It is important for the executive board and organization to allow members the opportunity to express their views. A good strategy is to provide an issue forum as an agenda item at some point during a meeting. The issue forum allows members to address a concern that is of interest to them. The time allowed for an issue forum should be limited; if members desire additional time, a motion to extend the time could be in order. For an organization to prevent a potential problem caused by a member's possessing a strong opinion on an issue, it is important to provide the member with an opportunity to speak.

PART THREE

Supporting and Improving Practice

CHAPTER 10

Ensuring Quality
in Advising

Ensuring whether or not students have high-quality experiences on college campuses is of widespread concern in contemporary society. Consider the following observation from the Wingspread Group on Higher Education (1993, p. 1): "A disturbing and dangerous mismatch exists between what American society needs of higher education and what it is receiving." Although we are not prepared to claim that the future of higher education rests on the quality of advising provided to student organizations, we are quite sure that all aspects of higher education should be of high quality, from the courses students enroll in to the services available on campus. As Upcraft and Schuh (1996, p. 13) observe, "It is a fundamental responsibility of student affairs to provide services, programs and facilities that are of high quality, however quality might be defined and for whomever."

There is no point in having individuals advise organizations unless the advice and counsel provided by these individuals is of high quality. But how do we know whether the advising is of high quality? How can we determine whether the organization is benefiting from advising? How does the adviser know whether the organization is functioning at a high level of effectiveness? These and other questions form the basis for this chapter. We propose to address issues related to ensuring quality in advising; to this end, we look at different kinds of evaluation approaches, briefly describe various evaluation methods, and then introduce some evaluation techniques that you can use to evaluate both your group and the job you are doing.

Evaluation can be quite complicated, and a number of excellent books have been written on this topic. We realize that most advisers have a full-time work assignment in addition to their work with a student group. Brown and Podolske (1993a) point out that there are appropriate times for both informal and formal evaluations. Our view is that the evaluation of the adviser and the organization is an ongoing process that is informal for the most part but requires formal evaluation at times, so we provide information that will meet both needs. Our approach is to introduce some tools for you that can be used to address the topic of evaluation without becoming so burdensome that you will never want to address this issue except in the most cursory way. Although we do not attempt to transform you into an expert evaluator, we trust that the ideas we present will help you make informed judgments about the quality of support you are providing to the organization you advise.

Evaluation Defined

To establish a common point of departure, we begin with a definition of evaluation: "Evaluation is any effort to use assessment evidence to improve institutional, department, divisional, or agency effectiveness" (Upcraft and Schuh, 1996, p. 19). This definition was originally developed to apply to units within student affairs. With a bit of modification it can be applied to organizations and their advisers. We propose to define evaluation for the purpose of this discussion as "any activity designed to improve the effectiveness of the organization or its adviser." Although we are primarily interested in providing tools to evaluate your work, it is also important that you be able to measure how well the organization is doing. Kuh and Hunter (1987, p. 183) add, "Evaluation becomes more useful when issues and activities are addressed that can help an adviser understand and design interventions to *improve group functioning*" (emphasis in the original).

Types of Evaluations

There are two common types of evaluation in higher education: formative evaluations and summative evaluations. "Formative evaluations are conducted periodically throughout the development phases of a program and are used to provide quick feedback to the program staff so changes can be made to improve the program as time passes" (Brown, 1979, p. 21). "If the reason for evaluating a program is to decide whether or not to terminate it or to assess which program among several to continue, a summative evaluation will be necessary, and decision makers are likely to be interested in the outcome" (Brown and Podolske, 1993b, p. 220). Brown and Podolske (1993b) also emphasize that evaluation has a political dimension, although in the context of looking at the effectiveness of an adviser, one would hope that the political nature of evaluation could be kept to an absolute minimum. Nevertheless, "Whose interests are served and how interests are represented in an evaluation are critical concerns" (House, 1994, p. 84).

In the context of evaluating your work as an organization's adviser, you could have the group's officers provide a formative evaluation in the middle of the year to give you feedback about how you are doing. You could conduct a summative evaluation at the end of the academic year; this could very well be a more formal process that involves many of the organization's members as well as the officers. The information generated by the evaluation could determine (1) whether or not you would wish to serve for another year, or (2) whether the members would like to invite you to serve again. For small clubs, these evaluations are likely to be very informal, but for a larger organization, a formal evaluation is in order.

Evaluation Questions

Before undertaking any evaluation, you need to answer a number of questions to help frame the evaluation; resolving these questions now will make the whole process go more smoothly. The following are adapted from the work of Upcraft and Schuh (1996).

1. Why is the group conducting the evaluation? Is it routine? Is it because members are dissatisfied with you? Do you want feedback? Are there other reasons? Your group must decide why it is conducting the evaluation. If people are not sure, the whole project could be a colossal waste of time.

2. What will be evaluated? Are there aspects of your performance that need to be evaluated, or is this a comprehensive look at everything you do? For example, if you primarily work with the treasurer on financial matters but also lend general support to all aspects of the organization, will just the financial work be evaluated, or will all aspects of your work be studied? Will the evaluation cover the entire academic year or just a portion of it?

3. How will you be evaluated? Will this be a paper and pencil instrument? Will members be interviewed? These questions address the techniques your group will employ. We provide a brief overview of techniques later in this chapter.

4. Who will conduct the evaluation? Will the officers conduct the evaluation? How will you be involved in the collection of information? Should your group use an external person? Will a single person or a committee conduct the evaluation? How much expertise is needed? The matter of who will do the work is a thorny problem, potentially full of controversy. If your work has been criticized openly by some members, completing an evaluation that appears to be honest and accurate may be quite challenging.

5. How will the results be analyzed? Who gets to decide what the data mean? What is the context for the analysis? If you take issue with the evaluation, will the group provide an opportunity for rebuttal?

6. How will the results be communicated, and to whom? Will the data be handled informally, or will someone write a report? Will the information go only to you? Will the officers get the results? What about the members? If the results are sensitive, just how far does the group go? Nobody wants to be embarrassed by the findings of an evaluation, so the officers may need to communicate the results to you privately in the case of a very unfavorable evaluation, rather than hanging you out to dry.

Again, we want to remind you that your role as adviser and the nature of the organization will have a great deal to do with how you are evaluated. In a small departmental club, the evaluation may be very informal and could involve everyone in the organization sitting down with you and visiting over refreshments. If you are the adviser to the student government association, on the other hand, you may need to be evaluated much more formally and on a regular basis because this assignment very well could be part of your full-time job assignment at the institution. In this case, evaluation could be tied to salary adjustments, a continuing appointment, and career advancement.

Evaluation Techniques

We can categorize evaluation methods as either quantitative or qualitative; each method employs very different techniques for providing information. Both methods require considerable rigor to be done well. Simply setting out to conduct an evaluation without considerable background and experience using either approach would be an exercise in folly. If you or your group is inexperienced with evaluation techniques, we suggest that you seek help from the student activities office, the dean of students office, or perhaps a colleague in one of the social sciences who is knowledgeable about these techniques.

Quantitative Methods

Quantitative methods rely on numbers, instruments, and statistical techniques to answer evaluative questions. Rossman and El-Khawas (cited by Terenzini and Upcraft, 1996, p. 85) defined quantitative methodology as "the assignment of numbers to objects, events or observations according to some rule." Stage (1992, p. 7) adds that quantitative methods can be defined as "measures requiring that a numerical or other evaluative symbol be assigned to the construct of interest." Using this approach, whoever is conducting the evaluation would perhaps administer a questionnaire to the officers, the members, or some other set of individuals associated with the organization.

Qualitative Methods

Qualitative methods employ detailed description of situations, events, people, interactions, and observed behaviors (Patton, 1990). Stage (1992, p. 7) defines qualitative methods as "techniques employing description of the constructs of interest (such as interviewing, document analysis, or observation)." "Qualitative inquiries are also called naturalistic inquiries or ethnographies and are traditionally identified with sociology, cultural anthropology, political science and education" (Erwin, 1996, p. 420). This approach uses interviews, focus-group discussions, observations of people's behavior, and review of documents.

Evaluating the Adviser

To begin evaluating your work, you might first consider thinking in a broad way about how your interaction with the organization is progressing. Kearney (1993) provides a series of questions that are particularly appropriate for creating this general framework.

- What are your accomplishments?
- What are your current strengths?

- What are your uncertainties and misunderstandings?
- What obstacles are in your way?
- Are there any specific goals or action steps that you would like to formulate as a result of your self-appraisal?

We provide several tools in this chapter to help you and your organization conduct evaluations. First, there is the Adviser's Self-Evaluation Checklist (Exhibit 10.1), which you can self-administer at almost any point during the academic year. You answer the questions yes or no based on your opinion of yourself and your work. You or your organization can add other questions, and you can skip any questions that you believe do not pertain to your work.

The Adviser's Log (Exhibit 10.2) illustrates a way for you to keep track of your interactions with members of the organization over a period of time. This log, in which you note the purpose of the interaction, what resulted from the interaction, and what the student(s) learned, will provide a record of your work with the organization over the course of an academic term or year.

The Adviser's Evaluation Checklist (Exhibit 10.3) is a tool similar to the self-evaluation in Exhibit 10.1; it can be administered to officers, members, or both. As is the case with the self-evaluation, you or the group can add or delete items, and you can administer the checklist during the academic year or at the end.

The purpose of each of these tools is to give you feedback regarding activities and traits that are central to your relationship with the organization. If you or your organization want to conduct a more formal evaluation, you can use these instruments in conjunction with other strategies, but only after you and the group have answered the questions introduced earlier in this chapter (Why is the evaluation being conducted? What will be evaluated? and so on).

If your organization would prefer to work with a discussion format, you can use the questions in Exhibit 10.4. These questions pertain to the heart of your relationship with the organization. Depending on the needs of the group, you or members might add or delete questions. Because leading such a discussion requires considerable skill, your group might prefer to have a person external to the group lead the discussion. Whether or not you are present depends on the nature of the evaluation. Once again, you and the group should address the framing questions so as to avoid making embarrassing mistakes.

Exhibit 10.1. Adviser's Self-Evaluation Checklist

Please answer the following questions as they relate to your role as an organization adviser:

Yes	No	Item
____	____	I actively provide motivation and encouragement to members.
____	____	I know the goals of the organization.
____	____	I know the group's members.
____	____	I attend regularly scheduled executive board meetings.
____	____	I attend regularly scheduled organizational meetings.
____	____	I meet regularly with the officers of the organization.
____	____	I attend the organization's special events.
____	____	I assist with the orientation and training of new officers.
____	____	I help provide continuity for the organization.
____	____	I confront the negative behavior of members.
____	____	I understand principles of group development.
____	____	I understand how students grow and learn.
____	____	I understand the principles that lead to orderly meetings.
____	____	I have read the group's constitution and by-laws.
____	____	I recommend and encourage without imposing my ideas and preferences.
____	____	I monitor the organization's financial records.
____	____	I understand the principles of good fundraising.
____	____	I understand how issues of diversity affect the organization.
____	____	I attend conferences with the organization's students.
____	____	I know the steps to follow in developing a program.
____	____	I can identify what members have learned by participating in the organization.
____	____	I know where to find assistance when I encounter problems I cannot solve.
____	____	_____
____	____	_____
____	____	_____
____	____	_____
____	____	_____

Exhibit 10.2. Adviser's Log

Date	Name of Student(s)	Purpose of Interaction	What Resulted	What Student(s) Learned

Exhibit 10.3. Adviser's Evaluation Checklist

Please answer the following questions about your organization's adviser:

Yes	*No*	*Item*
___	___	The adviser provides motivation and encouragement to members.
___	___	The adviser knows the goals of the organization.
___	___	The adviser attends regularly scheduled executive board meetings.
___	___	The adviser attends regularly scheduled organizational meetings.
___	___	The adviser meets regularly with the officers of the organization.
___	___	The adviser attends the organization's special events.
___	___	The adviser assists with the orientation and training of new officers.
___	___	The adviser helps provide continuity for the organization.
___	___	The adviser confronts the negative behavior of members.
___	___	The adviser understands principles of group development.
___	___	The adviser understands how students grow and learn.
___	___	The adviser understands the principles that lead to orderly meetings.
___	___	The adviser has read the group's constitution and by-laws.
___	___	The adviser understands the principles of good fundraising.
___	___	The adviser understands how issues of diversity affect the organization.
___	___	The adviser attends conferences with the organization's students.
___	___	The adviser knows the steps to follow in developing a program.
___	___	The adviser can identify what members have learned by participating in the organization.
___	___	The adviser knows the members.
___	___	_____
___	___	_____
___	___	_____
___	___	_____
___	___	_____
___	___	_____
___	___	_____
___	___	_____

Exhibit 10.4. Discussion Questions for Evaluating the Adviser

1. How well do you know the adviser, and in what context?

2. Do you know how to contact the adviser other than at meetings?

3. Does the adviser attend your events?

4. Is the adviser interested in your organization? How do you know this?

5. For officers: Is the adviser approachable? Is the adviser available to provide advice and counsel to you when you have problems?

6. Does the adviser know the goals of the organization? What evidence do you have to support this?

7. What does the adviser do at meetings? Is the adviser an active participant in discussions or a passive observer?

8. Does the adviser help clarify what you have learned by participating in the organization? In what ways?

9. What role does the adviser play in the financial management of the organization? What advice has the adviser provided about fundraising?

10. When it is clear that the adviser has ideas that differ from those of the group about how to handle something, what happens?

11. What do you like best about your adviser?

12. If there was one thing you could change about your adviser's performance, what would that be?

Evaluating the Organization

In addition to evaluating your own work, you may want to employ one or more of the several specific tools available to evaluate how well the organization is functioning. Obviously, you can ask general questions: Is the organization meeting its goals? What are students learning? Are students having fun? You and the group need to consider these and other questions periodically.

Although we did not intend this chapter to provide a comprehensive approach to program evaluation, it is useful to include one example of an approach to evaluating specific programs, such as a speaker, a workshop, or a social activity. Exhibit 10.5 is an all-purpose evaluation form that was developed by M. Lee Upcraft, assistant vice president emeritus at Penn State University; it can be used with a wide variety of programs. It is machine readable and seeks basic demographic information about program participants in addition to their opinions about the program. The form not only elicits student opinions but also asks questions related to how the student was affected by the program. Your group can develop a similar generic evaluation form to meet the specific needs of individual campuses. We think a generic form is far more useful than a specific one developed on a program-by-program basis.

Organizational Goals and Objectives

One of the best ways to look at an organization is to review its stated goals and objectives. These are articulated in the constitution and by-laws and should be used to frame the activities of the group. Is the group concerned with campus governance, such as a student government association? Is the group primarily a special-interest group that provides programs for members, such as a departmental club, sports club, or performance group? Does the organization have a service function, which would include service clubs and some honorary societies? You can measure the activities of the organization against its goals and objectives and determine, in a general sense, whether the organization is engaged in activities consistent with its purpose. For example, a service club whose members spend most of their time having parties and social events may have strayed from its stated purpose. You can then ask, Why is this occurring?

Breadth of Participation

The appropriate size of an organization will vary dramatically with the organization's goals and objectives, but regardless of its purpose, for an organization to be viable over time it must have an adequate number of members who participate regularly in events. A water polo sports club, for example, does not need one hundred members, but it certainly needs enough members to enable participants to practice and play games.

Beyond having enough members, organizations should also have wide participation so that not just two or three people are doing all the work, particularly when they need help from many members. The officers should not have to handle all the organizational responsibilities, pull together various events, arrange for transportation, and so on. One of the best ways for you to measure the health of your organization is to determine whether enough people are members of the organization and whether the responsibility for keeping the organization going is spread among the members.

Exhibit 10.5. Generic Evaluation Form

STUDENT NUMBER

PRESENTATION EVALUATION
Office of the Vice President for Student Affairs

PRESENTATION CODE

Presentation Title _____
Presentation Date _____
Presentation Topic _____
Presenter _____
Student Affairs Unit _____
CoSponsor _____

Information regarding individuals will be held in strict confidence, and will not be revealed under any circumstances.
USE NO. 2 PENCIL ONLY.

1. Gender ○ Female ○ Male

2. My local residence is ○ On campus ○ Off campus

3. Ethnicity ○ American Indian ○ Hispanic/Latino ○ White
○ Asian American/Pacific Islander ○ African American/Black ○ International
○ Other _____

4. Age ○ 17 or younger ○ 18 - 19 ○ 20 - 21 ○ 22 - 23 ○ 24 or older

5. If undergraduate indicate semester standing
○ 1 ○ 2 ○ 3 ○ 4 ○ 5 ○ 6 ○ 7 ○ 8 ○ 9 ○ 10
○ 11 ○ 12 ○ 13

Please indicate your agreement/disagreement with the following:	STRONGLY DISAGREE	DISAGREE	NEUTRAL	AGREE	STRONGLY AGREE
6. Purpose was clearly identified	○	○	○	○	○
7. Purpose was achieved	○	○	○	○	○
8. My expectations were met	○	○	○	○	○
9. I have learned new skills	○	○	○	○	○
10. What I have learned I can apply	○	○	○	○	○
11. My attitudes were changed	○	○	○	○	○
12. I expect to change some of my behaviors	○	○	○	○	○
13. I now have greater knowledge of the subject	○	○	○	○	○
14. Different points of view were encouraged	○	○	○	○	○
15. Material was clear and well organized	○	○	○	○	○
16. There were opportunities for participation	○	○	○	○	○
17. Presenters were prepared and knowledgeable	○	○	○	○	○
18. Presenters were interesting and enthusiastic	○	○	○	○	○
19. Presenters communicated well	○	○	○	○	○
20. Handouts were helpful	○	○	○	○	○
21. Visual aids were helpful	○	○	○	○	○
22. Facilities were adequate	○	○	○	○	○

23. I rate this program as ○ Poor ○ Fair ○ Average ○ Good ○ Excellent

24. Number of other Student Affairs Presentations attended this year
○ None ○ One ○ Two ○ Three ○ Four or more

25. Presenters were sensitive to students with diverse backgrounds (race, gender, religion, cultural, or sexual orientation)
○ Strongly Disagree ○ Disagree ○ Neutral ○ Agree ○ Strongly Agree

Finances

We have discussed financial issues elsewhere in this book, but here let us say that if the organization experiences chronic financial problems, these problems will distract the members from the primary goals of the group. Thus a quick review of the organization's balance sheet will help you evaluate the organization's success in terms of its financial well-being.

Learning

Perhaps the most important criterion of organizational success for you to review is what the members are learning as a result of their participation in the group. Are officers learning management skills? Is leadership being developed? Are members learning to work cooperatively? Is creativity being encouraged? Do routine tasks, such as preparing financial statements, become easier over time? You can consider these questions and others idiosyncratic to the group as part of an informal evaluation.

Yardsticks of Success

Exhibit 10.6 includes many of the characteristics of a successful organization. Compare these characteristics to those of your organization to measure the group's effectiveness. Not all of the items will apply to your group, and you can add other measures, but in general the list will help you get a sense of the group's level of health. If some of the areas appear to be weak, they might provide the basis for discussion with the officers or members. Areas of strength should generate notes of congratulations or affirmative comments in meetings. These items are a quick yet effective way of measuring organizational success.

Other Evaluation Techniques

Two additional techniques for evaluating the organization are the exit interview and a third-party review. You can conduct exit interviews with members as they leave the organization or when officers leave their posts (Prus and Johnson, 1994). The interview can include a series of standard questions, free-flowing discussion, or a combination of both, focusing on the experiences of the students and what they learned from their experiences with the organization.

Another approach is to bring in a third party (Prus and Johnson, 1994) to observe the organization informally for a period of

Exhibit 10.6. Yardsticks for Organizational Success

Goals and objectives

- Members understand the purpose of the organization.
- The constitution and by-laws are current.
- Members have read the organization's constitution and by-laws.
- Members understand how to amend the constitution and by-laws.

Membership

- Membership is stable or growing.
- Few members drop out.
- Recruitment of new members is well organized.
- Recruitment of new members is shared by the membership and is not only the responsibility of the membership chair.
- Members know what is going on in the organization.

Meetings

- Meetings are held regularly.
- Meetings begin on time.
- Meetings are run using Robert's Rules of Order or a similar approach.
- Members attend the meetings regularly.
- Officers attend the meetings regularly.

Leadership

- Students have learned leadership techniques.
- A variety of people provide leadership for the group.
- Officers complete their terms.
- Elections are contested.
- Officers have read the organization's constitution and by-laws.
- Communication mechanisms, such as a newsletter or Web page, have been established and are used regularly.

Finance

- Dues are paid on time.
- Financial reports are accurate and produced with regularity.
- Long-term debt is kept to a minimum.

- Self-financing events are successful.
- Multiple sources of financing exist.

Special Events

- Special events are planned with the needs of the members in mind.
- Special events are self-financed.
- Special events are well attended.
- Members have an opportunity to suggest and plan special events.

Learning

- Members can identify what they have learned by participating in the organization.
- Members learn to work cooperatively.
- Members' leadership skills have improved over time.
- Members can identify skills that are transferable to their careers after college.

time. A third party presumably can offer an unbiased opinion about the group, which is a real strength of this approach. This outsider's view can often yield unexpected insights into how your group is functioning. But it is possible that third parties can be biased or that they can misinterpret the activities of the organization. Still, these two alternatives can be useful.

CHAPTER 11

Developing and Increasing Personal Effectiveness

In this final chapter, we address three issues related to the practice of advising student groups: additional recommendations for professional practice, some thoughts about keeping advising activities rewarding, and suggestions for continuing education.

Recommendations for Professional Practice

Four areas of professional practice are worthy of additional comment. These are developing a philosophy of advising, emphasizing learning, securing administrative support for advising activities, and forming coalitions on campus.

Philosophy

The focus of this book has been on the technical side of advising student organizations. From time to time we have referred to institutional philosophy, values, and beliefs. We want to emphasize that you too need to develop your own philosophy of advising and advising style, within the philosophical frameworks of the campus.

In describing student affairs practitioners, Young (1996, p. 83) quite perceptively states: "More comfortable with practice than philosophy, members of the profession spend a great deal of time developing programs, services, and procedures and much less time musing about values that support all those activities." We use

Young's observation as a point of departure in suggesting that you develop a philosophy about working with student groups that will then guide your practice.

No one can tell you that there is one best way to go about working with student organizations. Some advisers are more comfortable taking a very active role with their organization—attending all the organization's meetings and events, having frequent meetings with the officers, and visiting with members regularly. Others prefer to take a more passive role with the organization— waiting to be contacted for advice, attending events on an irregular basis, and spending little time with individual members or officers.

Either approach can work, depending on the needs of the campus, the needs of the officers and the members, the nature of the organization, and the degree of comfort you feel in establishing a relationship with the organization. Our view is that you need to develop an advising style that fits best with all these factors. Although advising style is important, the values and philosophy that undergird it are the critical factors in developing relationships with students.

Commitment to Learning

Why do colleges and universities have student organizations? This question can be answered in a variety of ways, all of which could be right. Students need to have fun, they need to learn to work within complicated organizations, and, at public institutions, they could not be prohibited from forming organizations even if the institution wished to do so. Perhaps the most crucial reason for student groups is that student learning is enhanced by membership in campus organizations.

In looking at issues of the future, Komives and Woodard (1996) suggest that student affairs staff "must become experts at identifying the developing and learning experiences inherent in student employment, community service, cooperative education and other forms of experiential learning and link those to students' academic experience" (p. 549). Obviously, we believe that students have much to learn from their experiences as members and leaders of organizations, and you can play an important role in making sure that these experiences are meaningful.

You can expedite the learning process by asking key strategic questions through the course of the academic year. Among these are, What have you learned as a result of [a specific experience]? What have you learned in class that you can apply to that situation? If you were to summarize for an employer what you have learned from this experience, what would you say? If you were faced with this situation in the future, what would you do differently? There are many other questions you can ask of students that will help them think reflectively about their experiences, apply their classroom experiences in the out-of-class environment, and grow as learners.

Administrative Support

We have described a variety of very difficult situations that have significant ramifications not only for the organization and its students but for the institution as a whole. Make a mistake about how best to plan and supervise a trip, and the consequences could be dramatic and perhaps tragic. Fail to provide adequate oversight for the student treasurer, and all kinds of problems can arise.

It is therefore essential that you know administrative support is available, and where to obtain that support; we have provided suggestions throughout this book about where to find legal advice (Chapter Eight), help with financial matters (Chapter Seven), and assistance from various units throughout the institution.

Early in your advising experience, you need to make sure that such support is available. Having to function without it would put you in an untenable position. If support is not available, we question quite seriously whether you should accept an invitation to serve as an adviser; in our view, administrative support is essential to your success. No adviser should ever have to deal with problems, large or small, without help.

Forming Coalitions

Another key form of support comes from your relationships with colleagues who can provide you assistance and counsel. Among these colleagues are student affairs professionals, those who provide administrative support on campus, and other advisers.

Coalitions can be beneficial in a number of ways (see Komives and Woodard, 1996). They bring out the best thinking on issues of mutual interest and tend to result in stronger voices on campus. A coalition with those who provide administrative support makes the interchange between you and the support person natural and easy, and helps break down whatever barriers may exist. People begin to develop rapport, anticipate each other's needs, and freely exchange ideas and information.

Times may arise when those who provide administrative support to you will need your help, because as an adviser you will get to know students and their needs. As was pointed out in Chapter Six, students are frequently called on to participate in institutional activities, and there are times when those who provide administrative support will need your help in arranging student involvement. If the legal counsel, for example, were to host a meeting on campus for colleagues throughout the state to discuss legal issues related to students, how better to find student panelists for a discussion session than through student group advisers?

Another coalition is that of advisers themselves. As institutions continue to grow in complexity, and faculty and staff become more specialized, it becomes increasingly difficult for people from disparate disciplines to get to know each other well on campus. But advisers who work with student groups—whether the debate team, the history club, or the association of future accountants— share common issues and experiences. One effective way to meet informally to discuss these common concerns is to organize (with the help of the student activities office) a monthly advisers' forum.

Keeping the Work Rewarding

Having offered some thoughts about improving your professional practice as an adviser, we now move on to discussing several ideas about how to keep your work as an adviser rewarding. Experiences with students can be both exhilarating and discouraging, and it is very important to develop ways to stay enthusiastic about working with student groups.

Watching Students Grow

Sanford (cited by Pascarella and Terenzini, 1991) describes how students grow by facing and responding to challenges, and students' being involved in campus organizations is undoubtedly one of the best ways for them to experience such growth. For this reason, we urge you to remind yourself that the work is highly rewarding and will pay off in the long run as students learn and grow. Knowing that students grow and learn from their organizational experiences should be a strong incentive for you in difficult moments.

It was no accident that we decided to identify rewards for advisers in the very first chapter of the book, because you need to remind yourself that in spite of all the rough spots, long hours, and challenges you face, working with students individually and in groups as part of the advising experience is thoroughly rewarding. You may find it useful to reread the section on the rewards of advising from time to time, particularly in challenging situations for the adviser.

Enjoying Students

Barr (1993) also reminds us to *enjoy* our students. She writes, "It would behoove all of us to take time to enjoy the wonder of learning that many students experience and appreciate their enthusiasm" (p. 526). Too often one can find it all too easy to fall into the trap of characterizing students as doing not much more than creating problems. At times students make uninformed decisions, poor choices, or silly commitments, all of which result in the adviser having to intervene to "clean things up." In some ways, this cleanup work is what our job is about: when our organizational leaders make mistakes, it is our job to work with students so that they can learn from their errors and not repeat these mistakes in other circumstances where the ramifications could be far more serious. Most of us decided to pursue careers in higher education, whether in teaching, research, or administration, because we wanted to be associated with students. Serving as organizational advisers allows us to develop ongoing relationships with our students, and in that respect we are quite fortunate to have such an opportunity.

Maintaining Perspective

It is also important for you to maintain your perspective about your organization and your students. For many of the students, the roles they play within their organizations will be their first as leaders. They will make mistakes. One of the best ways to think about this aspect of advising is to remember that the college theater troupe, newspaper staff, or track team will not perform nearly as well as what you would expect from professional actors, the working press, or professional athletes.

Members of our organizations are students preparing for fulfilling lives as citizens, and only a few may move into positions directly related to their student organizational experience. Advisers need to realize that organizations will bounce along with imperfections and challenges; problems large and small are the natural order of the day. A healthy dose of realism will help you get through difficult times.

Recommendations for Continuing Professional Education

On the assumption that you are interested in staying active professionally and learning more about working with students, we conclude this chapter with some thoughts about continuing professional education. The three main ways to pursue your professional education are by becoming involved with professional organizations, reading, and attending training workshops and seminars.

Professional Organizations

Several professional associations provide good opportunities for inservice education for organization advisers. The National Association of Campus Activities, an organization of individuals whose careers tend to be focused on student organizations and their activities, would be a natural affiliation for you. In addition, the American College Personnel Association, which has a committee (technically called a commission—Commission IV. Students, Their Activities and Their Community) devoted to student activities, would be a logical affiliation for you. The Association of College and University Housing Officers-International has a committee on educational programs that includes leadership development and working with residence hall associations. The Association of College Unions-International has a student activities component that is concerned at least in part with student organizations and advisers.

Advisers of Greek letter organizations will have resources available through individual fraternities and sororities as well as the Association of Fraternity Advisors. The National Interfraternity Conference is also a useful resource.

All these organizations have annual conferences, and in some cases they offer regional conferences as well. The challenge is to find an organization that best meets your specific needs, which obviously will vary depending on your level of expertise as an adviser, your interest in the association, and other factors that encourage your active involvement. Nuss (1993, p. 376) observes that "there is no one best association, and you should feel comfortable exploring alternatives at various points in your career." She adds, "Whether you are a new professional, someone who has made a recent career change, or a senior student affairs officer, associations should play a meaningful and significant part in your development. It is never too early or too late to consider and reconsider the variety of associations and the forms of participation and involvement available" (p. 377).

Professional Reading

In addition to sponsoring conferences, the associations we just mentioned publish materials on a regular basis, and at times these materials include information for organization advisers. We also recommend the *NASPA Journal*, published by the National Associa-

Exhibit 11.1. Additional Resources

American College Personnel Association
One Dupont Circle, NW, Suite 300
Washington, DC 20036–1110

Association of College and University
    Housing Officers-International
364 W. Lane Avenue, Suite C
Columbus, OH 43201–1062

Association of College Unions-
    International
1 City Centre, Suite 200
120 W. 7th Street
Bloomington, IN 47404–3925

Association of Fraternity Advisors, Inc.
3901 W. 86th Street, Suite 390
Indianapolis, IN 46268–1977

ERIC-CASS
Counseling and Student Services
    Clearinghouse
School of Education
101 Park Avenue
University of North Carolina
Greensboro, NC 27412–5001

Jossey-Bass Inc., Publishers
350 Sansome Street, 5th floor
San Francisco, CA 94104–1342

National Association for Campus
    Activities
13 Harbison Way
Columbia, SC 29212–3401

NASPA Journal
National Association of Student Personnel
    Administrators, Inc.
1875 Connecticut Avenue, NW
Suite 418
Washington, DC 20009–5728

National Interfraternity Conference
3901 W. 86th Street, Suite 390
Indianapolis, IN 46268
SACSA Journal

Dr. Diane Cooper
Editor, SACSA Journal
College of Education
University of Georgia
Athens, GA 30602–7142

tion of Student Personnel Administrators, and the *SACSA Journal*, published by the Southern Association for College Student Affairs.

The annual Pfeiffer training and consulting series published by Jossey-Bass provides wonderful resources. You will find these materials particularly useful; they cover a myriad of topics that apply directly to organizational development. Exercises, questionnaires, and other training activities are part of this resource.

The World Wide Web (WWW) and the ERIC CASS (Educational Resources Information Center, Counseling and Student Services Clearinghouse) document repository are both valuable tools for locating published materials about student organizations. The WWW and ERIC will have such materials as unpublished campus reports and training materials, which you may find useful throughout the course of your work. Exhibit 11.1 includes the addresses of the resources we have mentioned in this chapter.

Training Opportunities

Professional organizations, such as those we have listed here, and individual campuses provide a variety of workshops, short courses, and other training opportunities for advisers. Frequently, professional associations offer preconference workshops that explore various issues in depth. Regional and statewide professional associations offer one-day "drive-in" conferences that can be very helpful to your professional development. It is also common for the student activities office, the residence life office, or other campus agencies to sponsor weekend, half-day, and other types of intensive workshops for advisers.

A Final Word

We conclude this book where we began, with a word about students, reminding you that student growth and learning is a fundamental part of organizational membership. We referred to the work of Astin, Pascarella, and Terenzini, and to others who have pointed out how valuable organizational membership is for students. We think that quality advising enriches students' experiences substantially.

We dedicate our book to the thousands of advisers on college campuses throughout the country who are committed to enhancing the lives of students. Whether you are a beginning adviser or a veteran with years of experience with student groups, we hope that this book will help you advance your work. Your students will be the beneficiaries of your efforts.

REFERENCES

American College Personnel Association. *The Student Learning Imperative.* Washington, D.C.: American College Personnel Association, 1994.

Archer, J. "Campus in Crisis: Coping with Fear and Panic Related to Serial Murders." *Journal of Counseling and Development,* 1992, *71,* 96–100.

Army ROTC. *The Facts About Army ROTC.* Ellicott City, Md.: Army ROTC, 1991.

Army ROTC. *Cadet Handbook.* Gainesville: Army ROTC, University of Florida, 1996.

Astin, A. W. *Achieving Educational Excellence: A Critical Assessment of Priorities and Practices in Higher Education.* San Francisco: Jossey-Bass, 1985.

Astin, A. W. *What Matters in College? Four Critical Years Revisited.* San Francisco: Jossey-Bass, 1993.

Barr, M. J. "Preface." In M. J. Barr and Associates, *Student Services and the Law: A Handbook for Practitioners.* San Francisco: Jossey-Bass, 1988a.

Barr, M. J. "Institutional Liability: What Are the Risks and Obligations of Student Services?" In M. J. Barr and Associates, *Student Services and the Law: A Handbook for Practitioners.* San Francisco: Jossey-Bass, 1988b.

Barr, M. J. "Becoming Successful Student Affairs Administrators." In M. J. Barr and Associates, *The Handbook of Student Affairs Administration.* San Francisco: Jossey-Bass, 1993.

Barr, M. J. "Legal Foundations of Student Affairs Practice." In S. R. Komives, D. B. Woodard, Jr., and Associates, *Student Services: A Handbook for the Profession.* (3rd ed.) San Francisco: Jossey-Bass, 1996.

Barrow, N., and Martin, S. B. "Student Organizations and Institutional Legal Liability." *Journal of Student Affairs,* 1996, *5,* 63–71.

Bayless, K. G., Mull, R. F., and Ross, C. M. *Recreational Sports Programming.* North Palm Beach, Fla.: Athletic Institute, 1983.

Beabout, G., and Wenneman, D. J. *Applied Professional Ethics.* Lanham, Md.: University Press of America, 1994.

Beck, R. C. *Motivation Theories and Principles.* Englewood Cliffs, N.J.: Prentice Hall, 1983.

Blake, R. R., and Mouton, J. R. "Don't Let Group Norms Stifle Creativity." *Personnel,* 1985, *62*(8), 28–33.

Blanchard, K., and Peale, N. V. *The Power of Ethical Management.* New York: Morrow, 1988.

Blank, M. A., and Kershaw, C. "Promote School Renewal: Plan a Retreat." *Clearing House,* 1993, *66,* 206–208.

Bloland, P. A. "Introduction." In J. H. Schuh (ed.), *A Handbook for Student Group Advisers*. Alexandria, Va.: American College Personnel Association, 1987.

Boatman, S. A. "Astin's Theory of Student Involvement: Implications for Campus Activities." Paper presented at the National Association for Campus Activities national convention, Washington, D.C., 1986.

Boatman, S. A. "Strong Student Governments . . . and Their Advisement."*Campus Activities Programming*, 1988, *20*(9), 58–63.

Boyer, E. L. *Campus Life: In Search of Community*. Princeton, N.J.: Carnegie Foundation, 1987.

Boyer, E. L. *Scholarship Reconsidered: Priorities of the Professoriate*. Princeton, N.J.: The Carnegie Foundation, 1990.

Brown, M. T. *Working Ethics: Strategies for Decision Making and Organizational Responsibility*. San Francisco: Jossey-Bass, 1990.

Brown, R. D. "Key Issues in Evaluating Student Affairs Programs." In G. D. Kuh (ed.), *Evaluation in Student Affairs*. Cincinnati, Ohio: American College Personnel Association, 1979.

Brown, R. D., and Podolske, D. L. "Strengthening Programs Through Evolution and Research." In R. B. Winston, Jr., S. Anchors, and Associates, *Student Housing and Residential Life: A Handbook for Professionals Committed to Student Development Goals*. San Francisco: Jossey-Bass, 1993a.

Brown, R. D., and Podolske, D. L. "A Political Model for Program Evaluation." In M. J. Barr and Associates, *The Handbook of Student Affairs Administration*. San Francisco: Jossey-Bass, 1993b.

Buchanan, E. T., III, "Constitutional Issues: Protecting the Rights and Interests of Campuses and Students." In M. J. Barr and Associates, *Student Services and the Law: A Handbook for Practitioners*. San Francisco: Jossey-Bass, 1988.

Burgoyne, R. A. "The Copyright Remedy Clarification Act of 1990: State Educational Institutions Now Face Significant Monetary Exposure for Copyright Infringement." *Journal of College and University Law*, 1992, *18*, 368–379.

Carr, J. "The Art of Supervision." Presentation at the National Housing Training Institute, Gainesville, Fla., 1995.

Cartwright, D. "Achieving Change in People: Some Applications of Group Dynamics Theory." *Human Relations*, 1951, *4*, 381–392.

Correnti, R. J. "How Public and Private Institutions Differ Under the Law." In M. J. Barr and Associates, *Student Services and the Law: A Handbook for Practitioners*. San Francisco: Jossey-Bass, 1988.

Country Kickers Dance Club. *The Constitution of the Ball State University Country Kickers Dance Club*. Muncie, Ind.: Country Kickers Dance Club, 1997.

Cowley, W. H. "The Disappearing Dean of Men." Paper presented at the 19th annual conference on the National Association of Deans and Advisors of Men, Austin, Tex., 1937.

Craig, D. H., and Warner, T. R. "The 'Forgotten Majority' of Student Organizations and Campus Activities." *Campus Activities Programming*, 1991, *23*(9), 42–46.

Cuyjet, M. "Student Government: The Nature of the Beast." *Programming*, May 1985, *18*, 25–31.

Cuyjet, M. "Student Government as a Provider of Student Services." In M. C. Terrell and M. J. Cuyjet (eds.), *Developing Student Government Leadership*. New Directions for Student Services, no. 66. San Francisco: Jossey-Bass, 1994.

DeCoster, D. A., and Brown, R. D. "Mentoring Relationships and the Educational Process." In R. D. Brown and D. A. DeCoster (eds.), *Mentoring-Transcript Systems for Promoting Student Growth*. New Directions for Student Services, no. 19. San Francisco: Jossey-Bass, 1982.

Douglas, D. O. "Fiscal Resource Management: Background and Relevance for Student Affairs." In T. K. Miller, R. B. Winston, Jr., and Associates, *Administration and Leadership in Student Affairs.* (2nd ed.) Muncie, Ind.: Accelerated Development, 1991.

Dumhart, H., and Schoen, M. "Corporate Fund Raising." In N. W. Dunkel and C. L. Spencer (eds.), *Advice for Advisors: The Development of an Effective Residence Hall Association.* Columbus, Ohio: Association of College and University Housing Officers-International, 1993.

Dunkel, N. W. "Supervision: Creating a Relationship for Advancement, Progressivity, and Education." Presentation at the annual meeting of the Association of College and University Housing Officers-International, Providence, R.I., 1996.

Dunkel, N. W., Bray, K., and Wofford, A. *Training and Raising Awareness in Career Knowledge (TRACK).* Gainesville: Division of Housing, University of Florida, 1989.

El-Khawas, E. "Student Diversity on Today's Campuses." In S. R. Komives, D. B. Woodard, Jr., and Associates, *Student Services: A Handbook for the Profession.* (3rd ed.) San Francisco: Jossey-Bass, 1996.

Erwin, T. D. "Assessment, Evaluation and Research." In S. R. Komives, D. B. Woodard, Jr., and Associates, *Student Services: A Handbook for the Profession.* (3rd ed.) San Francisco: Jossey-Bass, 1996.

Etzioni, A. *A Comparative Analysis of Complex Organizations.* New York: Free Press, 1961.

Fantasy Roleplaying Club. *Constitution of the Fantasy Roleplaying Club (Formerly the Fantasy Wargames Club).* Gainesville, Fla.: Fantasy Roleplaying Club, 1992.

Feldman, K. A., and Newcomb, T. M. *The Impact of College on Students,* Vol 1: *An Analysis of Four Decades of Research.* San Francisco: Jossey-Bass, 1969.

Fine, S. A. *Benchmark Tasks for Job Analysis: A Guide for Functional Job Analysis (FJA) Scales.* Hillsdale, N.J.: Erlbaum, 1985.

Florida Association of Residence Halls. *Constitution of the Florida Association of Residence Halls.* Gainesville: Florida Association of Residence Halls, 1996.

Franck, B. "Conflict: Is It Tearing Your Organization Apart?" *Campus Activities Programming,* 1983, *16*(5), 26–29.

Fraternity Insurance Purchasing Group. *Risk Management Manual.* Indianapolis, Ind.: Fraternity Insurance Purchasing Group, 1994.

Fried, H. J. "Teaching and Training." In U. Delworth, G. R. Hanson, and Associates, *Student Services: A Handbook for the Profession.* San Francisco: Jossey-Bass, 1989.

Gehring, D. D. "Legal Rights and Responsibilities of Campus Student Groups and Advisers." In J. H. Schuh (ed.), *A Handbook for Student Group Advisers.* (2nd ed.) Alexandria, Va.: American College Personnel Association, 1987.

Gehring, D. D. "Legal Issues in the Administration of Student Affairs." In T. K. Miller, R. B. Winston, Jr., and Associates, *Administration and Leadership in Student Affairs.* (2nd ed.) Muncie, Ind.: Accelerated Development, 1991.

Gehring, D. D. "Understanding Legal Constraints on Practice." In M. J. Barr and Associates, *The Handbook of Student Affairs Administration.* San Francisco: Jossey-Bass, 1993.

Geomatics Student Association. *Geomatics Student Association Constitution.* Gainesville, Fla.: Geomatics Student Association, 1996.

George Mason University. *Moving On: A Guide for Career Planning and Job Search.* Fairfax, Va.: George Mason University, 1988.

Gilligan, C. *In a Different Voice.* Cambridge, Mass.: Harvard University Press, 1982.

Glanz, E. C., and Hayes, R. W. *Groups in Guidance.* Needham Heights, Mass.: Allyn & Bacon, 1967.

Gugerty, C. R, and Swezey, E. D. "Developing Campus-Community Relationships." In B. Jacoby and Associates, *Service-Learning in Higher Education: Concepts and Practices.* San Francisco: Jossey-Bass, 1996.

Hennessy, T. J., and Lorenz, N. "Budget and Fiscal Management." In J. H. Schuh (ed.), *A Handbook for Student Group Advisers.* (2nd ed.) Alexandria, Va.: American College Personnel Association, 1987.

Hersey, P., and Blanchard, K. H. *Management of Organizational Behavior.* Englewood Cliffs, N.J.: Prentice Hall, 1988.

Horowitz, H. L. *Campus Life: Undergraduate Cultures from the End of the Eighteenth Century to the Present.* Chicago: University of Chicago Press, 1987.

House, E. R. "Trends in Evaluation." In J. S. Stark and A. Thomas (eds.), *Assessment and Program Evaluation.* New York: Simon & Schuster, 1994.

Hudson, M., and Hudson, D. T. "The Money Management of RHAs." In N. W. Dunkel and C. L. Spencer (eds.), *Advice for Advisors: The Development of an Effective Residence Hall Association.* Columbus, Ohio: Association of College and University Housing Officers-International, 1993.

Jacoby, B. J. "Service-Learning in Today's Higher Education." In B. J. Jacoby and Associates, *Service-Learning in Higher Education: Concepts and Practices.* San Francisco: Jossey-Bass, 1996.

Janes, S. S. "Administrative Practice: A Day-to-Day Guide to Legal Requirements." In M. J. Barr and Associates, *Student Services and the Law: A Handbook for Practitioners.* San Francisco: Jossey-Bass, 1988.

Jardine, C. "Staff Supervision and Appraisal." Presentation at the National Housing Training Institute, Gainesville, Fla., 1996.

Johnson, D. W., and Johnson, F. P. *Joining Together Group Theory and Group Skills.* Needham Heights, Mass.: Allyn & Bacon, 1991.

Kaplin, W. A., and Lee, B. A. *The Law of Higher Education.* (3rd ed.) San Francisco: Jossey-Bass, 1995.

Kearney, P. A. "Professional Staffing." In R. B. Winston, Jr., S. Anchors, and Associates, *Student Housing and Residential Life: A Handbook for Professionals Committed to Student Development Goals.* San Francisco: Jossey-Bass, 1993.

Keppler, K., and Robinson, J. "Student Governments: What Are the Issues of the Day?" *Campus Activities Programming,* 1993, 25(9), 36–46.

Kitchener, K. S. "Ethical Principles and Ethical Decisions in Student Affairs." In H. J. Canon and R. D. Brown (eds.), *Applied Ethics in Student Services.* New Directions for Student Services, no. 30. San Francisco: Jossey-Bass, 1985.

Kohlberg, L. *The Psychology of Moral Development.* New York: HarperCollins, 1984.

Komives, S. B. "Increasing Student Involvement Through Civic Leadership Education." In C. C. Schroeder, P. Mable, and Associates, *Realizing the Educational Potential of Residence Halls.* San Francisco: Jossey-Bass, 1994.

Komives, S., and Tucker, G. L. "Successful Residence Hall Government: Themes from a National Study of Select Hall Government Structures." In N. W. Dunkel and C. L. Spencer (eds.), *Advice for Advisors: The Development of an Effective Residence Hall Association.* Columbus, Ohio: Association of College and University Housing Officers-International, 1993.

Komives, S. R., and Woodard, D. B., Jr. "Building on the Past, Shaping the Future." In S. R. Komives, D. B. Woodard, Jr., and Associates, *Student Services: A Handbook for the Profession.* (3rd ed.) San Francisco: Jossey-Bass, 1996.

Kouzes, J. M., and Pozner, B. Z. *The Leadership Challenge.* San Francisco: Jossey-Bass, 1987.

Kowalski, G. J., and Conlogue, J. A. "Advising and Supervising: A Comparison of Unique Job Elements." Program presented at the annual meeting of the Association of College and University Housing Officers-International, Providence, R. I., 1996.

Kuh, G. D. "The Demographic Juggernaut." In M. J. Barr, M. L. Upcraft, and Associates, *New Futures for Student Affairs: Building a Vision for Professional Leadership and Practice.* San Francisco: Jossey-Bass, 1990.

Kuh, G. D. "Characteristics of Involving Colleges." In G. D. Kuh and J. H. Schuh (eds.), *The Role and Contribution of Student Affairs in Involving Colleges.* Washington, D.C.: National Association of Student Personnel Administrators, 1991.

Kuh, G. D., and Arnold, J. C. "Liquid Bonding: A Cultural Analysis of the Role of Alcohol in Fraternity Pledgeship." *Journal of College Student Development,* 1993, *34,* 327–334.

Kuh, G. D., and Hunter, D. "Using Evaluation Principles with Student Groups." In J. H. Schuh (ed.), *A Handbook for Student Group Advisers.* (2nd ed.) Alexandria, Va.: American College Personnel Association, 1987.

Kuh, G. D., and Lund, J. P. "What Students Gain from Participating in Student Government." In M. C. Terrell and M. J. Cuyjet (eds.), *Developing Student Government Leadership.* New Directions for Student Services, no. 66. San Francisco: Jossey-Bass, 1994.

Kuh, G. D., Schuh, J. H., Whitt, E. J., and Associates. *Involving Colleges: Successful Approaches to Fostering Student Learning and Development Outside the Classroom.* San Francisco: Jossey-Bass, 1991.

Lawrence, G. *People Types and Tiger Stripes.* Gainesville, Fla.: Center for Applications of Psychological Type, 1995.

Lifton, W. *Working with Groups: Group Process and Individual Growth.* New York: Wiley, 1967.

Magee, K. "To Pay or Not to Pay: The Questions of Student Stipends." *Campus Activities Programming,* 1994, *27*(6), 30–33.

Maloney, G. W. "Student Organizations and Student Activities." In M. J. Barr and Associates, *Student Services and the Law: A Handbook for Practitioners.* San Francisco: Jossey-Bass, 1988.

McCarthy, M. D. "One-Time and Short-Term Service Learning Experiences." In B. J. Jacoby and Associates, *Service-Learning in Higher Education: Concepts and Practices.* San Francisco: Jossey-Bass, 1996.

McKaig, R., and Policello, S. "Group Advising—Defined, Described and Examined." In J. H. Schuh (ed.), *A Handbook for Student Group Advisers.* Alexandria, Va.: American College Personnel Association, 1987.

Medieval Recreations. *The Constitution of the Ball State University Medieval Recreations.* Muncie, Ind.: Medieval Recreations, 1997.

The Merriam-Webster Dictionary. Springfield, Mass.: Merriam-Webster, 1995.

Mitchell, S. E. "Motivation of Paid and Volunteer Students." In N. W. Dunkel and C. L. Spencer (eds.), *Advice for Advisors: The Development of an Effective Residence Hall Association.* Columbus, Ohio: Association of College and University Housing Officers-International, 1993.

Miyamoto, T. "Liability of Colleges and Universities for Injuries During Extracurricular Activities." *Journal of College and University Law,* 1988, *15,* 149–176.

Mueller, K. *Student Personnel Work in Higher Education.* Boston: Houghton Mifflin, 1961.

Munschauer, J. L. *Jobs for English Majors and Other Smart People.* Princeton, N.J.: Peterson's Guides, 1986.

Murray, H. A. *Explorations in Personality.* New York: Oxford University Press, 1938.

Napier, R. W., and Gershenfeld, M. K. *Groups Theory and Experience.* Boston: Houghton Mifflin, 1989.

National Association for Campus Activities. *About Your Association.* Columbia, S.C.: National Association for Campus Activities, 1996.

National Interfraternity Conference. "Risk Management Policy." In J. L. Anson and R. F. Marchesani, *Baird's Manual of American College Fraternities.* Indianapolis: Baird's Manual Foundation, 1991.

National Intramural-Recreational Sport Association. "Holsberry Announces Retirement as NIRSA Executive Director." *NIRSA Newsletter,* 1996a, *48*(1).

National Intramural-Recreational Sport Association. *NIRSA Mission Statement.* Corvallis, Oreg.: National Intramural-Recreational Sport Association, 1996b.

National Residence Hall Honorary. *96 Ways to Recognize.* Macomb, Ill.: National Residence Hall Honorary, 1996.

Navy–Marine Corps ROTC. *Navy–Marine Corps ROTC: College Scholarships Bulletin.* Arlington, Va.: Navy–Marine Corps ROTC, 1997.

Nuss, E. M. "The Role of Professional Associations." In M. J. Barr and Associates, *The Handbook of Student Affairs Administration.* San Francisco: Jossey-Bass, 1993.

Osteen, J. M. "Advising Model for Residence Halls." Unpublished manuscript, Student Activities, University of Maryland, College Park, 1988.

Osteen, J. M., and Tucker, G. L. "Authority, Accountability, and Advice: Understanding the Unique Roles of Residence Life Staff and Hall Government Leaders." *Journal of College and University Student Housing,* (forthcoming).

Owen, K. C. "Reflections on the College Fraternity and Its Changing Nature." In J. L. Anson and R. F. Marcheson, Jr. (eds.), *Baird's Manual of American College Fraternities.* Indianapolis, Ind.: Baird's Manual Foundation, 1991.

Pascarella, E. J., and Terenzini, P. T. *How College Affects Students: Findings and Insights from Twenty Years of Research.* San Francisco: Jossey-Bass, 1991.

Patton, M. Q. *Qualitative Evaluation and Research Methods.* (2nd ed.) Thousand Oaks, Calif.: Sage, 1990.

People for Animal Liberation. *Constitution of the People for Animal Liberation.* Boone, N.C.: People for Animal Liberation, 1996.

Prus, J., and Johnson, R. "A Critical Review of Student Assessment Options." In J. S. Stark and A. Thomas (eds.), *Assessment and Program Evaluation.* New York: Simon & Schuster, 1994.

Public Relations Student Society of America. *Constitution of the ASU Public Relations Student Society of America.* Boone, N.C.: Public Relations Student Society of America, 1996.

Ramirez, B. V. "Adapting to New Student Needs and Characteristics." In M. J. Barr and Associates, *The Handbook of Student Affairs Administration.* San Francisco: Jossey-Bass, 1993.

Rest, J. *Moral Development: Advances in Research and Theory.* New York: Praeger, 1983.

Richmond, D. R. "Institutional Liability for Student Activities and Organizations." *Journal of Law and Higher Education,* 1990, *19,* 309–344.

Robert, H. M. *Robert's Rules of Order.* Glenview, Ill.: Scott, Foresman, 1996.

Rogers, C. *Dealing with Social Tensions.* Danville, Ill.: Interstate, 1948.

Rudolph, F. *The American College and University: A History.* New York: Knopf, 1962.

Saddlemire, G. L., and Rentz, A. L. (eds.). *Student Affairs Functions in Higher Education.* Springfield, Ill.: Thomas, 1988.

Sampson, K. "Group Development Concepts." In N. W. Dunkel and C. L. Spencer (eds.), *Advice for Advisors: The Development of an Effective Residence*

Hall Association. Columbus, Ohio: Association of College and University Housing Officers-International, 1993.

Sandeen, A. "Legacy of Values Education." In J. Dalton (ed.), *Promoting Values Development in College Students.* Washington, D.C.: National Association of Student Personnel Administrators, 1985.

Scheuermann, C. D. "Ongoing Curricular Service-Learning." In B. J. Jacoby and Associates, *Service-Learning in Higher Education: Concepts and Practices.* San Francisco: Jossey-Bass, 1996.

Schuh, J. H. "Current Fiscal and Budgetary Perspectives." In J. H. Schuh (ed.), *Financial Management for Student Affairs Administrators.* Alexandria, Va.: American College Personnel Association, 1990.

Schuh, J. H. "Making a Large University Feel Small: The Iowa State University Story." In G. D. Kuh and J. H. Schuh (eds.), *The Role and Contributions of Student Affairs in Involving Colleges.* Washington, D.C.: National Association of Student Personnel Administrators, 1991.

Schuh, J. H. "Planning and Finance." In S. R. Komives and D. B. Woodard, Jr., and Associates. *Student Services: A Handbook for the Profession.* (3rd ed.) San Francisco: Jossey-Bass, 1995.

Schuh, J. H., and Carlisle, W. "Supervision and Evaluation." In T. K. Miller, R. B. Winston, Jr., and Associates, *Administration and Leadership in Student Affairs.* (2nd ed.) Muncie, Ind.: Accelerated Development, 1991.

Schuh, J., and Ogle, T. "Legal Issues." In N. W. Dunkel and C. L. Spencer (eds.), *Advice for Advisors: The Development of an Effective Residence Hall Association.* Columbus, Ohio: Association of College and University Housing Officers-International, 1993.

Sherif, M., and Sherif, C. *Reference Groups: Exploration into Conformity and Deviation of Adolescents.* New York: HarperCollins, 1964.

Smith, M. C. "Students, Suds and Summonses: Strategies for Coping with Campus Alcohol Abuse." *Journal of College Student Development,* 1989, *30,* 118–122.

St. John, W. D. "You Are What You Communicate." Personnel, 1985, *64*(10), 40–43.

Stage, F. K. "The Case for Flexibility in Research and Assessment of College Students." In F. K. Stage (ed.), *Diverse Methods for Research and Assessment of College Students.* Alexandria, Va.: American College Personnel Association, 1992.

Stoner, K., Spain, J., Rasche, C., and Horton, R. "History and Services of NACURH, Inc." In N. W. Dunkel and C. L. Spencer (eds.), *Advice for Advisors: The Development of an Effective Residence Hall Association.* Columbus, Ohio: Association of College and University Housing Officers-International, 1993.

Student Government. *Constitution and Statutes of the University of Florida Student Body.* Gainesville: Author, 1996.

Super, D. E. "A Life-Span, Life-Space Approach to Career Development." *Journal of Vocational Behavior,* 1980, *16,* 282–298.

Terenzini, P. T., and Upcraft, M. L. "Using Qualitative Methods." In M. L. Upcraft and J. H. Schuh (eds.), *Assessment in Student Affairs: A Guide for Practitioners.* San Francisco: Jossey-Bass, 1996.

Tuckman, B. "Developmental Sequence in Small Groups." *Psychological Bulletin,* 1965, *63,* 384–399.

Tuckman, B., and Jensen, M. "Stages of Small Group Development Revisited." *Group and Organizational Studies,* 1977, *2,* 419–427.

United States Air Force. *USAF Fact Sheet.* Maxwell AFB, Maxwell, Ala.: United States Air Force, 1996.

University of Wisconsin-LaCrosse American Marketing Association Collegiate Chapter. *The Constitution of the University of Wisconsin-LaCrosse AMA Collegiate Chapter.* LaCrosse: University of Wisconsin-LaCrosse American Marketing Association Collegiate Chapter, 1996.

University of Wisconsin-LaCrosse Women's Rugby Football Club. *The Bylaws of the University of Wisconsin LaCrosse Women's Rugby Football Club.* LaCrosse: University of Wisconsin-LaCrosse Women's Rugby Football Club, 1996.

Upcraft, M. L., and Schuh, J. H. *Assessment in Student Affairs: A Guide for Practitioners.* San Francisco: Jossey-Bass, 1996.

Verry, B. "The Organizational Structures of RHAs." In N. W. Dunkel and C. L. Spencer (eds.), *Advice for Advisors: The Development of an Effective Residence Hall Association.* Columbus, Ohio: Association of College and University Housing Officers-International, 1993.

Weathersby, R. P., and Tarule, J. M. *Adult Development: Implications for Higher Education.* Washington, D.C.: American Association for Higher Education, 1980. (ED 191 382)

Wechsler, H., Kuh, G. D., and Davenport, A. E. "Fraternities, Sororities and Binge Drinking: Results from a National Study of American Colleges." *NASPA Journal,* 1996, 33, 260–279.

Whipple, E. G. "Student Activities." In A. L. Rentz and Associates, *Student Affairs Practice in Higher Education.* (2nd ed.) Springfield, Ill.: Thomas, 1996.

Wingspread Group on Higher Education. *An American Imperative: Higher Expectations for Higher Education.* Racine, Wis.: Johnson Foundation, 1993.

Winston, R. B., Jr., Bonney, W. C., Miller, T. K., and Dagley, J. C. *Promoting Student Development Through Intentionally Structured Groups: Principles, Techniques, and Applications.* San Francisco: Jossey-Bass, 1988.

Woodard, D. B., Jr. "Budgeting and Fiscal Management." In M. J. Barr and Associates, *The Handbook of Student Affairs Administration.* San Francisco: Jossey-Bass, 1993.

Woodard, D. B., Jr. "Leadership Challenges, 2002." In M. C. Terrell and M. J. Cuyjet (eds.), *Developing Student Government Leadership.* New Directions for Student Services, no. 66. San Francisco: Jossey-Bass, 1994.

Young, R. B. "Guiding Values and Philosophy." In S. R. Komives, D. B. Woodard, Jr., and Associates, *Student Services: A Handbook for the Profession.* (3rd ed.) San Francisco: Jossey-Bass, 1996.

Legal References

Baldwin v. *Zoradi,* 123 Cal. App. 3d 275; 176 Cal Rptr 809 (1981).

Beach v. *University of Utah,* 726 P.2d 413 (Utah, 1986).

Bradshaw v. *Rawlings,* 612 F.2d 135 (3rd Cir., 1979).

Healy v. *James,* 92S.Ct. 2338 (1972).

INDEX

10; in career development, 108; code
of conduct in, 197; in crisis intervention, 11–12; in funding collection and
disbursement, 142–143; governing
student behavior, 173; group framework and, 135, 139–146; of group regulation, 5, 19, 140–141, 171–172; of
judicial process, 68
Institutional recruitment and retention,
student group involvement in, 11,
136–137
Institutional role, challenges and
rewards in, 4–6

J

Jacoby, B. J., 137
Janes, S. S., 181
Jensen, M., 87
Johnson, D. W., 83
Johnson, F. P., 83, 84
Johnson, R., 221
Jung, C. G., 205

K

Kaplin, W. A., 170, 172, 181, 183, 184
Kearney, P. A., 213
Keppler, K., 19, 20
Kershaw, C., 50
Kitchener, K., 113
Komives, S., 26, 188, 192, 226, 227
Komives, S. B., 75
Kouzes, J. M., 74
Kowalski, G. J., 45
Kuh, G. D., 10, 15, 136, 173, 177, 182, 210

L

Lawrence, G., 205
Leadership: civic, 75; development,
73–75; followers' expectations of,
75–77; power bases in, 74. *See also* Student group leadership
Lee, B. A., 170, 172, 181, 183, 184
Legal counselors, 170
Legal issues, 4, 7, 169–185; Constitutional
right to organize and, 171–172; copyright law and, 181; federal and state
compliance and, 173; finances and,
180–181; hazing and, 182; in public versus private institutions, 170–171; in
registration and recognition processes,
172; student-institution contract and,
171; students with disabilities and, 184;
tort law on negligence and, 173–174
Liability and risk management, 7; adherence to industry standards and,
175–176; alcoholic beverages and,
182–184; high-risk behaviors and, 175;
insurance coverage and, 178–180;
transportation and, 176–177; waivers
and, 178

Lifton, W., 93, 94
Lorenz, N., 155
Lund, J. P., 10, 15

M

Magee, K., 80
Maloney, G. W., 180
Martin, S. B., 172
McCarthy, M. D., 137
McKaig, R., xiii
Memos formats, 57, *59*, 204–205
Mentors, 13–14, 42–45
Miller, T. K., 91, 93
Mitchell, S. E., 80
Miyamoto, T., 177
Moral development: case study, *118*;
models, 114–117
Motivation, extrinsic and intrinsic, 77–82
Mouton, J. R., 85
Mull, R. F., 31, 32, 33
Munschauer, J. L., 124
Murray, H. A., 81
Myers-Briggs Type Indicator (MBTI),
205–206

N

Napier, R. W., 83, 99
NASPA Journal, 230–231
National Association for Campus Activi-
ties, 18
National Interfraternity Conference
(NIC), 22–23, 198
National Intramural-Recreational Sport
Association (NIRSA), 32–33
National Pan-Hellenic Conference
(NPC), 23
National Pan-Hellenic Council (NPHC),
23
Navy-Marine Corps ROTC (NROTC),
28–29
Negligence, tort law on, 173–174
Networking, 14, 127, *128*
Newcomb, T. M,. 93
Nuss, E. M., 230

O

Ogle, T., 174
Osteen, J. M., 26
Owen, K. C., 22, 23, 24, 25, 27

P

Parliamentary procedure, 59
Pascarella, E. J., xiii, 4, 15, 136
Patton, M. Q., 213
Peale, N. V., 114
Peer groups, functions and influence of,
12, 93, 99
Peer mentors, 44
Personality conflicts, 205–206